UNSET
ACCOUNTS

Anthem Nineteenth Century Studies

Series Editor: Robert Douglas-Fairhurst

Other titles in the series:

Jane Austen and the Morality of Conversation, by Bharat Tandon

Outsiders Looking In: The Rossettis Then and Now, edited by David Clifford
and Laurence Roussillon

UNSETTLED ACCOUNTS

MONEY AND NARRATIVE IN THE NOVELS OF GEORGE GISSING

SIMON J JAMES

Anthem Press

This edition first published by Anthem Press 2003

Anthem Press is an imprint of
Wimbledon Publishing Comapny
75–76 Blackfriars Road
London SE1 8HA

Our Mutual Friend Advertiser (Figure 1, p. 25) reprinted by permission of
the Syndics of Cambridge University Library.
'Paris and Helen' (Figure 2, p. 145) reprinted by permission of
HarperCollins Publishers Ltd. © Walter Crane 1978.

British Library Cataloguing in Publication Data
Data available

Library of Congress Cataloging in Publication Data
A catalog record has been applied for

1 3 5 7 9 10 8 6 4 2

ISBN 1 84331 107 0 (hbk)
ISBN 1 84331 108 9 (pbk)

Typeset by Regent Typesetting, London

Printed by Bell & Bain Ltd., Glasgow

CONTENTS

ACKNOWLEDGEMENTS

Gissing's writing is so concerned with the solitude and the alienation involved in literary labour that to open a study of his work with such a due list of thanks to others feels somewhat inappropriate. However, without the following, this book would never have appeared.

The most important of all these acknowledgements must be to the graciousness, wisdom, patience and good humour of Dr Adrian Poole, who has been even more than a model PhD supervisor. It would be impossible to complete any work on Gissing without recognition of the achievement of the scholarship of Professor Pierre Coustillas; in my own case, the debt is greater still, for Pierre and Hélène Coustillas's kindness, erudition and generosity have enabled this project to be completed sooner and to a higher standard than would otherwise have been possible.

I would like to thank those who have commented on the text in its various and feckless stages: Gillian Beer, Robert Douglas-Fairhurst, Juliet John, Rod Mengham, Patrick Parrinder, Katie Ray, Elinor Shaffer and Andrew Sanders. I have had useful and stimulating discussions about various aspects of this work with colleagues at seminars and conferences over the past ten years, and in particular with Phil Connell, Lucy Crispin, Robin Dix, Rory Drummond, Chris Greenwood, Karen Harman, Liz Hedgecock, Matthew Lee, Emma Jane Liggins, Scott McCracken, Bharat Tandon and Jane Waller. I have also benefited from the advice and support of the following, whose help at times has been beyond the call of friendship: Marita Grimwood, Chris and Penny Hamlin, Jonathan Long, Toby Martinez de las Rivas, Fiona Price, Mark Sandy, James Thraves, Liz Williams and my family.

Tom Penn's energy and thoroughness as an editor have provided me with encouragement at the times when I have needed it most. I would also like to thank my colleagues in the Department of English Studies at the University of Durham; and students at each of the establishments where I have taught, especially those students who have followed a similar path and taken me along routes I would never have explored. Long may we all continue to learn from those whom we teach.

I am grateful to Mitsuharu Matsuoka's excellent Gissing web page, and to various internet resources which make some of the more mechanic aspects of this exercise less wearisome. I am also grateful to the staffs of the Cambridge University, British, Durham University, Bodleian and, especially in the work's early stages, English Faculty Libraries.

The completion of this book was made possible by Research Leave granted by the University of Durham, and by an award from the Arts and Humanities Research Board of Great Britain.

A version of the section on *The Whirlpool* appeared in *The Gissing Journal*, and some of this book's words appeared in the essay, 'Experiments in Realism: How to Read a George Gissing Novel', in *A Garland for Gissing* (Amsterdam: Rodopi, 2002), ed. Bouwe Postmus.

This book is dedicated to my grandmother, who first taught me to love Dickens.

1

INTRODUCTION: TELLING MONEY

One would have asserted without scruple that if Mr Pecksniff's conscience were his bank, and he kept a running account there, he must have overdrawn it beyond all mortal means of computation.

Martin Chuzzlewit, Chapter 20

Hundred pence are eight and fourpence,
    Never learn to cheat or swear.
Hundred and ten pence are nine and two pence,
    With bad companions take no share.
Hundred and twenty pence are ten shillings
    Learn to be both meek and mild.
Hundred and thirty pence are ten and tenpence,
    God never loves a wicked child.

From *The Archer Alphabet* (n.d.)[1]

Unsettled Accounts: Money and Representation

Unsettled Accounts is a book about the novels of George Gissing, but it is also about the representation of money in Victorian fiction. The subject of money preoccupies Gissing more than it does any other novelist in English literature. Daniel Defoe, Charles Dickens and many other writers have their claims; money inescapably underlies the fiction of Gissing's contemporaries such as Henry James and Thomas Hardy. However, in no other writer is the presence of money and the universalizing hold of commodity relations on modern social life so continually present, so insisted on both by the language of the narration and by the shape of the plot.

Gissing wrote to Edward Clodd in 1898, 'I am so preoccupied by the accursed struggle for money that nothing metaphysical seems to me of primary importance.'[2] No matter how the different voices of Gissing's fiction may protest against it, the power of money over the material world is so great that for Gissing the realist mode of fiction seems virtually the only possibility for a serious literary artist. He confessed to Clara Collet, 'I am never quite at ease save in dealing with forms of life where there enters pecuniary struggle. I think it will always be so. I find it a great effort to understand the daily life of people free from money cares. Never for one hour since I was out of boyhood have I been free from that harassing thought, & of course it affects my imagination.'[3] Gissing complained that Ruskin's imagination was adversely affected by his possession of independent wealth; Gissing's imagination was in turn conditioned by his own poverty.[4] He shared the post-Romantic artist's tendency to valorize high culture and to express distaste for commercial values, but contested literary culture's claim to autonomy from the profit-motive, insisting that the enjoyment of Art, and that indeed anything else that is worth having, such as a comfortable home, moral independence or even love, is dependent on the income necessary to fund it. 'Put money in thy purse,' warns the narrator of *A Life's Morning*, 'and again, put money in thy purse; for, as the world is ordered, to lack current coin is to lack the privileges of humanity, and indigence is the death of the soul.'[5]

As a result of conflicting loyalties both to cultural value and to realistic representation, Gissing's novels often appear contradictory and confusing. For him, late Victorian society's separate attitudes to money and to culture are contradictory; in Gissing's work, the internal contradictions of his form mimetically stand in for the incoherences and ideological censorings of the social world. In order to characterize Gissing's technique as a novelist, therefore, I will examine in turn the novels' images of money and of art. I will also consider subjects that, for Gissing, intersect with that of money: class, education, gender, politics, literature; and specific manifestations of late-Victorian economic life, such as the city, advertising, prostitution and imperialism.

Resisting Capital

Of the enormous corpus of Victorian fiction, there is barely a single novel whose contents remain untouched by money: John Vernon has suggested that money is 'the most common theme in nineteenth-century fiction.'[6] While Victorian literature tries to resist the idea of money as a moral *telos* for its characters, it is rarely able to establish an imaginative world that is capable of functioning entirely without money. Money may be, like the first pound notes that Pip receives from Magwitch, greasy from circulation in the public world, but it is still needed by realist fiction to oil the wheels of its plot mechanics. George Orwell, realist novelist and an emphatic admirer of Gissing, adapted I Corinthians 13 for the epigraph to his novel *Keep the Aspidistra Flying*, itself a twentieth-century reimagining of Gissing's *New Grub Street*.[7]

Though I speak with the tongues of men and of angels, and have not money, I am become as a sounding brass, or a tinkling cymbal. And though I have the gift of prophecy, and understand all mysteries, and all knowledge; and though I have all faith, so that I could remove mountains, and have not money, I am nothing. And though I bestow all my goods to feed the poor, and though I give my body to be burned, and have not money, it profiteth me nothing. Money suffereth long, and is kind; money envieth not; money vaunteth not itself, is not puffed up, doth not behave unseemly, seeketh not her own, is not easily provoked, thinketh no evil; rejoiceth not in iniquity, but rejoiceth in the truth; beareth all things, believeth all things, hopeth all things, endureth all things... And now abideth faith, hope, money, these three; but the greatest of these is money.[8]

The presence of money in a narrative almost functions as a kind of index of fidelity to real life, filthy lucre a guarantee of grimy realism.[9] Realistically portrayed fictive worlds have to possess economies of some kind, whether more or less visible, and modern economies require money. Even in one of Vladimir Propp's examples of pre-capitalist narrative in *The Morphology of the Folktale*, a bag of money occupies the function of 'reward'.[10] Victorian fiction frequently substitutes a legacy for the treasure or half a kingdom traditionally awarded to the hero of a fairy tale: Pip in *Great Expectations* (1860–1) mistakenly believes himself to be the hero of this kind of narrative, as if money were the means of bringing about his desired fairy-tale ending. While the representation of money has tended to be associated more with mimetic realism than with wish-fulfilling romance, money remains the site where realism and romance frequently compete. Money is simultaneously attractive and repulsive; money's illimitable translateability into power or commodities make it a powerful force for good or for evil. Shirley Keeldar claims cheerfully of the fortune that she inherited:

I can do a good deed with my cash. My thousand a year is not merely a matter of dirty bank-notes and jaundiced guineas (let me speak respectfully of both though, for I adore them); but, it may be, health to the drooping, strength to the weak, consolation to the sad. I was determined to make something of it better than a fine old house to live in, than satin gowns to wear; better than deference from acquaintance, and homage from the poor.[11]

Little that is good can be achieved without money; money also lies at the heart of much that is evil, whether as poverty or excessive pursuit of riches. Money can appear as the just restoration of the Dickensian ending, or equally as the origin of social ills; in the Victorian age money is a potent source of cultural anxiety.[12] While this is undoubtedly the case for eras before and since, Grahame Smith suggests that:

> What is new in the nineteenth century is the notion that greed for money lies at the very heart of almost all personal and social evil, that other forms of wrongdoing are superstructures erected upon this one essential foundation, and that it is diffused throughout the whole of society.[13]

In Victorian texts from *Our Mutual Friend* to *Capital*, such is the power of money that it even seems to possess a will of its own, accomplishing changes in the social world without human agency.

Novels therefore rarely feel entirely comfortable when handling money. In everyday life one needs money to exist, but would not wish one's whole existence to be consumed by thoughts, worries, desires or fantasies about money. Similarly, novels must deal with money, but struggle against being overpowered by an economic logic which would obliterate the meanings of their narrative. An unmediated mimetic representation of the market might preclude narrative entirely; if the dictates of the market are obeyed exclusively, moral narrative is elided, as characters obey economic logic alone, to the exclusion of individual conscience.

Thomas Carlyle's hugely influential comparative history *Past and Present* (1833) voiced resistance to the increasing dominance of the financial motive on the nation's moral life: 'We have profoundly forgotten everywhere that *Cash-payment* is not the sole relation of human beings.'[14] Carlyle's attempts to demonstrate the moral fissure between the increase of the nation's wealth and the inequity of its distribution is echoed throughout Victorian discourse, from the debate over whether ethics had any place in economic theory (a case made by John Stuart Mill, for example, but opposed by WS Jevons) to fiction's protests against the naked pursuit of capital.[15] Carlyle, Mill, Ruskin and other Victorian writers were aware that theirs was a protest that swam against the tide within 'a moral and religious ethos that stressed such virtues as hard work, thrift, and accumulation of wealth as intrinsic goods to be sought for their own sake.'[16] Uriah Heep, perhaps with some justice, complains that he was taught at school 'from nine o'clock to eleven, that labor was a curse; and from eleven o'clock to one, that it was a blessing and a cheerfulness, and a dignity, and I don't know what all'.[17] The life of a gentleman, to which David Copperfield virtuously and Heep transgressively aspire, requires a minimum level of income, but at the same time the ideals of gentlemanliness affect to repudiate the possessive individualism that ideologically powered Victorian economic growth.[18]

The novels of such Victorian writers as Dickens, Elizabeth Gaskell, Gissing and HG Wells contest the ideology that the general pursuit of enlightened monetary self-interest would lead to an increase in individual moral happiness. Even Malthus criticized such a belief, arguing in 1798 that 'the wealth of a society may increase [...] without having any tendency to increase the comforts of the labouring part of it.'[19] For socially concerned novelists, the visible presence in real life of the poor who populate their fiction is proof that the distribution of wealth in Victorian society could not be viewed as morally legitimate; liberal sympathies do not necessarily harmonize with classically liberal economics.[20] Such novelists were aware that theirs was an age of genuinely increasing and unprecedented prosperity, but were concerned that existing structures of social relations were failing to adapt to the rapidly changing nature of their economic base, that economic value and social or moral value could not coincide.[21]

Money and the Shape of Belief

As Walter Benjamin, among many others, has argued, narrative has its origins in social use, in the desire to instruct.[22] If stories do indeed teach, they accomplish this function by implying a shape of belief, by constructing an analogical relationship between the fictive universe in which they take place, and an ideal moral universe in which correct actions are rewarded and sinful conduct punished.[23] The following brief and slightly oversimplified account of Dickens (an author I have chosen as an example here partly because of his special significance for Gissing, and partly because of the conspicuity of money in his work) is intended as a kind of case study for the relationship between money, morality and ending in Victorian fiction. Peter Brooks suggests that 'narrative must tend towards its end, seek illumination in its own death. Yet this must be the right death, the correct end.'[24] Narratives that include money, therefore, construct a shape of belief towards money and its correct use: in Victorian fiction, for instance, it is a repeated *topos* that while the pursuit of money for its own sake is morally reprehensible, the self should also learn how to use money correctly. Harriet Martineau's *Illustrations of Political Economy* (1834), for instance, and Millicent Garrett Fawcett's *Tales of Political Economy* (1874) attempt to use narrative responsibly to instruct their readers.

Attempting to locate the place of the love of money in human happiness, John Stuart Mill warns that '[w]hat was once desired as an instrument for the attainment of happiness, has come to be desired for its own sake.'[25] Money, Victorian fiction repeatedly states, should be the means to an end, and not an end in itself; frequently, however, if money cannot be an end it is still an ending, in the form of the protagonists' reward for the virtue that they have displayed in the course of the narrative. Money's underwriting of the material reality in which the plot occurs makes money, or things purchasable with money, almost the only possible reward for a protagonist after love, and perhaps not even then. One of the most frequently employed endings in Victorian fiction is thus the unexpected inheritance. This convention can be seen as a fictive strategy to restore the desired link between moral action and economic existence, between deserts and possession. Such a relationship is also embodied in the extremely popular Victorian anthology of true-life 'success stories', Samuel Smiles's *Self-Help* (1859), in which the protagonists' display of the correct moral value of hard work is rewarded by deserved success in their chosen sphere of action. In the chapter on 'Money – Its Use and Abuse', Smiles claims:

> How a man uses money – makes it, saves it, and spends it – is perhaps one of the best tests of practical wisdom. Although money ought by no means to be regarded as a chief end of man's life, neither is it a trifling matter, to be held in philosophic contempt, representing as it does to so large an extent, the means of physical comfort and social well-being.[26]

In the classic novel, moral value and money are both weighed and calculated in the final reckoning of the ending, its ultimate judgement on the characters providing an image, perhaps, of the Last Judgement that will ultimately apportion punishment and reward.[27] The moral accounting of the classic novel's ending calls upon the reader's own faculty of ethical judgement to infer a relationship between the fates of the characters and a system of moral judgement, and implies thereby a kind of 'moral grammar' for interpretation of their actions.[28]

The financial preconditions of life as represented in the Victorian novel thus translate the mechanics of narrative, and of narrative closure in particular, into a pseudo-economic form. 'Yes, reader, we must settle accounts now', writes Charlotte Brontë's narrator, beginning *Shirley*'s final chapter, 'The Winding-Up'.[29] John R Reed suggests that for Dickens, 'the language of money and commercial exchange easily comes to signify the accumulation of moral debt and the need to have that debt repaid or forgiven.'[30] Moral values are incorporated within, even reified by, the internal economy of the novel; the moral universe created by the novel's plot settles scores with the characters, finally balancing the book. Roland Barthes has read the classic text as a relay of economies which are resolved by narrative closure, the internal exchanges of capitalist economics thus mimicked in the art form which is most closely associated with the rise of capitalist economics, the novel.[31] (The metaphor 'economy' has indeed recently become very popular in critical terminology to characterize such textual circulations, as in 'economies of the body', 'economies of taste', and so on.)

Debts, both literal and metaphorical, are therefore an obstacle to traditional narrative closure. For the narrative to end, nothing must still be owing or remain unaccounted for; money that has circulated through the plot must come to rest in the right place. After they have received their legacy in *Our Mutual Friend* (1864–5), 'Mr. and Mrs. Harmon's first delightful occupation was, to set all matters right that had strayed in any way wrong'.[32] Although the virtue that the ending rewards has often been demonstrated by resistance to the profit impulse, the very weighing-up of deserving qualities at the ending of the classic text, satirically described by Henry James as 'a distribution at the last of prizes, pensions, husbands, wives, babies, millions, appended paragraphs, and cheerful remarks', makes closure a form of financial calculation.[33] If, as Vernon suggests, to write a realist novel in the nineteenth century is virtually to be obliged to write about money, money itself becomes a part of narrative technique, arguably with greater force later in the century. Monetary metaphors blur the boundary between the metaphorical and the literal: if monetary relations ultimately underlie the forms of social life in the nineteenth century, generic terms such as 'debt', 'payment', 'fortune' and 'account' half-acknowledge the existence of an economic superstructure beneath the narrative's apparent freedom. Fredric Jameson has suggested that, ideologically, texts uniformly possess a 'political unconscious'; one might add that indeed all texts possess an 'economic unconscious' as well, and in nineteenth-century realist fiction this unconscious can never be successfully repressed. Money circulates through novels; it underwrites their represented truths; it funds their assertions of moral value; it is the text beneath the text. Gissing may be more specific than most about his characters' financial situation, but protagonists from Moll Flanders to Leopold Bloom are capable of producing a balance sheet of their income and expenditure when their stories end.

Paper Fictions: Money and the Novel

Victorian fiction warns against incorrect or immoral uses of money, but as the century progressed, the novel itself registered increasing anxiety about its own role as a benign influence. The Education Act of 1870 created a much larger reading public for fiction, but also made the correlation between artistic value and commercial success less clear; on the contrary, the novel's visibility as a commodity exchanged for money became more and more apparent. Patrick Brantlinger argues:

> Money and fiction, both representational systems relying on credit, are also often interchangeable: money as the fiction of gold or of absolute value; fiction as a commodity, exchangeable for money. And from Defoe onwards, realistic fiction, at least, is always in some sense about money.[34]

The self-image of writers as benign influences on their public was threatened by an increasingly spectacular, less verifiably real or reliable economy of literature which did not seem to reward diligent, authentic work with corresponding financial reward. For John Vernon, 'culture could hardly function as an alternative to the economic or the commercial when it, too, was relentlessly undergoing commodification, as was obviously the case with the novel.'[35] *Fin de siècle* writers such as Gissing, James and Robert Louis Stevenson fretted that the novel's moral and artistic value was inherently compromised by its association with the vulgar, commercial values of its newly expanded, less-discriminating mass audience. Writers who valorized the novel as a serious art form felt increasingly that the moral or artistic value of the novel was lessened by its exchange value as a commodity, that the ethics, or rather, lack of them, of the commercialized market for literature were antithetical to the intended 'use-value' of the morally or politically committed work of art.

Often in narrative, a character's moral authenticity is demonstrated by the legibility of his self to the reader; a villain, conversely, presents a false self to the world for the sake of his own advancement. (Gissing's *Born in Exile* parodies this kind of plot.) The plot ultimately exposes and punishes the villain's deception, and rewards the hero's transparency. Realist narration, however, also has to acknowledge the actual nature of the economic world and is therefore obliged to represent the higher priority that commodity culture places on attractive appearances ahead of a true signifier. Realist economic novels, therefore, tend to demonstrate scepticism about the truth of representations, even their own. The brilliant money-narratives of, for instance, *Washington Square*, *The Portrait of a Lady*, *The Wings of the Dove* and *The Golden Bowl* are generated in part from James's sense of the disparities between true moral nature and attractive appearances.[36] Although virtue may be valuable in another register than the economic, a complete legibility of the self to the outside world is anti-economic: virtue may be dangerous if displayed too openly in a realistically represented, hostile struggle for economic existence.[37] For

Gissing, the presentation of a wholly authentic moral self to the world is made impossible by the demands of economic life.

Much work in recent years on the relationship between the historical reality of money and its representations in fiction has thus focused upon the tensions created by the novel's claim to be an autonomous, independent work of art, and its status as a commodity object, itself a part of the lived, real transactions of everyday capitalist life.[38] Many writers seem to feel that resistance to capital by the novel, the nineteenth century's quintessential artwork-as-commodity, must by necessity be limited. In late nineteenth-century fiction that is especially preoccupied with money, and in Gissing's work in particular, the exchangeability of art for money, and vice versa, must inevitably weaken culture's social mission to counteract the values of the marketplace. Economic activity that is dependent on the production not of things, but of signifiers, such as the writing of novels, threatens the possibility of an inflationary representational economy in which the real cannot make good the paper promises of written language. Even Trollope, who in his demystifying *Autobiography* was candid about the economics of literary production even to the detriment of his posthumous reputation, was concerned that money's dematerialization in the late nineteenth century called the truth of its representation into question: 'As for many years past we have exchanged paper money instead of actual money for our commodities, so now it seemed that, under the new Melmotte regime, an exchange of words was to suffice.'[39] David Musselwhite identifies a similar anxiety in the economics of William Thackeray's *Vanity Fair*.

> At another level, of course, this breakdown of representation means that it is wholly appropriate that Becky's household should survive on 'nothing a year': credit, like language and like desire, must thrive in an inflationary economy where it is never called to account.[40]

The late Victorian novel's critique of capital is thus a rather uncomfortable one, caught as it is between the claims to truth of its own assertions, and the fictional medium in which such assertions are made. Patrick Brantlinger has argued (perhaps at times overemphatically) that the claims of the realist novel to portray reality with both mimetic accuracy and moral force are undermined by its necessarily fictional status, and by its association, both literal and literary, with money:

> The realistic novel is a form of frustration" because [...] as a commodity exchangeable for money, in its own terms its ultimate value is no more or less than the price that it sells for in the literary marketplace. [...] The frustrating failure of mimesis is often most

evident when money is the theme or when money is at stake. Then
a novelist's debts to the real are apt to seem most irredeemable
and the novel itself most insolvent. Recognition of the novel's commodity status – that is, of the novel's exchangeability through the
literary marketplace into money – was the primary theme or trope
through which writers of realistic fiction registered their frustration
with the always-already failure of mimesis.[41]

Philosophical writing on money such as Jacques Derrida's *Given Time* also
stresses the ontological correspondences between money and fiction, both
requiring a form of 'suspension of disbelief' or 'credit' in order to function.
The textual and imaginative nature of both money and the novel weaken the
claim to truthfulness by either kind of representation.[42] Neither novels nor
money can ever be unproblematically 'real'; just as novels are invented from
the material of life, money too is something else before it becomes money.
However, it remains something else even after: an object, a round of metal, a
printed piece of paper. Marx observed: 'we cannot tell from the mere look of
a piece of money, for what particular commodity it has been exchanged.
Under their money-form all commodities look alike. Hence, money may be
dirt, although dirt is not money.'[43] An early article in *Household Words* by
Harriet Martineau details the process by which sweepings from a gold workshop floor are turned back into gold (interestingly, given Eugene Wrayburn's
final transformation in *Our Mutual Friend*, this process includes immersion in
water). WH Wills 'reviews' a new banknote as if it were a much-desired new
novel before giving an account of the note's manufacture, including its origin
as rags. Dickens himself described the Bank of England as a huge circulating
library.[44]

Money partly shares fiction's imaginary status; in particular, 'paper money
is a fiction with its roots in the actual – but a fiction nonetheless.'[45] Marc Shell
identifies in the early nineteenth century an anxiety that the relationship
between the signifier of paper money and the signified of value is functionally
imperfect, or even delusive.[46] The reader knows that fiction is not 'real', but
disbelief must be partially suspended to allow the experience of reading to
function satisfactorily. Money is also an imaginary contingency: the mind
knows that money is not 'real' either, but for ordinary economic life to function normally, this knowledge must be repressed.

Money is itself a signifier, and by no means a reliable one; fictional money
is thus doubly removed from the real. Like a novel, a coin is worth more than
the material from which it is made; it is 'both a proposition and a thing.'[47]
Since the value of a piece of currency is no longer guaranteed by its weight in
gold, money's real value is remote, inaccessible, unseen in a bank vault. As a

signifier of value elsewhere, rather than something that embodies value intrinsically, money itself is thus an absence as much as it is a presence. Perpetually absent, but omnipresent in society's conversion of everything into monetary value, money is both nowhere and everywhere.[48] In its ideal state, money is simultaneously the signifier of a certain amount of real gold in the Bank of England, and an undisputed token of exchange. Money is seen as an evil when it becomes the signified as well, an object of desire in itself, rather than a way of achieving desires. Mill insisted that money exists neither as capital nor as wealth, but as a medium of exchange, and that this was in fact the nature of money's power.

> One whose fortune is in money, or in things rapidly convertible into it, seems both to himself and others to possess not any one thing, but all the things which the money places it at his option to purchase. The greatest part of the utility of wealth, beyond a very moderate quantity, is not the indulgences it procures, but the reserved power which its possessor holds in his hands of attaining purposes generally; and this power no other kind of wealth confers so immediately or so certainly as money.[49]

According to Kurt Heinzelman, 'Money not only mediates between necessities and their obtainability, but also becomes desirable in itself, a signifier whose signified content is itself.'[50] Carlyle had prophesied that 'the symbol shall be held sacred, defended everywhere with tipstaves, ropes and gibbets; the thing signified shall be composedly cast to the dogs.'[51] Fawcett also makes the distinction: 'There are many excuses for the persons who made the mistake of confounding money and wealth. Like many others they mistook the sign for the thing signified.'[52] George Eliot's miser Silas Marner has been desocialized by his inability to make the hermeneutic leap from money's material existence to its intended social function:

> For twenty years, mysterious money had stood to him as the symbol of earthly good, and the immediate object of toil. He had seemed to love it little in the years when every penny had its purpose for him; for he loved the *purpose* then. But now, when all purpose was gone, that habit of looking towards the money and grasping it with a sense of fulfilled effort made a loam that was deep enough for the seeds of desire.[53]

Ruskin complained in his lecture on 'The Political Economy of Art', 'money doesn't mean money: it means wit, it means intellect, it means influence in high quarters, it means everything except itself.'[54] In a wholly commodified world, everything is convertible into money: the true referent of money is thus simultaneously only itself, and everything that is not itself. A truly universal signifier has no stable signified if its referent is, ultimately, everything; it cannot have a meaning if there are no boundaries to what it might mean. For Jacques Lacan, as a consequence, money is 'the signifier most destructive of all signification'.[55] If, as Shell suggests, money is a 'universal signifier', then it can stand for anything, hence the unanswerability of Paul Dombey's famous question about the nature of money.[56] The answers to Paul's question are, as his father implies, numerous, and none can possibly be definitive.

> "Papa! What's money?" [...]
> Mr Dombey was in a difficulty. He would have liked to give him some explanation involving the terms circulating-medium, currency, depreciation of currency, paper, bullion, rates of exchange, value of precious metals in the market, and so forth; but, looking down at the little chair, and seeing what a long way down it was, he answered: "Gold, and silver, and copper. Guineas, shillings, half-pence. You know what they are?"[57]

This does not answer Paul's question: in fact he knows what money materially *is*: what he wants to know is what it can and can't do, and his father's answer to this is not satisfactory either. Money is a commodity; Adam Smith argues in 'The Origin and Use of Money' that the commodity is ideally a representation of labour, but immediately has to explain why this perfect condition is not in fact the case. 'Though labour be the real measure of the exchangeable value of all commodities, it is not that by which their value is commonly estimated.'[58] In fact, however, the value of a commodity is pragmatically modified by the market through money; a commodity's value in labour is its real value, and its value in money only its nominal value. In practice, it is surely the case that the 'nominal' takes precedence over the 'real'. 'Labour [...] is the only universal, as well as the only accurate measure of value, or the only standard by which we can compare the values of different commodities at all times and places', Smith claims, but one might, like Orwell, substitute 'money' for 'labour' to make this statement more accurate.[59] *Capital* is in one sense Marx's lengthy continuation of Smith's attempt to answer why money has come to represent itself rather than labour.[60] (Indeed, for Jean Baudrillard, it is Marx's failure to transcend the inherited linguistic categories of Political Economy that is the central weakness of his work.)[61]

Late-nineteenth-century discussion of money thus tends to focus less on money's essential nature than on its effectiveness as a means of exchange, such as in the debate over international exchange centred on 'bimetallism' (a topic excluded from discussion in Alfred Yule's planned impractical literary journal in *New Grub Street*).[62] Money cannot have value if the state whose name it bears is insolvent. As Brantlinger has demonstrated at length in *Fictions of State*, the value of currency is intimately connected to questions of national identity:

> The Victorian novel simultaneously registers both the substantiality of British power and prosperity and its insubstantiality, its basis only in "credit" and "debt," in part by metaphorizing its own lack of reality (its fictionality) as no different from that of money (always a form of debt).[63]

Even the guarantee of the British Empire is insufficient to ensure fictional money's substantiality. David Trotter has suggested that in late-Victorian popular fiction, British hallmarks are a trustworthy signifier of value, but in 'serious' literature, the reliability of currency is frequently questioned.[64] Since Britain is an Empire, even the pound is not a self-sufficient entity, but is underwritten by the Empire (displaced Dickensian heroes such as Joe Willett, Walter Hartright and Pip all work there). Once again, wherever value may lie, it is not present, not tangible, but deferred elsewhere.

Telling Tales: Money and Narrative

As I have suggested, in Victorian fiction, the effectiveness, or even the suitability of money to perform its narrative functions can rarely be established without difficulty. Money is simultaneously ever-present and elusive. While nothing can be achieved without money, plot can 'do' nothing with it either: the existence of money in itself does not constitute a narrative. DA Miller usefully identifies the condition of 'narratability' as being for unstable, or 'narratable' elements, 'the instances of disequilibrium, suspense, and general insufficiency from which a given narrative appears to arise', to disrupt a previously stable continuum.[65] In the openings of numerous novels from Marie Corelli's *The Sorrows of Satan* to Knut Hamsun's *Hunger*, the narratable is constituted by lack of money or property. From Oliver Twist and Nicholas Nickleby through to John Harmon, the stories of Dickens's more virtuous heroes often begin when they are deprived of what is rightfully theirs. The plot dramatizes the hero's eventual regaining of his patrimony, thus re-establishing equilibrium: 'the first act of Nicholas, when he became a rich and prosperous merchant, was to buy his father's old house'.[66] The possession of financial means is a precondition of the stability needed for realistic closure. A secure income, ideally independent wealth, guarantees immunity from the threatening, unstable, narratable elements that have generated the plot. The inheritance is thus the ideal Victorian narrative ending, the protagonist's family wealth restoring a link with newly restabilized origins. Inheritance gives wealth the permanence and moral value that money does not intrinsically possess: money is neither unstable nor corrupting if it is passed onto one's children, nor is it anonymous if it becomes, in this sense, a part of the family.[67] Jane Eyre's reunion with her family leads to her discovery of her inheritance, for example, and she unifies her 'wealth of the heart' with her fortune by sharing the latter with her cousins.[68]

Only rarely in the classic realist text does the, usually middle-class, protagonist end his narrative without the visible means to continue a more than comfortable financial existence (George Eliot's 1866 novel *Felix Holt* provides a characteristic exception). The strength of what, after Fredric Jameson, might be called 'narratemes' such as the inheritance-plot, is demonstrated by their persistence through to the end of the century and into the twentieth.[69] The device of the inheritance adapts, often in parodic and distorted forms, in such novels as George Eliot's *Felix Holt* (1866), *Middlemarch* (1871–2) and *Daniel Deronda* (1876), Henry James's *The Portrait of a Lady* (1881), *The Spoils of Poynton* (1897), *The Wings of the Dove* (1902), George Gissing's *Demos* (1886), *Isabel Clarendon* (1886), *The Nether World* (1889), Marie Corelli's *The Sorrows of Satan* (1895), HG Wells's *Kipps* (1905) and *Tono-Bungay* (1909), Joseph Conrad's *Nostromo* (1903) and even, as Reed observes, HG Wells's *When the Sleeper Wakes* (1899) and EM Forster's *Howards End* (1910). As late as 1920, Lily Bart's plot in Edith Wharton's *The House of Mirth* is shaped by her expectation of a legacy of which, like Pip, she proves unworthy (although nor does she deserve the ending that she does receive); Charles Palliser's pastiche of Victorian narrative conventions *The Quincunx* (1989) makes brilliant use of the legacy device.

Although, as I have suggested, money must be incorporated within a realistic plot, political economy's base units of capital and labour are not in themselves easily narratable. Possession can be represented, but as nonnarratable description of property such as land, houses and material objects rather than as narration. Land, hitherto the most common stable signifier for wealth and power, had begun to decline in value by the generation after the repeal of the 1846 Corn Laws, and the value of what it produced was undercut by imports of cheaper food from abroad.[70] Land is by its nature static; even monetary wealth hardly changes except as capital accumulation, altering in quantity but not in nature. Capital does not have a *telos* or an ending. In *The Mill on the Floss*, Tom realizes that he will not find the narrative that he desires by working in a bank: 'there seemed so little tendency towards a conclusion in the quiet monotonous procedure of these sleek, prosperous men of business.'[71] The possession of property or a four-percent bond does not in itself constitute a plot, as is demonstrated by the failure of the narrative told by Thomas Leaf at the end of Thomas Hardy's *Under the Greenwood Tree* (1872):

> "Once," said the delighted Leaf, in an uncertain voice, "there was a man who lived in a house! Well, this man went thinking and thinking night and day. At last, he said to himself; as I might, 'If I had only ten pound, I'd make a fortune.' At last by hook or by crook, behold he got the ten pounds! [...] In a little time he made that ten pounds twenty. Then a little time after that he doubled it, and made it forty. Well, he went on, and a good while after that he made it eighty, and on to a hundred. Well, by-and-by he made it two hundred! Well, you'd never believe it, but – he went on and made it four hundred! He went on, and what did he do? Why, he made it eight hundred! Yes, he did," continued Leaf in the highest pitch of excitement, bringing down his fist upon his knee with such force that he quivered with the pain; "yes, and he went on and made it A THOUSAND!"[72]

Manufacturing, since the Industrial Revolution Britain's source of economic supremacy, became less conspicuous later in the century as a signifier of wealth than finance, as dramatized in novels such as Dickens's *Little Dorrit* (1855–7), and Anthony Trollope's *The Way We Live Now* (1874–5). Yet finance's power to signify money was unstable, as a series of highly public bank scares and financial crises proved, most notoriously the collapse of the discount house of Overend & Gurney in 1866, which captured the imagination of novelists.[73] (Ranald C Michie suggests, however, that novelists were not especially well informed about how finance actually worked.[74]) When capital does become narratable in Victorian literature, it is usually in the dramatically sudden expansions and deflations of speculation; in such cases, capital may be erratic and singular enough to generate narrative.[75] The vulgar advertising broker Luckworth Crewe in Gissing's *In the Year of Jubilee* finds such romance in the streets of the City of London:

> Crewe had stories to tell of this and that thriving firm, of others struggling in obscurity or falling from high estate; to him the streets of London were so many chapters of romance, but a romance always of to-day, for he neither knew nor cared about historic associations. Vast sums sounded perpetually on his lips; he glowed with envious delight in telling of speculations that had built up great

fortunes. He knew the fabulous rents that were paid for sites that looked insignificant; he repeated anecdotes of calls made from Somerset House upon men of business, who had been too modest in returning statement of their income; he revived legends of dire financial disaster, and of catastrophe barely averted by strange expedients.[76]

Speculation tends to be associated in Victorian narratives with hypocrisy and the creation of false appearances: much of the anxiety that Melmotte generates in *The Way We Live Now* is caused by the fact that, like international capital, nobody knows where he comes from; for all his conspicuous wealth what Melmotte really means is not legible. Fraud in fiction seems to be made endemic by the money-getting nature of society. As Reed expresses it:

> What seemed to be secure, if hope in the next world was not, was greed in this world. Financial grappling, rapine, deceit were regularly attributed to the commercialised society of Victorian England. Writers persistently deplored and attacked the debasement of values to a cash level. From the fiery Carlyle, to an indignant Dickens, or a milder Trollope, accusations of cupidity accompanied lamentations on the sad degradation of moral values until, in these writers and others, swindling became not merely a realistic ingredient of their narratives, but a symbol of a moral bankruptcy as well.[77]

Labour, supposedly the source of wealth, is only barely easier to dramatize; Pip's work in Cairo, for example, is not actually narrated in the ending(s) of *Great Expectations*. Alexander Welsh has suggested that Dickens's novels 'espouse work as a value, but not as an experience'.[78] Under the conditions of industrial capitalism, labour is both repetitive and reproducible, like the commodity object of the novel, but unlike the singular narrative contained within. At its simplest, labour in an industrialized society consists of the same action performed repeatedly over fixed lengths of time, and the labourer, the 'hand', can be replaced by somebody with the same skills; industrial capitalism, William Morris argues, makes labour innately tedious.[79] The classic novel, by contrast, tends to describe an individual 'case', an action taking place over a period of historical time. In Mrs Gaskell's *Mary Barton* (1848) and *North and South* (1854–5), for instance, it is the uncertainties of accidents and unemployment, events which are *not* themselves labour, that make labour narratable: Gaskell writes in the Preface to *Mary Barton* of finding 'romance' in the 'strange alternations between work and want'.[80] Narrative takes place within the only at best liminal realm that Marx characterizes as 'freedom', the unalienated sphere of human action that is not reified and codified into labour. Capital, labour, or a combination of the two (as in *Shirley* and *North and South*), are more likely to be the ending of a plot than to provide the substance of a plot themselves.[81] George Eliot provides a characteristic variation in *Silas Marner* (1861), the ending of which demonstrates the victory of productive, virtuous labour over sterile, hoarded capital.

In his working notes for *Our Mutual Friend*, Dickens plans that Bella 'comes into no end of money', but this is exactly what she does *not* come into.[82] Since the power of money opens up the vertiginously limitless possibilities of the Harmons' desires being all deservedly fulfilled for the rest of their lives, the narrative has to end there. The protagonists and their capital are all safely banked in order to avoid the risks associated with circulation. George Orwell famously complained that when Dickens's protagonists receive inheritances, they do nothing with them.[83] Tom Winnifrith acerbically notes a similar pattern in Mrs Henry Wood:

> Unrealistically, if moralistically, the virtuous are usually rewarded with wealth, while the wicked are usually ruined. The preaching of this pious moral is rendered slightly less impressive by the failure of the virtuous to be very generous with their money.[84]

Narration, therefore, must occupy itself with the transactions between the economic world and the self, with different kinds of exchanges between labour and property, with negotiation. Since this study will be concerned with specific manifestations of money in the novel, it will thus be concerned less with debates within the specialized discourse of Political Economy, and more with economics as experienced in the transactions of everyday life, hence the prominence of Gissing in this project. If neither labour nor capital can easily be manipulated to form the material of plot, then narration must concern itself with spending or the lack of it, more than with getting. Negotiation in its various moral registers can be honest or dishonest; plots can hinge on whether a purchase is made or resisted, on whether a character possesses sufficient funds to continue on a particular path or is obliged by lack of funds to choose another.

Through dealing with the market, through exchange, the self can be tested; through the plot's charting of characters' negotiation of the contingent economic realities of everyday life, their moral worth can be made visible to the reader. As each novel implies a different shape of belief, each novel has a distinct economy; 'the market' is both a mimesis of the economics of real life and specific to an individual novel.[85] Although the self cannot choose whether to live with money or without, money does provide the opportunity for other kinds of choice, especially when mediated through the family. Oliver resists market values and is rewarded with an inheritance and relations; Pip succumbs to the lure of excessive purchase and is punished with exile from his family. Dora Copperfield proves a bad wife in her inability to manage household expenditure; she dies to be replaced by the competent housekeeper-wife, Agnes. The Crawleys irresponsibly generate debts they can never pay; Dobbin honourably settles his own and others' debts. Heathcliff takes revenge on Hindley by usurping his inheritance; *The Warden* and *Orley Farm* both turn on the interpretation of a will. The aristocrat Sir Willoughby Patterne oppresses those around him with the power of his inherited wealth; Victor Radnor fails in business as his family disintegrates. Esther Lyon renounces her legacy for a life of modest usefulness in a marriage that is, in terms of class, beneath her, but morally and emotionally right. Fred Vincy's poor management of his finances impoverishes both himself and those he loves; by learning the virtue of hard work he is finally able to make good the debt. Rosamond Lydgate refuses to moderate her expenditure to match her husband's dwindling income; both Lydgate and Bulstrode are compromised by the settling of Lydgate's debt. Dorothea Casaubon finally renounces her fortune to marry the man she loves, promising to 'learn what everything costs'; Gwendolen Grandcourt is trapped by marrying for money.[86] Michael Henchard trades in his family for money, but later tries to settle all his debts honestly; while under the necessity of labouring to earn a living Jude Fawley will never achieve the education for which he longs. (Gissing literalizes this trope when characters are tempted by pieces of currency in *A Life's Morning* and 'Our Mr Jupp').[87]

Money is a powerful sign, but morally an empty one. Ruskin claims:

> It is impossible to conclude, of any given mass of acquired wealth, merely by the fact of its existence, whether it signifies good or evil to the nation in the midst of which it exists. Its real value depends on the moral sign attached to it, just as sternly as that of a mathematical quantity depends on the algebraical sign attached to it. Any given accumulation of commercial wealth may be indicative, on the one hand, of faithful industries, progressive energies, and productive ingenuities: or, on the other, it may be indicative of mortal luxury, merciless tyranny, ruinous chicane. Some treasures are heavy with human tears, as an ill-stored harvest with untimely rain; and some gold is brighter in sunshine than it is in substance.[88]

The overlapping of moral choice with economics in the Victorian novel allows the inscription of ethical values upon money's surface; money used in this way by a narrative ceases to be anonymous, and can indeed become money that means something.

Moral Economies: Charles Dickens

In Charles Dickens especially, money's nature is conspicuously polysemic, as both moral corruptor and reward for good deeds. The plots of Dickens's novels repeatedly operate a moral economy in which the deserving establish their virtue through resistance to the values of the market, and are finally rewarded with enough accumulated capital to relieve them of future want; an independence, therefore, brings resolution. Protagonists are circulated to demonstrate their value; at the end of the narrative they are withdrawn from circulation and safely banked, often in a location away from the dangerous city in which the plot has occurred. As long as they have proved themselves to be virtuous, hero and heroine are thus permitted to retain their value, and are both redeemed and rewarded with interest; the 'account' they are able finally to give of themselves is both a story, and a financial reckoning, a correct valuation.[89] Some characters, such as Nancy or Smike, may prove their virtue only to be sacrificed by the plot for the sake of pathos; however, the majority of the other characters are reckoned with according to their deserts. The cast of *Martin Chuzzlewit*, for example, is theatrically assembled at the novel's close to be rewarded or punished in mathematical proportion to the extent they have helped or hindered the hero and heroine; a draft version of its title is *The Life and Adventures of Martin Chuzzlewit / His relatives, friends, and enemies. Comprising all His Wills and His Ways, With an Historical record of what he did and what he didn't; Shewing moreover who inherited the Family Plate; who came in for the Silver spoons, and who for the Wooden Ladles. The whole forming a complete key To The House of Chuzzlewit.*[90] Characters who have openly pursued economic motives are punished or made to reform, most famously in what is now Dickens's most popular story, *A Christmas Carol* (1843). Scrooge is warned by his former business-partner Marley, who is fettered with a chain 'of cash-boxes, keys, padlocks, ledgers, deeds, and heavy purses wrought in steel.'[91] Scrooge is then presented with a ghost-narrative of his possible future, in which narrative rewards will be denied him because of his pursuit of profit. Charity and family relationships, for Dickens the antitheses of commercial values, allow Scrooge to redeem what remains of his life, and pledge himself to an emotional life that is separate from (albeit still apparently underwritten by) his labour in the counting-house.

In *Oliver Twist* (1837–9), by contrast, the hero displays his virtue by always resisting capital; Oliver's preternaturally developed moral sense shies away from economic exchange in almost every form in which he encounters it. The plot seems to prove that he is right to do so. Oliver's first experience of supposedly legitimate commerce, the delivery of books to a binder, returns him to the criminal environment: the 'accidental display' of his old clothes in a shop window allows Fagin's gang to trace him.[92] Oliver is too childlike and virtuous to be polluted by success as a thief; had he permanently become even a chimney sweep or an undertaker's mute, his narrative would have been stillborn, the *tabula rasa* of his virtue irrevocably smirched by the economic process of labour. In this novel, virtue appears to be characterized throughout by aversion to all financial transaction. Brownlow forgets to pay for the book that he is reading when the Dodger picks his pocket; Harry Maylie demonstrates his goodness and earns a happy ending by giving up worldly success for the love of Rose. Nancy signals her reform by withdrawing her already-commodified body from the marketplace:

> "This purse, cried [Rose]. "Take it for my sake, that you may have some resource in an hour of need and trouble."
> "No!" replied [Nancy]. "I have not done this for money. Let me have that to think of." '[93]

Little Nell and her grandfather in *The Old Curiosity Shop* (1840–1) are forced away from London by Quilp's appropriation of their livelihood; their escape is away from capitalism into a kind of barter economy.[94] It also seems to be proof of virtue in Dickens to undertake a journey without means to pay for it – as well as Little Nell and her grandfather, Oliver Twist, Nicholas Nickleby, Dick Swiveller, Martin Chuzzlewit, Mark Tapley, Tom Pinch, Florence Dombey, David Copperfield, Lady Dedlock, Stephen Blackpool and Betty Higden all do so. Virtue is constituted in early Dickens by distance, or even removal, from economic circulation.[95] One might think of the unsuccessful businesses owned by virtuous characters in Dickens: the Old Curiosity Shop, Sol Gill's marine stores, Mr George's shooting gallery, Clennam and Doyce's works, or even the Cheerybles' warehouse, Joe's Forge and Mr Venus's shop, which, it is claimed, are successful, but which are rarely seen to be troubled by customers. Visibly successful businessmen are instead characterized by greed and duplicity: Ralph Nickleby, Gride, Quilp, Scrooge, Dombey, Carker, the Smallweeds, Merdle, Bounderby, Fledgeby and nearly all of the lawyers.[96]

Oliver's inheritance is explicitly identified as a reward for his resistance to money by the terms of his father's will, which stipulates a condition that 'in his minority he should never have stained his name with any act of dishonour, meanness, cowardice or wrong.'[97] Oliver has unknowingly obeyed his father's will to the letter even before knowing of its existence; his virtue and his ending appear to be in perfect balance. Dickens revealed in the 1841 Preface to

Oliver Twist that he 'wished to shew, in little Oliver, the principle of Good surviving through every adverse circumstance, and triumphing at last.'[98] Oliver's plot resembles the demonstration of inviolable heroic nature that Georg Lukàcs attributes to epic. Lukàcs's description of the epic world recalls the attempt in Dickens's endings to create a perfect form of fictional justice:

> The epic world is either a purely childlike one in which the transgression of stable, traditional norms has to entail vengeance [...] or else it is the perfect theodicy in which crime and punishment lie in the scales of world justice as equal, mutually homogeneous weights.[99]

Such an ending, however, must be neither anticipated nor expected. Nicholas Nickleby rebukes his mother for expressing a desire for the ending that the novel will actually endorse: his marriage to Madeleine, Kate's to Frank and a substantial gift from the Cheerybles.[100] Nicholas's virtue is demonstrated by his attempting not to fulfil, but rather to negate or at least postpone, his own desires.[101] The novel's other characters, by contrast, can hardly stop themselves from always wanting. Satisfaction of desire of course requires financing: *Nicholas Nickleby* in particular is awash with discounted bills, as if the morally flawed characters are unable to defer gratification of any kind. The virtuous resist fulfilment of their desires, then finally 'cash in' their narrative freedom in exchange for lasting happiness.[102]

Dickens's later novels warn emphatically against a premature expectation of this kind of ending; according to Anny Sadrin, 'in 1860, [Pip] is chastised for the unpardonable anachronism of taking himself for Oliver Twist'.[103] In *Bleak House* (1852–3), Harold Skimpole parodies the romantic wish-fulfilment of Dickens's earlier endings by expecting to be provided for as if he were Nicholas Nickleby:

> "There should be no brambles of sordid realities in such a path as that. It should be strewn with roses; it should lie through bowers, where there was no spring, autumn, nor winter, but perpetual summer. Age or change should never wither it. The base word money should never be breathed near it!"[104]

A legacy must not be expected or anticipated, as Pip does his; John Harmon is paradoxically rewarded with his inheritance after having demonstrated his virtue by strenuously attempting to avoid it. In *Little Dorrit*, Dickens even parodies his own use of the convention, when William Dorrit behaves as if he has deserved his legacy when he plainly has not, exhorting the Collegians 'to follow his example – which at least so far as coming into a great property was concerned, there is no doubt they would have gladly imitated.'[105]

Although, as I have suggested, labour itself cannot constitute a narrative, adult heroes from Nicholas onwards can establish their virtue by working. (David's aunt withholds two thousand pounds of his inheritance for the explicit purpose of testing him through the obligation to work.) For flawed characters not virtuous or high-caste enough to be permitted the utopian ending of an inheritance, labour can prove the means by which sufficient virtue for a happy ending is established. A prefiguring of flawed later heroes such as Pip, Dick Swiveller in *The Old Curiosity Shop* initially believes that one 'may be good and happy without riches' because he does not feel obliged to pay for anything.[106] To deserve a happy ending he must learn to rework this maxim in a way that Little Nell would understand. Honourably employed at the end, Dick only consumes what he can afford, and pays what he owes. His debts finally settled, Dick is permitted a happy ending, consumption and payment now balancing each other in the novel's accounts. Dick's rebirth into full responsibility takes place, like Pip's, after temporary loss of self through illness, and the permanent loss of all the belongings owned by his previous, unreformed self. Reborn into the world, naked once more after the sale of his clothes, Dick inherits a patrimony mediated by his past actions: "If you had been another sort of nephew, you would have come into possession (so says the will, and I see no reason to doubt it), of five-and-twenty thousand pounds. As it is, you have fallen into an annuity of one hundred and fifty pounds a year".[107] Partly good, Dick comes into a part of his legacy. His virtue is confirmed by his discovery of charity, which allows a moral payment against the balance of his past misdeeds. Dick's gifts of food and sixpences to the Marchioness function as redress for her exploitation by the Brasses, and his benevolence eventually allows them to continue their story as far as the eventual happy ending of their marriage:

> It is but bare justice to Mr. Swiveller to say, that, although the expenses of her education kept him in straitened circumstances for half a dozen years, he never slackened in his zeal, and always held himself sufficiently repaid by the accounts he heard (with great gravity) of her advancement.[108]

Pip in *Great Expectations* is more honest than any previous Dickens hero about his desire for money and what it can purchase. Temporarily at least, the world does not refuse Pip's desires. Often, in novels such as Samuel Warren's 1839–41 novel *Ten Thousand a Year*, *Great Expectations*, *The Sorrows of Satan* (even more explicitly a version of Faust than many of these nineteenth-century money-narratives), or Gissing's *Demos*, the heroes' initial poverty is contrasted with their subsequent dangerously wish-fulfilling wealth. Like many Victorian protagonists who come into their legacy too early, Pip overconsumes, acquiring conspicuous symbols of wealth such as linen, jewellery and even a better education, which previously had foundered for lack of money. Once he loses his legacy, the process is reversed, and Pip converts 'easily spared articles of jewellery into cash' via the pawn-shop exchange of the downwardly mobile, a pattern which is repeated throughout Gissing's work.[109] For Pip to have a happy ending, he must also settle the financial and familial debts he has incurred, and acknowledge the connection to his family that his fortune encouraged him to deny. Money seems to give Pip the power to create false appearances, such as his passing as a gentleman. According to Herbert Pocket's father, however:

> "No man who was not a true gentleman at heart, ever was, since the world began, a true gentleman in manner. He says, no varnish can hide the grain of the wood; and that the more varnish you put on, the more the grain will express itself."[110]

Pip's rowing teacher later comments that the heavily varnished Pip has 'the arm of a blacksmith' – perhaps, like the Veneerings' furniture, there is too much of the smell of the workshop to him.[111] Making futile attempts to disguise Magwitch, Pip finds that 'from head to foot, there was Convict in the very grain of the man.'[112] Pip's anxiety about class is located particularly in personal appearance. He is alarmed that in comparison with his friend the real gentleman, Herbert 'carried off his rather old clothes, much better than I carried off my new suit'; Trabb's boy, for one, is not deceived by Pip's appearance in his gentleman's outfit.[113] Only when these false money-created signifiers are stripped away can the true meanings below outward reality be revealed, such as the source of the wealth and Estella's real parentage, and closure take place.

In his last completed novel, *Our Mutual Friend*, Dickens was evidently greatly troubled by the shift in the nature of wealth in the nineteenth century away from traditionally solid signifiers such as land towards the more imaginary representations of finance; at the same time, his confidence in a national community of shared values seems to wane. The source of the money at the heart of *Our Mutual Friend* is dust-heaps: in this novel especially, money, fiction and rubbish are circulated within an entropic, unproductive economy:

> That mysterious paper currency which circulates in London when the wind blows, gyrated here and there and everywhere. Whence can it come, whither can it go? It hangs on every bush, flutters in

every tree, is caught flying by the electric wires, haunts every enclo-
sure, drinks at every pump, cowers at every grating, shudders upon
every plot of grass, seeks rest in vain behind the legions of iron
rails.[114]

Our Mutual Friend at the same time both accurately represents the world and
unpicks the fabric of material reality. Nowhere in Dickens is the hold of
money stronger, but this novel's money has an abject and arbitrary existence
as the wealth that originates from the dust-heaps. While Dickens's docu-
mentary realism is at its most literally 'grimy' in *Our Mutual Friend*, this novel
simultaneously points to its own flimsy unreality. Fictions dominate the plot:
Boffin's pious defrauding of Bella, Harmon's masquerading as Rokesmith, the
Veneerings' pedigree, Bradley's disguise. Lady Tippins sustains the 'grisly
little fiction' of her love affairs; Blight keeps his sanity with a 'fiction of an
occupation'. Eugene and the Inspector toy with the 'lime fiction' of Eugene's
respectable trade; Fledgeby's supposing Riah growing rich at his expense is a
'very convenient fiction'. Wegg's wooden leg is a 'timber fiction'; Miss Peecher
makes a 'fiction of conducting the examination'. Veneering signals a wealth
that he does not in fact possess by displaying a 'quantity of plate-glass window
and French-polished mahogany partition, and a gleaming and enormous
door-plate.'[115] Twemlow is misled both by Veneering's glowing social advertisements and the false representation that is Veneering's stock-in-trade:

> Mr Twemlow feels a little queer [...] in consequence of having
> taken two advertised pills at about mid-day, on the faith of the
> printed representation accompanying the box (price one and a
> penny halfpenny, government stamp included), that the same "will
> be found highly salutary as a precautionary measure in connection
> with the pleasures of the table."[116]

If 'printed representation' cannot be trusted, whether as the disposable
'paper currency' of London's litter, as advertising (whose promises of gratified
desire enclosed the original serial numbers of *Our Mutual Friend* – see Figure 1
opposite (p. 25)) or as the story itself, the reader might well doubt the truths
advertised by the paper fiction of Dickens's novel.[117] In the presentation of the
idealized Lizzie, for example, Dickens seems to doubt the truth of his own
assertions:

> But ladies in carriages would frequently make purchases from her
> trifling stock, and were usually pleased with her bright eyes and her
> hopeful speech. In these and her clean dress originated a fable that
> she was well to do in the world: one might say, for her station, rich.

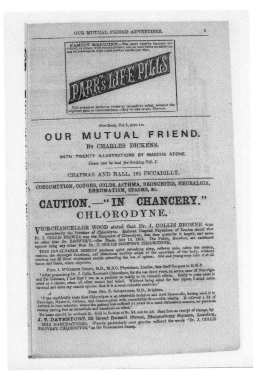

Figure 1. **Reality meets fiction in the *Our Mutual Friend Advertiser*. Mr Twemlow's 'advertised pills', with their promises of gratified desire, jostle for attention with an announcement for a new edition of *Our Mutual Friend*.**

> As making a comfortable provision for its subject which costs nobody anything, this class of fable has long been popular.[118]

Such a rewarding class of fable had kept Dickens, fond of stating how 'rich' his poorer characters can be without financial wealth, rich for the previous thirty years. Yet if such fiction can cost nothing, it is unlikely to be valued by the society portrayed in the novel. Dickens's objection to the *nouveau riche* type embodied in the Veneerings seems to be that capital suddenly gained on dubious moral grounds evades the need for expiatory narrative, and that money gained in this way might obliterate surrounding meanings as well:

> As is well known to the wise in their generation, traffic in shares is the one thing to have to do with in this world. Have no antecedents, no established character, no cultivation, no ideas, no manners; have Shares. Have shares enough to be on Boards of Direction in capital letters, oscillate on mysterious business between London and Paris,

and be great. Where does he come from? Shares. Where is he going
to? Shares. What are his tastes? Shares. Has he any principles?
Shares. What squeezes him into Parliament? Shares. Perhaps he
never of himself achieved success in anything, never originated anything, never produced anything? Sufficient answer to all; Shares. O
mighty Shares![119]

It is written in the 'Book of the Insolvent Fates' that, after the novel finishes,
the Veneerings are to lose their money: the device of the smash, as in *Nicholas
Nickleby*, *Martin Chuzzlewit*, *Dombey and Son* and *Little Dorrit*, forces a false money-
generated signifier into reconciliation with a real signified. In *Our Mutual
Friend*, the Dickens novel closest in spirit to Gissing's pessimistic realism,
Dickens's vision of reality is at its most persistently commodified: surfaces take
precedence over reality and money has the power to rewrite the meanings of
the perceptual world. Consequently, even the most basic relationships
between individuals are threatened by a money-generated inauthenticity: for
example, the Lammles marry because each, wrongly, believes the other to be
rich. As Adrian Poole suggests, in *Our Mutual Friend*, 'the aspiration to a vision
of total human interdependence that had in various ways animated Dickens's
previous major novels, finally buckles under the pressure of a deepening
scepticism.'[120] The hero and heroine eventually come into their inheritance,
but only after making strenuous efforts to avoid it, as if they recognized their
reification by the power of old Harmon's supposedly 'dead' money. Bella
protests at being left 'in a will, like a dozen of spoons'; ' "Am I for ever to be
made the property of strangers?" '[121] Her cupidity at the beginning of the
novel is persuasive, since marriage for money is the best of her limited
options: 'It's not that I care for money to keep as money, but I do care so
much for what it will buy!'[122] Bella feels that the difficulty of managing even to
pay the rent alters the nature of her moral responsibilities, a claim with which
many of Gissing's protagonists would find themselves in agreement:

> "I grudge this money going to the Monster that swallows up so
> much, when we all want – Everything. And if you say (as you want
> to say; I know you want to say so, pa) 'that's neither reasonable nor
> honest, Bella,' then I answer, 'Maybe not, pa – very likely – but it's
> one of the consequences of being poor, and of thoroughly hating
> and detesting to be poor, and that's my case." '[123]

Although her mother provides Bella with a poor example of how best to
maintain a family and household, the maintained connection with her father
prevents Bella from actually behaving as immorally as she threatens to do.

Dickens's site of resistance to the money-ordered reality of the public world is the home and family, also, of course, the preferred site of reading.[124] Ideally for Dickens and for Ruskin, in the home the only economy is that of the *oikos* and the only production that of children; chrematistic wealth-getting is banished elsewhere.[125] Dickens's fiction usually promotes the family as an antonym of the market, generating parallel oppositions: private/public, gift/trade, connection with the childhood self/fraudulent denial of the past. *A Christmas Carol* usefully polarizes these oppositions: Scrooge's reform begins, of course, with a reminder of his past selves. One source of anxiety around money was that the impersonality, indeed anonymity, of monetary relations was eroding traditional structures of community. Following the 1844 Bank Charter Act, paper money becomes unidentifiable; it bears no proper names except that of the Bank of England, and is untraceable. Once money begins circulating in the world it has no identity, and thus its meaning is the opposite of that of home, where for Dickens, if not for every Victorian novelist, identity can be confirmed as real. Maurice Bloch and Jonathan Parry have suggested that 'one particularly prominent strand in Western discourse, which goes back to Aristotle, is the general condemnation of money and trade in the light of an ideal of household self-sufficiency and production for use.'[126] Dickens's domestic refuges constitute a realm where payment appears to be attenuated and indefinitely prolonged: ' "There was never such a Dame Durden" ', comments Jarndyce on the preternaturally competent Esther, ' "for making money last." '[127] Nonetheless, as *David Copperfield* shows, domestic bliss must still be underwritten by a steady income and by capable household management. Dickens frequently describes an efficient wife as a 'treasure', as if indicating that such a commodity is highly valuable, but never circulated. In the ending of *Our Mutual Friend*, the novel's language partly acknowledges what is owed to the economic foundations of middle-class marriage and its ideal home:

> For a City man, John certainly did appear to care as little as might be for the looking up or looking down of things, as well as for the gold that got taken to the Bank. But he cared, beyond all expression, for his wife, as a most precious and sweet commodity that was always looking up, and that never was worth less than all the gold in the world.

> "You have thrown yourself away," said Eugene, shaking his head. "But you have followed the treasure of your heart."

> "Would you not like to be rich now, my darling?"
> "How can you ask me such a question, John dear? Am I not rich?"[128]

In Dickens, it is as if money has to be handled capably, but its presence partially denied or ignored, like an open secret; family life suffers if money is spoken of too plainly, but also if it is not administered competently. Dickens's unhappiest families are often those in which the profit-motive has reified the domestic emotions: think, for instance, of Jonas and Anthony Chuzzlewit, or the Smallweeds. Arthur Clennam complains that ' "I am the only child of parents who weighed, measured, and priced everything; for whom what could not be weighed, measured, and priced, had no existence" '; that his parents had deliberately mortified the family's capacity for happiness as ' "a bargain for the security of their possessions." '[129] Dorrit, Ralph Nickleby and Dombey are punished for allowing the market to commodify the 'wealth of their hearts'. Dombey loses both domestic and commercial 'houses' as a result; Pip allows money to corrupt his family relationships and ends with 'bills up in the windows'.[130]

In Dickens, the domestic can provide a refuge from the threatening com-modified outside world. While Dickensian modes of the utopian and pastoral have a strong imaginative appeal to Gissing, such wish-fulfilment should be resisted. For Gissing's art to be sincere, it must articulate his perception of experience as an enforced condition of negotiation with an outside world that is intrinsically hostile to the development of a better self.

Looking at Things

Since realist fiction therefore concerns itself with the exchanges between money and the things that it can buy, wealth's visible presence in the classic novel tends to be as property, rather than currency, as the objects, clothing and environments which provide much of the fabric of realist narration. Externals exist both contingently and as indices of (economic) meaning. 'Everything looked like money – like the last coin issued from the Mint', notes Tess, admiring the landscape of the Chase.[131] In *S/Z*, Roland Barthes reads the appearances of the material world in novels in terms of simultaneously applied codes. In realist narration, economic codes overlap with hermeneutic codes; if, as Donald L McLoskey has suggested, applied economists are like realist novelists, realist novelists are also in a sense like economists.[132]

Although money may not be a reliable signifier of value, it is, worryingly, perhaps the only one in a material world that is undergoing relentless commodification. 'By being the equivalent to all the manifold things in one and the same way', fretted Georg Simmel, 'money becomes the most frightful leveler.'[133] Harry Levin characterizes Balzac's vision of equivalence between money and the world, a technique which Henry James found so overpower-ing, thus: 'So long as values are pegged to the gold standard, taste is ruled by pecuniary canons. Balzac's shrewd insight affixes to everything its plainly marked price tag. The cost of passion can be measured in cab fares and tailor bills.'[134] Realist fiction can only partially suppress its knowledge that in a material world everything is convertible into money; for money to be visible, it must be translated back into the things that it can be or do. Ruskin protested at this technique of imaginative transformation becoming a common practice in everyday life:

> Since this commercial wealth, or power over labour, is nearly always convertible at once into real property, while real property is not always convertible at once into power over labour, the idea of riches among active men in civilized nations, generally refers to commercial wealth; and in estimating their possessions, they rather calculate the value of their horses and fields by the number of guineas they could get for them, than the value of their guineas by the number of horses and fields they could buy with them.[135]

Grahame Smith has suggested that the presence of objects as commodities in this respect is new to nineteenth-century fiction: 'money should have value only because it represents objects, but it seems more in capitalist society as if objects come to have value only because they represent money.'[136] The commodification of reality into terms of monetary value may be a social evil but it can make the world representable for the novelist and intelligible to the reader. As Rachel Bowlby has expressed it:

> The commodity makes the person and the person is, if not for sale, then an object whose value or status can be read off with accuracy in terms of the things he has and the behavioural codes he adopts.[137]

Objects are rarely only contingent in realist novels: the reader they imply uses economic codes to interpret external appearances, a method that would reach its apotheosis at the *fin de siècle* in the long narratives extrapolated from found objects and visible bodies by Sherlock Holmes.[138]

As Fredric Jameson argues, for Gissing every environment, no matter how private, is legible in terms of commodities.[139] Dickens's opposition between the market and the home is also crucial in Gissing, for it establishes a boundary that Gissing is keen to blur. In the slum dwellings and bourgeois domestic hells of Gissing's fiction, the material realities of economic life are rarely made to seem invisible. Gissing's domestic interiors are always vulnerable to the forces of natural selection that make continued survival a battle. Characters can struggle to find even the barest level of existence, in the difficulty of find-ing labour, in the difficulty of establishing an environment that allows love to survive, in the constant vulnerability of all forms of property to loss or the pawn-shop. The values that Gissing inscribes on his heroes and on the things they cherish are always contested by the nature of the world they inhabit, a world in which the free movement of the protagonist is contextualized, checked, limited and directed by a tangible, visibly present, material totality. The material objects framed by Gissing's narrative vision always meto-nymically imply a larger reality. Habitually, the nature of this reality is an unjust economy in which individual natures are crushed by hostile circum-stances. Money, or its lack, is usually the medium of the world's incursions into the vulnerable self, which fails to reach its potential. Lukàcs identifies this technique as characteristic of pre-modernist literary realism:

> Abstract potentiality belongs wholly to the realm of subjectivity; whereas concrete potentiality is concerned with the dialectic between the individual's subjectivity and objective reality. The literary presentation of the latter thus implies a description of actual persons inhabiting a palpable, identifiable world. Only in the inter-action of character and environment can the concrete potentiality of a particular individual be singled out from the 'bad infinity' of purely abstract potentialities, and emerge as the determining poten-tiality of just this individual at just this phase of his development. This principle alone enables the artist to distinguish concrete poten-tial from a myriad of abstractions.[140]

Few other novelists catalogue the financial lives of their fictional creations in such precise financial detail as Gissing: *Demos* is cited by Charles Booth as a source for learning about working-class life.[141] Gissing's recognition of the stranglehold of the possession of money on the merely quotidian life, let alone the moral or intellectual, is the keynote of his fiction. This technique provides a way of dramatizing the relationship between the environment and the self, even his own self. 'He had always been excessively self-conscious,' wrote Gissing's son Alfred, 'and could regard his own circumstances with unusual detachment.'[142] Gissing introspectively examined the circumstances that had established his own consciousness: Thomas Gissing's willed isolation of his family from the rest of his class, Gissing's classical education, his imprison-ment, his failure to achieve a successful 'emigration-ending' in America, his desires for companionship and sexual fulfilment. Gabrielle Fleury complained to Clara Collet that this made the novelist difficult to live with:

With regard to practical life, everyday life, George is like a child. Nobody – even the most fortunate – can avoid many little worries which a day brings & another takes away, but as soon as George comes in contact – immediat [*sic*] or intermediate – with one, he thinks it is due to his actual circumstances, a part of them, a thing that wld never [have] happened [had] these circumstances altered. That is the constant delusion of his mind, a product of his bad health and his deep.unpracticality.[143]

In a similar way, Gissing's work extrapolates narratives from the material environment. His narrative eye passes from individual objects, to individuals, to environments, to a larger social totality. In Gissing's diary for 1888, he carefully describes the room in which his first wife Nell died: the pictures kept from their earlier life together, the shabby furniture, worn-out clothes, lack of food, pawn tickets and empty medicine bottles, concluding, 'henceforth I never cease to bear testimony against the accursed social order that brings about things of this kind.'[144] The technique that Gissing uses in this entry, one of the longest in his diary, is also employed throughout his fiction: an interior is realistically catalogued, from which description the reader can, by imaginative extension, infer an economic and social meaning. As John Goode suggests, 'Nell was for [Gissing] a direct connection with the world of poverty, and an ineluctable symbol of the way in which nineteenth-century society crushed the individual in its universal and anarchic struggle for wealth.'[145]

Writing on Charles Dickens, Gissing suggests that objects in Dickens's fiction are not merely self-sufficient, but connected to a larger imaginative reality beyond: 'The very building and its furniture fix themselves in the mind, so described that each room, each table, becomes symbolic, instinct with a meaning which the ordinary observer would never have suspected.'[146] Gissing's realist notations are always connected to a larger thesis: objects are contextualized and defined by their relationship to existing social conditions, inequable as they usually are. This mode of vision is a pessimistic, realist extension of the 'way of seeing' Raymond Williams also identifies in Dickens's social vision: Gissing's own vision focuses on both the single consciousness of the protagonist and the totality of the world that formed it.[147] In Dickens, however, while objects and appearances can be interpreted in an economic register, they are also described to express the characters pictorially, as if they existed autonomously; a character is portrayed in terms of their clothing or their surroundings because such a description 'fits' them.[148] Such is the liberality of Dickens's imagination that there is narrative energy to spare to 'colour in' his descriptions beyond the indicial conveying of necessary information. Just as Gissing's characters are worn down by the petty contingencies of everyday economic life, so his narrative vision appears limited by a deliberate poverty of imagination, which almost exclusively denotes meaning in a specific register.[149] For Gissing, the conditions of existence translate clothing and possessions into terms of only monetary value; Gissing's characters are rendered unable to represent themselves through their appearance and their surroundings without the right sum of money that would make such self-expression possible.[150] Gissing wrote to his friend and biographer Morley Roberts:

> What I desire to insist upon is this: that the most characteristic, the most important, part of my work is that which deals with a class of young men distinctive of our time – well-educated, fairly bred, *but without money*. It is this fact (as I gather from reviews & conversation) of the *poverty* of my people which tells against their recognition as civilized beings. "Oh," said someone to Bullen, "do ask Mr. Gissing to make his people a little better off!"[151]

As the protagonists' self-expression is limited by poverty, objects that denote meaning in Gissing can be represented even as absence: the lack of a topcoat, a violin, an item of furniture or a shelf of treasured books, in the utter bareness of the destitute Candys' room, the gradual loss of objects from his lodgings noticed by Arthur Golding, or Edwin Reardon's sale of his furniture: 'These stripped rooms were symbolical of his life; losing money, he had lost everything. [...] Man has a right to nothing in this world that he cannot pay for.'[152] The pawnshop, visited by Pennyloaf Candy in an episode narrated in detail in *The Nether World*, is a frequent medium of transmission between the home and the market in Gissing's fiction. This exchange allows visible possession and currency to become the other: a French writer on London in 1888 observed that the pawnshop is 'the alpha and omega of Wapping existence – the place where you can obtain money, and the place where you can spend it.'[153] This repeated process of possession and loss is a parodic reversal of the conspicuous consumption of the upwardly mobile; money is lost on interest each time the transaction takes place.[154]

Marx and Mill both employ clothing as a metaphor for the commodity, while Carlyle, in *Sartor Resartus*, also cites the attention that society pays to clothes as evidence of its overdependence for meaning on the outwardly material.[155] Gissing is especially fond of writing his characters' clothing in the economic register, since clothes can proclaim not only wealth, poverty or mere respectability, but also movement between these states: Biffen's utterly shabby gentility, Daniel Dabbs's sudden, vulgar prosperity, Louise Derrick's obviously new bourgeois equipping of her body for entry into society.[156] One need only think of the role of clothing in *New Grub Street*, for example, as a commodity that can nearly always be exchanged with the market. To reduce expenditure, Amy refrains from purchasing needed clothing; Mrs Yule is repeatedly seen sewing. Biffen pawns his topcoat and sits indoors in his overcoat. Whelpdale's 'consumptive' bride raises funds by selling 'all she could of her clothing'. In the opening pages of the novel, Jasper's clothes are 'of expensive material, but had seen a good deal of service'; as he succeeds, he acquires better ties and a silk hat. The same significant piece of headgear is also sported by the more well-to-do Carter and young John Yule. Whelpdale's professional breakthrough is marked by 'delicate gloves; prosperity breathed from his whole person.' While John Yule harangues him, Reardon envies 'the perfection of the young man's boots and trousers.' Reardon and Biffen are unable to apply for almost any respectable job without suitable tailoring; when they receive money from Carter and Biffen's brother respectively, their first purchases are clothes. Dora and Maud are restricted in society by their small number of dresses; as a prospective heiress and a fiancée, Marian increases her attention to her appearance. The story of Biffen's friend Allen, 'who lost the most valuable opportunity of his life because he hadn't a clean shirt to put on', ominously foreshadows the money-enforced separation of the Reardons:[157]

> He had made himself as decent as possible in appearance, but he must necessarily seem an odd Sunday visitor at a house such as Mrs Yule's. His soft felt hat, never brushed for months, was a greyish green, and stained round the band with perspiration. His necktie was discoloured and worn. Coat and waistcoat might pass muster, but of the trousers the less said the better. One of his boots was patched, and both were all but heelless.
>
> Very well; let her see him thus. Let her understand what it meant to live on twelve and sixpence a week. [...]
>
> Amy had meant to offer her hand, but the unexpected meanness of Reardon's aspect shocked and restrained her. All but every woman would have experienced that shrinking from the livery of poverty. Amy had but to reflect, and she understood that her husband could in no wise help this shabbiness; when he parted from her his wardrobe was already in a long-suffering condition, and how was he to have purchased new garments since then? None the less such attire degraded him in her eyes; it symbolised the melancholy decline which he had suffered intellectually. On Reardon his wife's elegance had the same repellent effect. [...] A man must indeed be graciously endowed if his personal appearance

can defy the disadvantage of cheap modern clothing worn into shapelessness.[158]

For Gissing, the permeability of the self to shaping by economic forces can go beyond even the outer layers of clothing. Circumstances are visible on the face as physiognomy; experience shapes the body and makes it a legible text.[159] In *The Emancipated* (1890), the success of the Mallards' marriage is dependent on Miriam's face becoming like the second portrait he sketches of her; her face is a text whose meaning is immanent. Gissing, like Marx, was fond of the metaphor of 'stamping' for this process, as if the metal of the self needed to be legibly minted for it to take part in the transactions of society. In *Isabel Clarendon*, Kingcote claims that 'Circumstances are the mould which give shape to such metal as we happen to be made of. The metal is the same always, but it may be cast for mean or for noble uses.'[160]

Gissing hated the extent to which money possessed so exclusive a hold on social relations, but felt obliged to recognize and represent it; consequently, his fiction can seem intentionally limited, self-negating, even perverse. Realism, for Gissing, must involve a sacrifice of the idea of living in the transcendent, however attractive the idea of a realm beyond the material may be. For one powerfully symbolic moment in *New Grub Street*, the struggling novelist Edwin Reardon almost pierces the veil of money's universal hold on signification when he borrows a five-pound note: 'The bit of paper was crushed together in his hand. Out in the street again, he all but threw it away, dreaming for the moment that it was a 'bus ticket or a patent medicine bill'.[161] However, Reardon can only transform the paper money into signs of debased forms of commercial transaction, mass transport or quack medicine. As in *Our Mutual Friend*, the suggestion is made that money is not 'true', but that it nonetheless increasingly orders and structures social life. Very little exists that money does not condition in some way: as Sidney Kirkwood puts it resignedly in *The Nether World*, 'the world is made so; everything has to be bought with money.'[162] However, making abuses of capital in life visible in art might still be a valid use for literature. Shelley, who greatly influenced the young Gissing, wrote in the *Defence of Poetry* that:

> Poetry, and the Principle of Self, of which money is the visible incarnation, are the God and Mammon of this world. [...] The cultivation of poetry is never more to be desired than at periods when, from an excess of the selfish and calculating principle, the accumulation of the materials of external life exceed the quantity of the power of assimilating them to the internal laws of human nature.[163]

Raymond Williams has argued that the connection between realism and reality is a communal one:

> When it was first discovered that man lives through his perceptual world, which is a human interpretation of the material world outside him, this was thought to be a basis for the rejection of realism; only a personal vision was possible. But art is more than perception; it is a particular kind of active response, and a part of all human communication. Reality, in our terms, is that which human beings make common, by work or language. Thus, in the very acts of perception and communication, this practical interaction of what is personally seen, interpreted and organized and what can be socially recognized, known and formed is richly and subtly manifested. [...] Reality is continually established, by common effort, and art is one of the highest results of this process.[164]

My project is obviously influenced by different types of Marxist thinking about the relationship between literature and money, a relationship often interpreted as synecdoche for the parallel relationship between art and life. Much twentieth-century Marxist criticism, however, seems limited by an over-materialist conception of literary discourse and its relationship to ideology. Art, as Williams indicates, is not merely a reflection of life, but an articulation of it, the characteristics of whose expression may be unique and specific to the individual text. Gissing complained when his books were read more as pamphlets than as works of art; I do not propose here a separation between the value of Gissing's novels as 'documents' and their formal qualities as literary texts.[165] I will certainly be concerned with the 'materiality' of literary production, with local historical circumstances that brought Gissing's work into existence; however, I will also be discussing the specific nature of his fiction as an aesthetic discourse, hence my concern with narrative form. Consequently, the first Gissing texts that I will consider are his writings on Dickens.

2

DICKENS IN MEMORY:
GISSING'S CRITICAL WRITING

"You are still in the happy years, Arthur, when the thoughts run
but little on riches or poverty. Should you be surprised if I told you
that I was a poor man – a very poor man?"

"I should be surprised if you told me you were very poor, sir."

"You would?" repeated the other, smiling. "Would you be sorry
to hear it?"

"Very sorry, for I am sure you do not deserve to be poor, sir,"
replied the boy.

Workers in the Dawn, I, Chapter 11

George Gissing claimed that he thought Thackeray a better writer than
Dickens, that his favourite English novelist was Charlotte Brontë, and that his
own literary models as a writer were the novelists of France and Russia.[1] In
one of two introductions he wrote to *David Copperfield*, Gissing suggested that
'it is only during the last five and twenty years that, under foreign influence,
English fiction has modified its constructive methods in the direction of what
we call realism.'[2] Gissing's assessment of Dickens as a writer who owed
nothing to novels in other languages is crucial in establishing a difference
between Dickens and himself. For Gissing, the influence of Continental
novelists, even more than that of Thackeray, encourages the contemporary
writer to write as he wants to, even if it will *épater les bourgeois*. In the absence of
this influence, Dickens's fiction is, for Gissing, too restricted by the nature of
the public's artistic tastes. It was Dickens, however, against whom Gissing had
to define himself as an author. Dickens was the figure that dominated the
image of the writer in the late nineteenth-century popular imagination, as Sir
Walter Scott had in Dickens's time, although both also provided a warning of
overworking and overcommercializing their genius. In his 1901 essay
'Dickens in Memory', Gissing acknowledges the debt he owes, especially to
Dickens's representations of London: 'We bookish people have our consolations for the life we do not live. In time I came to see London with my own
eyes, but how much better when I saw it with those of Dickens!'[3] Dickens's

'way of seeing' was to persist, albeit in distorted forms, throughout Gissing's career.[4]

In a letter to Amy Catherine Wells in 1897, Gissing describes the unfamiliar task of writing literary criticism on Dickens as an 'alien subject'.[5] However, he also admitted to Eduard Bertz that 'I shall enjoy the task', and to Clara Collet:

> Dickens has not wearied me; far from that. I think more highly of him than ever. In this book, "Little Dorrit," which I have often foolishly abused, I find most admirable things on all but every page. I am much less inclined to charge him with exaggeration in his characters. I see all his artistic faults, but there remains such splendid power, & such bright energy of temper! No man writing to-day has a shadow of a claim to speak contemptuously of Dickens. He belongs to a greater race.[6]

In *Charles Dickens: A Critical Study* (1898), Gissing warns against a judgement of Dickens formed only from a childhood reading of the novels; evidently he was surprised to enjoy rereading all of Dickens's novels during 1897 as much as he had.[7] Gissing wrote to Collet, 'your remark that one's impressions of Dickens are the reminiscences of childhood is very good, & must be borne in mind. It explains a great deal of ridicule by people who do not really know what they are criticizing.'[8] Arguably, Dickens remains English Literature's most evocative writer of childhood; Pierre Coustillas and Patrick Bridgwater have noted that, in the commonplace book of Gissing's father, Dickens is by far the most-quoted author.[9] Gissing associates Dickens with his own childhood and his father, Thomas Waller Gissing, who died in 1870, the same year as Dickens, when Gissing himself was thirteen.[10] (The other writer whom Gissing associates with childhood and the memory of his father is Wordsworth – I will return to this connection later.) In 'Dickens in Memory', Gissing recalls seeing one of the parts of *Our Mutual Friend* on his father's table: Dickens is closely associated not only with Gissing's self-formation as a writer, but, through the association with a parent, with his own existence.[11] (Interestingly, under the acknowledged influence of Robert Langton's *The Childhood and Youth of Charles Dickens*, Gissing's abridgement of the *Life of Dickens* softens some of Forster's harshness in judging Dickens's own father.)[12] Gissing's anxiety about his inheritance from his literary parent involves avoidance of the aesthetic mistakes and even betrayals of the father, but also the repayment of gratitude.[13] Meditating on the theme of the 'empty chair' hitherto occupied by Gissing's father, John Goode articulates the relationship thus:

[Gissing] is a novelist whose major point of reference is Dickens. I
don't mean by this that Dickens was the greatest influence on him.
But it is Dickens who represents the specific success in the face of
which Gissing has to define himself. […] We might say that Gissing
was Gissing precisely because he was not Dickens.[14]

The ways in which Gissing chooses not to be Dickens are crucial, for it is
the mid-Victorian novel embodied by the work of Dickens that provides
Gissing with his primary fictional model, however inadequate it seems to him.
According to Gissing's *Critical Study*, the English novelists of the eighteenth
century were Dickens's 'natural inheritance' – crude and morally wanting in
contemporary terms, but nonetheless the foundation of his fictional method;
Dickens's work served as a comparable legacy for Gissing.[15] Dickens stands as
the pre-eminent example of a novelist who produced fiction both realist and
ideologically engaged, like Gissing's – but at the same time commercially
successful, which Gissing's, crucially, was not. Both writers came from lower-
middle-class backgrounds: in spite of his later reservations about the aesthetic
consequences of Dickens's class, Dickens served for Gissing and many
Victorian novelists with similar class origins as a model of successful merito-
cratic rise. Declassing economic transactions had threatened the development
of both into writers: the blacking factory for Dickens, the theft of money at
Owens College for Gissing. Much like the typical Gissing narrative in which
the self's autonomous cultural growth is jeopardized by economic need, these
experiences might have prevented either man from becoming a writer at all.[16]

It is in the earlier novels, from *Workers in the Dawn* (1880) to *The Nether World*
(1889), that Gissing's engagement with Dickensian forms of narrative is most
strongly felt. As Peter Keating has noted, in Gissing's representation of
London and the urban working-class in particular he has to engage with
Dickensian modes: 'in time I came to see London with my own eyes'.[17]
Elements of Dickens's plots, often disordered or parodied, recur throughout
Gissing's novels; Stephen Gill writes in his introduction to *The Nether World*:

> *The Nether World* certainly has a plot […] and the plot is
> Dickensian. More exactly, it is like *Great Expectations* […] viewed
> overall it is clear that most of the ingredients of the Dickens plot
> figure in *The Nether World* – mystery, a missing will, machination, an
> heiress, disappointed claimants and dubious lawyers. […] The plot
> of *The Nether World*, however, systematically and discomfitingly
> denies its parentage. […]
> In a Dickens plot, gaining or losing money can both establish
> correct order and promote virtue. Oliver Twist comes into his

inheritance and Fagin and Monks are rightly destroyed. Pip loses his, again rightly. John Harmon becomes rich, while Silas Wegg ends up being pitched into a scavenger's cart. In every case the plot identifies a hierarchy of deserving and undeserving, humbles the proud, unmasks the hypocrite, and in at least one site of domestic virtue – the new Bleak House – establishes happiness. The plot of *The Nether World* refuses all of this.[18]

In Dickens's endings, as I have argued, the final domestic utopias of love and financial independence attempt to exclude the realist material contingencies, previously narrated by the plot, that might threaten their future stability. Although these acts of exclusion seem more provisional in later novels, such as *Little Dorrit* and *Our Mutual Friend*, the terminal classification of every protagonist comprises a reckoning with the virtues (charity, fellowship, domesticity) promoted by the narrative. Franco Moretti has argued that the characteristic pattern of the *Bildung*-narrative in the English literary tradition is for the protagonist to struggle with the disappointment of his wishes before he accepts the value and place the world assigns to him. Narrative and plot conspire together to ensure the seemingly perfect 'justice' of the ending; even Little Nell's death can be seen as transcendently happy.[19] The end-directed structure of Dickens's plots thus enables values to be created virtually separate from those of the money-ordered reality in which the plot occurs, a reality finally evaded by the hero and heroine.

Gissing deliberately resists the certainty of this model of closure. He writes sarcastically of Lady Dedlock's fate:

> It is all so satisfying; it so rounds off our conception of life. Nothing so abhorred by the multitude as a lack of finality in stories, a vagueness of conclusion which gives them the trouble of forming surmises.[20]

In Gissing's work, the protagonist's worth is proved, not by his acceptance of classification, but by a lengthy struggle with circumstances followed by denial or defiance; hence the perverse 'negative identification' between moral worth and an unhappy or undeserved ending.[21] In Moretti's terms, the ending and the aim of narration are not the same; put more simply, Gissing's characters rarely get what they deserve.[22] Jacob Korg argues that 'Gissing clearly perceived the dissonance between economic and intellectual life presented by modern society, and based his systematic view of reverse justice upon it.'[23] Gissing values as authentic not the quality of adapting to the contingencies of the hostile, vulgar world, but of resisting them, hence the number of his protagonists that appear to be failures. Authenticity means retaining an ideal of conduct as true as possible to an internal, rather than public, conception of value. Often in Gissing's fiction this authenticity *is* sacrificed under pressure of circumstances. Gissing's model of *Bildung* thus always contains a structural gap between potential and fulfilment, the former articulated in the discourse and the characters' own dialogue, the latter enacted by the plot.

However, unlike a number of Gissing's European fictional models, his protagonists' martyrdom 'by the fact of possessing uncommon endowments' does not in turn establish a condemnation of the world that has failed to reward them.[24] The hero's failure in the world may be a result as much of his inability as his unwillingness to adapt to it. Narrative possibilities are limited not only by external hostility but also by internal inflexibility, by the hero's own temperament, described by *New Grub Street*'s Harold Biffen as one's 'diathesis'.[25] A protagonist may see the most rational or rewarding course of action while recognizing himself to be constitutionally incapable of it. For instance, in *New Grub Street*, the contrasting values and aspirations of Edwin Reardon and Jasper Milvain are polarized, but along an identical realist axis – what Bertz objected to as 'the consensus among [Gissing's] characters on the subject of money'.[26] Both characters acknowledge the same truths about the nature of the literary market: the difference between them is their temperamental ability to act on such knowledge. John Middleton Murry suggests that 'lack of money is hardly more than the symbol of a deeper cause of frustration [...] what is peculiar about the heroes of those novels is that they are frustrated by something more (and less) visible than their poverty'.[27] Temperaments such as that of Edwin Reardon, who possesses 'moral weakness which was allied with his aesthetic sensibility', are ill-equipped for the universe in which they exist, yet Gissing can simultaneously value the inflexibility of this kind of temperament as proof of the character's worth.[28]

Only Gissing's younger and more naive heroines, such as Emily Hood, Adela Waltham, Cecily Baske, Amy Yule and Lilian Allen, whose upbringing initially keeps them ignorant, have any illusions about the hostile nature of the world they inhabit. Indeed, many protagonists are able through a fortunate upbringing – involving a scholarship, or artistically-minded parent-figure such as Mr Tollady – to perceive better than most the nature of the material forces ranged against their aspirations. Gissing's choice of heroes with 'superfluity of sensitiveness', protagonists who apprehend both social injustice and aesthetic beauty, enables him to expose the contradictions he perceives within late-Victorian cultural conceptions of value.[29] In Constance Harsh's words, Gissing's novels provide a critique of 'a cultural system that is intrinsically hostile to the human self-development its official ideologies ostensibly promote.'[30] Often Gissing's heroes possess an encultured imagination materially at odds with the economic status given them by that upbringing, an imagination that makes so many of these protagonists artists.[31]

Barbara Hardy has suggested that in a Dickens novel, much of the inclusively panoramic plot is excluded from the ending, which 'squeezes its solace through too narrow an exit', hence the familiar objection to Dickens's work that evils attacked in the novel such as Chancery and the Circumlocution Office are left unreformed by the utopian domesticity of the endings.[32] Unlike Dickens, Gissing will not allow himself to create a narrative (en)closure perfect enough to exclude an outside world where, although small acts of effective benevolence are possible, they are almost always overpowered by the Darwinian struggle for existence that takes place around them. The given certainties against which Gissing's heroes must struggle – the vulgarity of the commercial world, the impossibility of transcending sexual difference, the entropies of physical decay, disease and death – are shown as more powerful in Gissing than in the majority of Victorian fiction. His work's immediate loyalty is to the accurate representation of 'circumstances', even more potent a word in Gissing's fiction than in Thomas Hardy's. If what is cherished by the author – high culture, unwillingness to compromise – is valued little by the world as Gissing sees it, this disjunction must be represented within the text, particularly by its ending, as a condition of the novelist's realism. Gissing is thus committed to a more sincere, less providential mimesis of material reality in which the unstable narrative elements excluded by Dickens (in order, Gissing argues, for Dickens to ensure the approval of his readers) might be incorporated.

Although Gissing's artistic and moral convictions can seem to be in conflict, his work does not simply amorally reflect reality, all moral judgement suspended.[33] If moral values cannot be upheld by the realist plot, they may be expressed in the discourse, the language that narrates it.[34] Gissing's plots do imply a shape of belief, but inversely; his fiction is morally committed, but to showing that the world is not moral. Consequently, Gissing is usually read as a largely pessimistic writer, his most significant difference from Dickens. Gissing himself argued that his apparent tendency to pessimism was a consequence of artistic fidelity, even at cost to his own commercial success. He wrote to Gabrielle Fleury, 'The English public will never *like* my books. I have not the true English note – that foolish optimism that is indispensable to popularity.'[35] Optimism should never be blindly maintained in the face of convictions to the contrary: he wrote to Bertz, 'The condition of the mass of men is one of what may be called unconscious optimism. With *consciousness*, (in the strictest sense of the word,) I am beginning to believe that the possibility of *honest* optimism ceases.'[36] Gissing would no doubt have agreed with his friend Grant Allen's claim in *The Woman Who Did* that 'Pessimism is sympathy.

Optimism is selfishness. [...] All honest art is therefore of necessity pessimistic.'[37] Gissing's realism dramatizes simultaneously the idealist assertion of value, and the realist conviction that what is valued is declining. He observed to HG Wells: 'I have a conviction that all I love & believe in is going to the devil; at the same time, I try to watch with interest this process of destruction, admiring any bit of sapper-work that is well done.'[38] Gissing faithfully catalogues material phenomena he finds wholly inimical, a kind of narrative discourse in which hopes are articulated, only to be frustrated. One might crudely represent the dialectical structure of Gissing's novels thus:

Discourse	Story
Narrator	Ending
Past	Modernity
Romance	Realism
Individual	Society
Protagonist (sensitive)	World
Idealism	Practicality
Authenticity	Pragmatism
Art	Market
Edwin Reardon	Jasper Milvain

Variations on this kind of structure can be found in other *fin de siècle* literary fiction: one might think of the enthusiastic promotion of radical modes of life, in spite of their defeat by the plot, in the discourses of novels as different as *Dracula*, *The Woman Who Did* and *The Picture of Dorian Gray*.

This structural dissonance between discourse and story, what John Sloan calls the 'disturbing indeterminacy' of Gissing's work, can make it awkward, unsettling to read, and easy to misinterpret.[39] Many readers will no doubt be surprised to find such apparently highly opinionated writing as Gissing's being described as 'indeterminate', but the author's apparent sympathies can seem as inconsistent as he perceives the world to be. Such visible contradictions have led critics to adopt some unhelpful perspectives on the apparent instability of Gissing's work, and to conclude that the disturbing effects his work produces are unintentional or to ascribe them to the biographical fallacy that has plagued much work on Gissing, as though Gissing's desire to dramatize the circumstances of his own life is consistently stronger than the limits of his form or his artistic conscientiousness.[40] His fiction may draw on autobiographical material, but that does not make his art autobiography. In his lifetime, Gissing frequently expressed his frustration at being misread by readers and critics, complaining that his intentions were imperfectly understood, trying to rectify mistaken judgements in his letters. He wrote to Gabrielle Fleury, '*My motives are too subtle*. You know that I constantly use *irony*; & this is never understand [*sic*]; it is all taken in the most stupid literal sense.'[41] Partly for this reason I draw extensively here on Gissing's letters as a primary source; declared authorial intention is by no means an infallible guide to the success of a work, but it might at least help to guard against some fallacies of interpretation.

This difficulty of locating an authorized position in Gissing's work presents a crucial methodological hurdle to interpreting it. For instance, critics both in Gissing's own time and since frequently attribute views to Gissing which are expressed in a character's speech. Even HG Wells, who could perceive the distance between Gissing and *Born in Exile*'s Godwin Peak, failed to read as ironic Harvey Rolfe's celebration of Kipling at the end of *The Whirlpool* (1897).[42] Gissing, however, repeatedly avowed a separation between his personal voice and that of his text:

> The character Godwin Peak is obviously, in a great degree, sympathetic to the author. But you will not find that Peak's tone is to be henceforth mine – do not fear it. Indeed, it seems to me that the tone of the whole book is by no means identical with Peak's personality; certainly I did not mean it to be so. Peak is myself – one phase of myself. I described him with gusto, but surely I did not, in depicting the other characters, take *his* point of view?[43]

Gissing complained in a letter to the *National Observer* in 1894 that 'the novelist is often represented as holding an opinion which he has simply attributed to one of his characters.'[44] Gissing grants his characters full freedom of expression; while the conservative narrator can attempt to influence the reader by commenting on the other characters' dialogue, such pronouncements do not have the full force of an omniscient 'Voice of Authority'. Gissing's narrators and characters are given comparable autonomy; the former is never to be explicitly identified with the authorial position. Indeed, his narrators are rarely reliable judges of character and can even give the impression of actively disliking certain characters.[45] Christina Sjöholm rightly observes that Gissing's 'tendency to people his novels with representatives of different, juxtaposed or balancing opinions to ensure a many-sided treatment of an idea, without judging or overtly revealing where his sympathies lay, is still an overpowering problem to his critics.'[46] Fredric Jameson suggests of Gissing that 'it is as though, in a world of reified language, even the author's own personal language cannot be genuine any longer, and comes before us as virtually Flaubertian mimicry of received ideas of a disembodied, floating sort.'[47] Gissing's polyphony is thus another element of his work that can make it uncomfortable to read: Virginia Woolf noted the tendency of Gissing's work to leave the reader 'completely baffled'; Ruth Capers McKay observes that 'the reader is often in a quandary as to whether to applaud or condemn.'[48]

In *New Grub Street*, Edwin Reardon confesses to padding his novels with dialogue since it makes them easier to write quickly.[49] Nonetheless, the technique of granting the speech of his characters such freedom makes Gissing's imagination arguably more 'dialogic' than that of any other nineteenth-century English writer of fiction. Gissing was arguably the earliest English novelist to be influenced by Dostoevsky, whose *Crime and Punishment* he declared 'magnificent'.[50] Bakhtin's account of Dostoevsky's use of literary parody is reminiscent of Gissing's ironic narration of alienated heroes in parodic versions of Dickensian plots:[51]

> Literary parody, on the other hand, strengthens the element of literary conventionality in the narrator's discourse, depriving it even more of its independence and finalizing power in relation to the hero. In subsequent works as well, this element of literary conventionality, and the various forms used to expose it, always served to intensify greatly the direct and autonomous signifying power of the hero and the independence of the hero's position.[52]

Gissing's use of heteroglossic language allows him to dramatize differing perspectives on a subject (such as socialism, say, in *Demos*, or writing in *New Grub Street*) without producing an authorized, definitive conclusion. Gissing wrote to his sister Ellen, 'There is a satiric vein in "The Emancipated" which, to those conservatives who understand it, will make the book rather acceptable than otherwise. (This you evidently missed.) It comes of the fact that I am able to look at both sides, & to laugh at the weaknesses of both.'[53]

Gissing's narrative voice is certainly more heavily ideologically inflected than Mikhail Bakhtin seems to find Dostoevsky's; however, Gissing's work shares many of the qualities of the Dostoevsky novel lauded by Bakhtin in *Problems of Dostoevsky's Poetics*. Gissing's own views and those of a character can overlap, of course, but such a character is not a 'vehicle for the author's own ideological position'. Both novelists are concerned with 'the position of the déclassé intellectual and the social wanderer' and 'struggle against a *reification* of man, of human relations, of all human values under the conditions of capitalism.' Dostoevsky and Gissing perceive 'the contradictory nature of evolving social life': as I have suggested, contradiction is a principle of Gissing's representation of life, as long as he perceives life to be so. The voices of characters in a novel can be given equal weight to the author's own, and as a consequence of this polyphonic quality, the 'novel is *multi-accented* and contradictory in its values; contradictory accents clash in every word of his creations.'[54] Utterances within Gissing's multi-accented novels are contextual, and may be contradictory: 'is there such a thing in this world', the narrator of *The Nether World* wonders, 'as speech that has but one simple interpretation, one for him who utters it and for him who hears?'[55] Bakhtin also champions 'the organic combination of philosophical dialogue, lofty symbol-systems, the adventure-fantastic, and slum-naturalism' in the menippea; the first and last of these are especially prominent in Gissing's work.[56] (The other two elements are less visible perhaps due to their close association with Dickensian sentiment: carnival is also largely absent from Gissing, except ironically).[57]

Irony and parody are essential elements of Gissing's technique as a novelist. Narrative conventions that Gissing as a critic viewed as a means of social control are present in his fiction, but in a distorted shape. Virtuous characters are rarely protected and rewarded by Providence, but are either crushed by the unforgiving world, or made to barter their virtuous passivity for self-alienating, pragmatic activity. Bakhtin describes the change in the nature of the hero in the transition from epic to novel thus:

> The capitalist world is also not idealized, its inhumanity is laid bare, the destruction within it of all ethical systems (which had been formed at earlier stages of development), the disintegration of all previous human relationships (under the influence of money), love, the family, friendship, the deforming of the scholar's and the artist's creative work and so forth – all of these are emphasized. The positive hero of the idyllic world becomes ridiculous, pitiful and unnecessary, he either perishes or is re-educated and becomes an egoistic predator.[58]

Wills and legacies appear in nearly every Gissing novel, including the first seven, but usually do not reward protagonists, satisfyingly closing their narrative, but rather propel them into still greater instability.[59] The revelation of concealed parentage is always mis-timed, even irrelevant (*The Unclassed, In the Year of Jubilee, Sleeping Fires*). Philanthropic projects provide only partial or temporary relief against the totality of the social forces ranged against them, and may even cause harm rather than good (*Workers in the Dawn, Demos, Thyrza, The Nether World*). A couple may realize their love for each other but be divided by circumstance for a long time or even permanently (*Isabel Clarendon, Born in Exile, The Odd Women, Sleeping Fires*). As Fredric Jameson suggests, 'the early Dickensian "solutions" turn out to produce fresh problems and contradictions in their turn'; it is as if Gissing is directly addressing fictional conventions with the reasonable objection that real life, sincerely depicted, does not square deserts with reward.[60] For that reason, Gissing's work is perhaps at its strongest when it is engaging with the logic of failure rather than with the happy contingencies of success: AW Ward praised Gissing's 'infinite pity for those who fail'.[61] Gissing wrote in *The Private Papers of Henry Ryecroft*: 'I see no single piece of strong testimony that justice is the law of the universe; I see suggestions incalculable tending to prove that it is not.' Gissing shared in Hardy's belief that 'A perception of the FAILURE of THINGS to be what they are meant to be, lends them, in place of the intended interest, a new and greater interest of an unintended kind.'[62]

Gissing's negative model of closure is justified in his own critical writing as an artistic commitment to speaking the truth, a more authentic artistic technique than the insincere concealment of unpalatable truths committed not only by his successful predecessors Dickens and Thackeray, but also by his more commercially minded contemporaries. Gissing felt it the duty of the artist to represent life without such censorship, and was vexed by criticism of his choice of subject matter.[63] Frederick W Farrar, Archdeacon of Westminster, objected in his review of *The Nether World* to the defence that:

> such realistic pictures are excusable only on the plea of Art for Art's sake. That 'such things are' is not, in itself, an adequate excuse for dragging them into publicity. That a dunghill exists, or that a beggar's foot is dirty, is no sufficient reason for painting them.[64]

Gissing insisted that the choice should be that of the artist alone; the selection of an unpleasant aspect of real life should not detract from the value of the resulting work of art as long as the work of art has been expressed with sufficient truthfulness and craftsmanship. 'Sincerity I regard of chief importance', Gissing wrote in the 1895 essay 'The Place of Realism in Fiction': his ideal of 'sincerity' justifies Gissing's gloomy plotting and perplexing inversion of generic narrative conventions. In this essay, Gissing rejects both the adoption of deliberately congenial subjects and pseudo-scientific objectivity in favour of a (perhaps overstated) realism that is founded on the artist's faithful depiction of the material world he perceives around him:

> Realism, naturalism, and so on signified an attitude of revolt against insincerity in the art of fiction. Go to, let us picture things as they are. Let us have done with the conventional, that is to say, with mere tricks for pleasing the ignorant and the prejudiced. Let the novelist take himself as seriously as the man of science; be his work to depict with rigid faithfulness the course of life, to expose the secrets of the mind, to show humanity in its eternal combat with fate. No matter how hideous or heartrending the results; the artist has no responsibility save to his artistic conscience. The only

question is, has he wrought truly, in matter and form? The leaders of this revolt emphasised their position by a choice of vulgar, base, or disgusting subjects; whence the popular understanding of the term *realist*. [...] It is commonly supposed that novelists of this school propound a theory of life, by preference that known as 'pessimism.' There is but one way out of this imbroglio: to discard altogether the debated terms, and to inquire with regard to any work of fiction, first whether it is sincere, secondly, whether it is craftsmanlike.[65]

Realism is thus the accurate portrayal by the artist of the world as the artist sees it; if the resulting work is gloomy it is because the artist finds the world so. Gissing wrote to John Northern Hilliard, 'If my stories are pessimistic, it is because my life is such. My environments were sordid, the people were sordid, and my work is but a reflection of it all.'[66] This is a rather ingenuously narrow aesthetic, ruling out Dickensian use of coincidence, the supernatural or humour in order to secure a happy ending or other generic expectation should the artist not 'behold' such forms of success in reality. There are to be no easy escapes through coincidence or even benevolence in Gissing's own fiction, for he rarely saw such things in his own life, and used what he perceived as the actual contingencies of life to thwart the insincere conventions of art. Gissing's emphasis on personal sincerity, by definition subjective, rejects both the pure determinism of Zolaesque scientific objectivity and Flaubert's claims to have withdrawn personality from narration altogether:

What the artist sees is to him only a part of the actual; its complement is an emotional effect. Thus it comes about that every novelist beholds a world of his own, and the supreme endeavour of his art must be to body forth that world as it exists for him. The novelist works, and must work, subjectively. A demand for objectivity in fiction is worse than meaningless, for apart from the personality of the workman no literary art can exist. [...] What can be more absurd than to talk about the 'objectivity' of such an author as Flaubert, who triumphs by his extraordinary power of presenting life as he, and no other man, beheld it? There is no science of fiction. However energetic and precise the novelist's preparation for his book, all is but dead material until breathed upon by the 'shaping spirit of imagination,' which is the soul of the individual artist. Process belongs to the workshop; the critic of the completed work has only to decide as to its truth – that is to say, to judge the spirit in which it was conceived, and the technical merit of its execution.

Realism, then, signifies nothing more than artistic sincerity in the portrayal of contemporary life; it merely contrasts with the habit of mind which assumes that a novel is written 'to please people,' that disagreeable facts must always be kept out of sight, that human nature must be systematically flattered, that the book must have a 'plot,' that the story should end on a cheerful note, and all the rest of it.[67]

Gissing's formulation of literary production is both materialist ('workshop') – after reading Trollope's *Autobiography*, Gissing reportedly admitted that 'all artistic work is done, to a great extent, mechanically' – and romantic, echoing Coleridge in 'the "shaping spirit of imagination"'.[68] To bring about the material's 'emotional complement' in the reader, the author must tell the truth in a way that is both craftsmanlike and sincere:

> Reflect on the laws of fiction. Into a page the writer must concentrate what in nature is boundless; his business is not to report life *in extenso*, but to convey to another mind some impression which it has made upon his own. If he do this honestly and capably, then his work is "true".[69]

The form of Gissing's fiction is produced by the parodic interaction of narrative forms inherited, largely, from Dickens, with a 'sincere' representation of experience as the world's violation and limitation of the essential self, a process mediated largely through economic life.[70] Structurally, Gissing's fictions appear to be as end-directed as traditional English Victorian plots; yet the notorious unhappiness of Gissing's endings focuses the reader's attention more on the narrated social processes that bring such endings about. Unlike the typical Victorian narrative template suggested by Moretti, Gissing's evaluation of the worth of a particular individual is at odds with that of society; in Gissing's novels the classification enacted by the ending tends to dramatize the failure of the self to resist the narrow path marked out for it by the world. For Gissing, the valuation assigned by society (society in general, that is, rather than a cultured elite) is not, on the whole, to be trusted. If a protagonist is valued by the narrative, his interpellation by the external world is insufficient, and should be resisted (although this is less true of Gissing's later work). Gissing's dissonant model of *Bildung* draws more on a private than a public conception of value. He wrote in the Preface to his 1895 revision of *The Unclassed*:

With regard to the title, which has sometimes been misunderstood, I should like to say that by "unclassed" I meant, not, of course, *déclassé*, nor yet a condition technically represented by the heroine. Male and female, all the prominent persons of the story dwell in a limbo external to society. They refuse the statistic badge – will not, like Bishop Blougram's respectabilities, be "classed and done with."[71]

Society's habitual set of categories does not 'fit' Gissing's alienated protagonists; his endings in particular illustrate not harmony, closure and successful categorization, but dissonance, openness and instability.

Tonight I finish "Isabel Clarendon"! I have done my utmost to make the story as realistic as possible. The ending is as unromantic as could be, & several threads are left to hang loose; for even so it is in real life; you cannot gather up & round off each person's story.[72]

In the same novel, the narrator's voice makes an extraordinary disavowal of knowledge, offering a defence of a novelistic technique which can potentially leave the reader baffled and frustrated:

He who is giving these chapters of her history may not pretend to do much more than exhibit facts and draw at times a justifiable inference. He is not a creator of human beings, with eyes to behold the very heart of the machine he has himself pieced together; merely one who takes trouble to trace certain lines of human experience, and, working here on grounds of knowledge, there by aid of analogy, here again in the way of bolder speculation, spins his tale with what skill he may till the threads are used up. [73]

James Ashcroft in *The Academy* compared Gissing to James in his objection to the loose threads in the ending of *Isabel Clarendon*.[74] Gissing shared with James a distaste for the over-determinations of the endings of much nineteenth-century fiction, and for the omniscience of its narrators. (Interestingly, when James met Gissing he thought him 'quite particularly marked out for what is called in his and my profession an unhappy ending.' [75] James wrote this, unwittingly, on the day Gissing died.) While Gissing resisted Dickens's exclusion of material for reasons of self-censorship, like James he disliked fiction which provided too much unnecessary information. Gissing wrote to his brother Algernon in 1895:

It is fine to see how the old three-vol. tradition is being broken
through. [...] It is the new school, due to continental influence.
Thackeray & Dickens wrote at enormous length, & with profusion
of detail; their plan is to tell everything, to leave nothing to be
divined. Far more artistic, I think, is this later method, of merely
suggesting; of dealing with episodes, instead of writing biographies.
The old novelist is omniscient; I think it is better to tell a story
precisely as one does in real life, – hinting, surmising, telling in
detail what *can* so be told, & no more. In fact, it approximates to the
dramatic mode of presentment.[76]

In *Isabel Clarendon*, produced during the mid-1880s, when most of Gissing's
fiction had a proletarian setting, the characters' motives are frequently made
inaccessible to the reader. The novel's over-sensitive protagonist, Bernard
Kingcote, moves to the country to escape the vulgarity of the urban world,
but is soon bored by his solitude, until meeting the eponymous heroine. The
novel appears to become a love story, like, as David Grylls notes, nearly all of
Gissing's novels; however, its central characters are eventually divided by
both circumstances and temperament.[77] Isabel appears to be rich; in fact, her
dead husband's malicious will is going to disinherit her in favour of Ada
Warren, who may be Clarendon's illegitimate daughter. Kingcote has to
leave Knightswell to care for his sister when she is left penniless by the death
of her commercial-traveller husband; Isabel's essential worldliness and Kingcote's temperamental inability to act with masculine forcefulness eventually
bring the engagement to an end. Isabel marries instead the prosperous lawyer
Robert Asquith, and Kingcote becomes the manager of a bookshop owned by
his artist friend Clement Gabriel. Perhaps the central characters are better off
for ending apart: Isabel, who had grown up poor, confesses more than once
her weakness for preferring the kind of society life that requires a high
income. It is hinted that Kingcote might eventually marry Isabel's sullen ward
Ada Warren, who genuinely shares his cultural interests, and who finally gives
her inheritance back to Isabel, feeling that she neither deserves nor needs it.
Like the truth of Ada's parentage, whether their marriage takes place is not
definitely confirmed by the novel.

Like many of Gissing's heroes, Kingcote's education has made him a less,
rather than more, effective social being: he advises his sister against trying to
pay for an education for her children if they will never have the income to live
up to it. "Of no greater unkindness can parents be guilty than to train as if for
a life of leisure children whose lot will inevitably be to earn a livelihood by
day-long toil." Kingcote is both admirably and morbidly sensitive; his exclusion from the society of Knightswell proves, perversely, his worth. Kingcote's

good qualities and the qualities that cause him to suffer are the same; conventional novelistic notions of rewarding the just and punishing the wicked are thwarted. Society is portrayed in this novel as essentially violating the self; Gissing's use of paradigms that he inherits from such a society's literature is therefore parodic.

Kingcote, as with other of Gissing's protagonists, frequently perceives what his best course of action should be, but feels incapable of taking it: he is 'devoid of energy, and morbidly contemplative', suffering from 'dangerous passiveness'. He is estranged not only from society, but also from himself: 'there is nothing I hold more in horror than the ghost of my former self. I deny identity'.[78] Gissing perceives late-Victorian society to be unstable and contradictory; he views the self as similarly unstable, in spite of similar claims to consistency and wholeness. Even in a school essay written in his late teens, he censures Richardson's creation of Clarissa: 'Hers is a life conducted in unvarying obedience to principles laid down, and is therefore unnatural.'[79] In the notebook which he used in America after release from prison, Gissing wrote, '*Consistency* in a bad or foolish course is *not* meritorious. I had rather have a man who preaches an absurd doctrine and violates it in practice, than one who is consistent in following such a course.'[80] Michel Ballard suggests that in *Born in Exile* Gissing 'does not view man as a flat figure with clear-cut motives but as a complex knot of conflicting influences each striving for supremacy.'[81] Gissing's selves are thus not only in conflict with hostile external circumstances, but are internally divided, even stubbornly so. In *Heredity*, which Gissing read in 1889, Théodule-Armand Ribot claimed that:

> The person, the ego, the thinking subject, assumed as a perfect unity, is but a theoretic conception. [...] Our personality breaks up into an infinity of sensations, sentiments, images and ideas, past or future; it is only a synthesis, an aggregate, a sum that is ever undergoing addition and subtraction, but of which the whole reality is in the concrete events which compose it.[82]

The narrator writes of Bunce in *Thyrza*, 'like all who are most genuinely at odds with the world, the first head of his quarrel was with himself.'[83] The *Times* reviewer of *Born in Exile* was perplexed by the novel's lack of 'consistency of characterization'; for Gissing (especially in this novel), both a character's and the narrator's knowledge of the self is of necessity limited, and so the self does not appear consistent to either.[84] Omniscience must be artistically insincere, for it cannot really exist in life.

Revising Dickens: *Charles Dickens: A Critical Study*

Gissing began his work on Dickens when his own critical reputation had at last begun to improve, and as Dickens's continued to decline following attacks made in his lifetime by critics such as George Lewes, James Fitzjames Stephen and the young Henry James.[85] Yet Dickens was still being widely read, if not by professional literary critics, then by the succeeding generation of novelists and by large numbers of ordinary readers. George Ford has claimed:

> If even during the eighties and nineties (supposedly the nadir of Dickens' literary status), the sales increased rather than declined, the only real question was [...] by whom were the books being read? One could answer that they were being read by Gissing and Conrad, Kipling and Hopkins, Swinburne and Henley, the aging William Morris and the young George Bernard Shaw.[86]

Gissing read Dickens enthusiastically when young and he exhorted his siblings to do the same; according to one schoolfellow, he read *Nicholas Nickleby* in a single Sunday afternoon.[87] He bought *Barnaby Rudge* and *Martin Chuzzlewit* in parts in 1878, reread *Little Dorrit* and *Our Mutual Friend* in 1882, *Great Expectations* and *David Copperfield* in 1888 and *Dombey and Son* in 1889.[88] In spite of Gissing's disavowal of Dickens as a literary role model, and of the conspicuous differences between their oeuvres, the resemblances between the two writers are sufficiently evident that comparisons between them remain a commonplace. Gissing's first published novel, *Workers in the Dawn* (1880), heavily parodies Dickens; the uncharacteristically comic novel, *The Town Traveller* (1898), written immediately before *Charles Dickens: A Critical Study*, takes its title from a Dickens essay and heavily imitates Dickens's robust comic style.[89] Even eighteen years apart, both *Workers in the Dawn* and *The Town Traveller* have 'improbable' plots of the kind that Gissing the critic deplored in Dickens; the later book even uses a family resemblance like that in *Bleak House*. (The narrator's lack of sympathy for the characters and the ironic reversals of the ending are, of course, all Gissing's own.) Throughout his work, Gissing remains in dialogue with Dickens, creatively arguing with the tensions between Dickens's realism and moral purpose, particularly in fiction's representation of money, and in the final determinations of the ending.

In his excellent study of Gissing's literary context, Adrian Poole accounts convincingly for Gissing's declared preference for Thackeray.[90] Peter K Garrett has also suggested that:

> Thackeray and Dickens share a strong sense of conventional patterns, types, and forms, but Dickens's symbolic imagination

tends to work through inherited forms like the mystery plot, intensi-
fying and reinterpreting them, while Thackeray works against
them, resisting their clear arbitrariness and attempting to displace
and discredit them in his effort to reveal a truth they obscure.[91]

Gissing's ironic relationship to 'inherited forms' is much closer in this respect
to Thackeray's than Dickens's. Yet most Gissing critics, including Poole,
inevitably compare Gissing more frequently to Dickens than Thackeray, or
indeed to any other single writer. For all of Gissing's distaste for aspects of
Dickens's writing, it is Dickens to whom Gissing is closer in his choice of both
subject matter and moral purpose. Thackeray provides instead a model of
truthfulness in his pose of indifference to public reaction:

> The Art of Fiction has this great ethical importance that it enables
> one to tell the truth about human beings in a way which is
> impossible in actual life. [...] Thackeray's moral usefulness is
> especially great in that respect.[92]

Gissing's relationship with Thackeray is admiring but distant compared to
his closer, far more complex relationship with Dickens.[93] Thackeray's settings
in 'the world of rank and fashion and wealth' and ironizing self-dramatiza-
tions are far removed from Gissing's painstaking articulations of moral value
in the face of multiple, hostile, contradictory realist convictions.[94] Thackeray's
career as man of letters began after he had dissipated his aristocratic patrimony; Dickens's self-fashioning as a professional novelist began much closer
to Gissing's own lower-middle-class origins. The narrative of Dickens's own
life even served as a model of (artistic) virtue rewarded: Gissing claimed that
Forster's *Life*, which he later revised, had been a constant source of artistic
inspiration to him:

> Well, this it was that stirred me, not to imitate Dickens as a novelist,
> but to follow afar off his example as a worker. From this point of
> view the debt I owe him is incalculable. Among the best of my
> memories are those moments under a lowering sky when I sought
> light in the pages of a biographer, and rarely sought in vain.[95]

As Poole notes, the *Critical Study* and the collected Rochester Prefaces *The
Immortal Dickens* are 'as interesting for what they reveal to us of Gissing's own
point of view, prejudices, sympathies, as for their insight into Dickens.'[96]
For Gissing, to write about Dickens means writing about art, money, class,
morality, education and women, just as writing a novel involves addressing

the same themes. (Perhaps surprisingly, given the other preoccupations of Gissing's fiction, his critical writing contains no discussion of Dickens the popular journalist and editor, nor of the end of Dickens's marriage.)

For Gissing, the creation of a much larger reading public by the Education Act in the year of Dickens's death means that Dickens's popularity belongs to a different historical era entirely.[97] Gissing, as much as any writer of his generation, felt it impossible both to retain the artistic autonomy of the post-Romantic literary writer and to succeed as a producer of marketable commodities. He wrote to his first agent, William Morris Colles:

> The idea is to depict Dickens as a man of the early Victorian time –
> to estimate his work as an artist, as a philanthropist, as a democrat.
> For this judgement the time seems to have come. I may say that I
> shall write in a distinctly sympathetic tone, & be throughout very
> favourable to the *man*, though discreetly critical of the *novelist*.[98]

Nonetheless, Gissing does tend to write less sympathetically about Dickens and his audience than the authors of other contemporary studies.[99] Gissing's fiction set among the lower class often implies a reader who is more culturally sophisticated than its subject; in the *Critical Study*, he imagines Dickens writing for a public that is less discerning (at times, exaggeratedly so) than the implied reader of the *Critical Study*:

> We are educated, we are cultured; be it so; but, to say the least,
> some few millions of us turn with weariness from pages of concen-
> trated art. Fifty years ago the people who did *not* might have been
> gathered from the English-speaking world into a London hall, with-
> out uncomfortable crowding. [100]

Gissing's central difficulty in evaluating Dickens is the older writer's failure to match contemporary aesthetic standards. Gissing's historicizing of Dickens attempts to relativize him out of responsibility to such standards, to make him the artistic representative of an age 'clearly distinguishable from our own', yet to evolve more discriminating tastes.[101]

> So great a change has come over the theory and practice of fiction
> in the England of our times that we must needs treat of Dickens as,
> in many respects, antiquated. To be antiquated is not necessarily to
> be condemned, in art or anything else (save weapons of slaughter);
> but as the result of the last chapter we feel that, in one direction,
> Dickens suffers from a comparison with novelists, his peers, of a

newer day, even with some who were strictly his contemporaries. We have now to ask ourselves in what other aspects his work differs markedly from our present conception of the art of novel-writing. It will be seen, of course, that, theoretically, he had very little in common with the school of strict veracity, of realism – call it what you please; the school which, quite apart from extravagances, has directed fiction into a path it is likely to pursue for many a year to come.[102]

At the same time as Gissing finds fault with Dickens's numerous artistic failures, he attempts to do justice to Dickens's strengths within an alternative set of aesthetic categories. Dickens's genius is never questioned, especially when *The Pickwick Papers* is discussed. Gissing does portray Dickens as artistically sincere within a world view otherwise sadly limited by class, history and the prudish tastes of his audience. A constant in his account is Dickens's embodiment of the class for whom he writes.[103] Gissing imagines a lower middle-class Dickens eager to rise, who observes:

> in a spirit of lively criticism, not seldom of jealousy, the class so rapidly achieving wealth and rule. He lived to become, in all externals, and to some extent in the tone of his mind, a characteristic member of this privileged society; but his criticism of its foibles, and of its grave shortcomings, never ceased.[104]

Before the more polarized reading public that had transformed the conditions for literary production, it was economically and artistically possible for the most accomplished practitioner of the novel in England to be the most popular as well. The fissure between commercial success and artistic integrity, such an important theme in Gissing's own work and in *New Grub Street* especially, has yet to open. Dickens's successful internalizing of the values of his reading public accounts for both his refusal to challenge the agreed limits of literary decency and his popular success:

> Dickens […] never desired freedom to offend his public. Sympathy with his readers was to him the very breath of life; the more complete that sympathy, the better did he esteem his work. Of the restrictions laid upon him he was perfectly aware, and there is evidence that he could see the artistic advantage which would result from a slackening of the bonds of English delicacy; but it never occurred to him to make public protest against the prejudices in force. Dickens could never have regarded it as within a storyteller's

scope to attempt the conversion of his readers to a new view of
literary morals. Against a political folly, or a social injustice, he
would use every resource of his art, and see no reason to hesitate;
for there was the certainty of the approval of all good folk. To write
a novel in a spirit of antagonism to all but a very few of his country-
men would have seemed to him a sort of practical *bull*; is it not
the law of novel-writing, first and foremost, that one shall aim at
pleasing as many people as possible?[105]

Dickens's polemics on, say, child labour, which Gissing applauds, surely
contradict his supposed representativeness of a bourgeois-industrial class;
however, Gissing's conception of Dickens's 'instinctive sympathy with the
moral (and therefore the artistic) prejudices of the everyday man' allows him
partially to excuse Dickens for failing to challenge the boundaries of what it is
permissible to show in literature.[106] The gulf between what is congenial for the
artist and what is congenial for the public was painfully felt by Gissing,
especially at the beginning of his career; for Gissing's Dickens, such a gulf
simply did not exist. (The controversy with Thackeray over the accuracy of
Oliver Twist and the satirizing of Podsnap's literary tastes would in fact seem to
suggest otherwise, however.) The Dickens imagined by Gissing sees no
contradiction between artistic and commercial considerations, since sales are
the criterion of artistic success: Gissing cites Forster's *Life* on Dickens finding
fault in himself, rather than the public, for the relative failure of *Martin
Chuzzlewit*.[107] In contrast to Gissing's claim that the duty of the artist is to
represent reality accurately even at the cost of affronting bourgeois taste,
Dickens's main aim is to entertain his public. Gissing notes with his habitual
later distaste for the theatre Dickens's youthful desire to become an actor, and
attributes to this aspect of his personality Dickens's unfortunate need for 'the
stimulus of praise.'[108] Several times Gissing effectively impugns Dickens for
betraying the duty of the artist by softening the fidelity of his representations
rather than offend his readership (Thackeray and 'the great big stupid public'
thus being a useful contrast); but such charges are usually mentioned only for
them to be immediately withdrawn.[109] Especially in the more generous
Rochester Prefaces, collected in *The Immortal Dickens*, Gissing seems resigned
to the power of Dickens's writing in spite of his aesthetic strictures against its
weaknesses. Art, after all, can only ever be art and not life.

As soon as a writer sits down to construct a narrative, to imagine
human beings, or adapt those he knows to changed circumstances,
he enters a world distinct from the actual, and, call himself what he
may, he obeys certain laws, certain conventions, without which the

art of fiction could not exist. Be he a true artist, he gives us pictures which represent his own favourite way of looking at life.[110]

Compared to present-day fiction, Dickens's art is narrower but deeper: even within self-imposed limits on the portrayal of what he sees, he still 'saw more than ordinary people.'[111] Like Robert Buchanan, another less than whole-hearted admirer, Gissing continually praises Dickens nonetheless for the magnificence and power of his vision:[112]

> Assuredly few men have known so well how to use their eyes. A student is commonly inobservant of outward things; Dickens, far from a bookish youth, looked about him in those years of struggle for a livelihood with a glance which missed no minutest feature of what he saw. We are told that his eyes were very bright, impressing all who met him with a sense of their keenness. Keen they were in no ordinary sense; for they pierced beneath the surface, and (in Lamb's phrase) discerned the *quiddity* of common objects. Everything he looked upon was registered in his mind, where at any moment he could revive the original impression, and with his command of words, vital, picturesque, show the thing to others.[113]

If Dickens, albeit mistakenly, believed that this penetrating but limited vision constituted 'reality', then Gissing can permit the novelist's mimesis of this vision to be, at least, 'sincere', and hence artistically acceptable. 'Dickens's art is consistent with itself. And arts mean illusion, in different degrees, of various kinds.'[114] Dickens is thus reconstructed as an antirealist, or even aesthete:

> Our "realist" [...] holds that truth, for the artist, is the impression produced on *him*, and that to convey this impression with entire sincerity is his sole reason for existing. To Dickens such a view of the artist's duty never presented itself. Art, for him, was art precisely because it was not nature. [...] Admitting his limits, accepting them even gladly, he was yet possessed with a sense of the absolute reality of everything he pictured forth.[115]

Polemic may still be contained within these aesthetic limits if the novelist sees and represents something that is unfamiliar to Dickens's readership, such as abuses in Chancery, or Yorkshire Poor Schools (which Langton credits Dickens with single-handedly closing down).[116] Although one chapter of the *Critical Study* is entitled 'The Radical', Gissing does not overplay the egalitarianism of Dickens's politics, even claiming him as an antidemocrat.[117] Shrewdly, Gissing locates instead Dickens's impulse for change in ethics rather than politics: 'morally he would change the world; socially, he is a thorough conservative.'[118]

Such a vision of Dickens as a representative of his class is an enforced over-simplification, a monologic historicizing of the kind from which Gissing him-self would later suffer. However, he feels such reductivism necessary to make Dickens's writing palatable to the present-day reader with a stricter awareness of what 'our grave Art of Fiction' requires, as if, for Dickens, 'modern laws of fiction did not exist; a story was a story, not to be judged by the standard of actual experience'.[119] Weighed according to rules of late nineteenth-century realism such as organic unity, accuracy without caricature and minimal authorial intervention, Dickens's novels uniformly fail: *Martin Chuzzlewit*, for instance, shows 'how little the characteristic merit of Dickens's writings has to do with their completeness as works of art'.[120] Many passages of the *Critical Study* patronize Dickens's writing, or damn him with such faint praise. In a 1902 book review, however, Gissing recognized Dickens's unique separate-ness from such considerations, his effective immunity from dismissal by the cultural elite:

> By the multitude he is read as ever he was, with delight in his strong characteristics, regardless of his prominent defects; the intelligent read him, in spite of a severity of criticism such as no other novelist has undergone and survived.[121]

Since the passage of time has destroyed the perfect harmony between author and public of Dickens's own times, Gissing is left to explain how the novels continue to be read and enjoyed. In attempting to solve this dilemma, Gissing departs from his earlier historicized view of Dickens as a man of his time, lapsing into a clichéd appeal to Dickens's sense of 'universal humanity', praising his 'unexampled buoyancy of spirit, an unfailing flow of the healthiest mirth, the kindliest humour'.[122] A *fin de siècle* readership will indulge outdated social criticism and improbabilities as great as the plot of *Bleak House* or as pedantically mild as David Copperfield's fellow passengers believing him to have eaten all his 'cutlets', for the sake of Dickens's humour, 'the supreme quality of his genius'.[123] Gissing even laments the lack of humour in *Barnaby Rudge*, and, perhaps surprisingly, finds fault with Dickens's didacticism when moral purpose is *not* subordinated to amusement: 'It is when indignation gets the upper hand, and humour is lost sight of, that he falls into peril of uncon-sciously false sentiment.'[124] (Gissing does, however, praise parts of *Little Dorrit* for suggesting 'the kind of novels Dickens might have written without his humour'.[125])

Dickens's acceptance of the limits imposed on his fiction by the tastes of his audience ultimately proves a strength in respect of his use of humour. Self-censorship produces a comic vision whose formal method is the selective control of detail: 'novels such as those of Balzac are said to be remorseless studies of actual life; whereas Dickens, it is plain, never pretends to give us life itself, but a selection, an adaptation.'[126] Dickens's portrayal of Mrs Gamp entertains because it omits the lethal realities of her professional incompetence; we laugh at the Marchioness starving in a cellar because of the 'farcical extravagance' of the stray detail of ' "two square inches of cold mutton". [...] If he had avoided exaggeration, and shown us the ragged, starving child swallowing the kind of meal which was really set before her, who could have endured it?'[127] Dickens's selectivity is prevented from a fragmentary lack of unity by the individual vividness of the parts:

> Language cannot do more in the calling up of a vivid image before the mind; and this result is mainly traceable to the writer's humorous insight. There could be no better illustration of the difference between Dickens's grasp and presentment of *a bit of* human nature, *a bit of* observable fact, and that method which the critics of to-day, inaccurately but intelligibly, call photographic.[128]
> (italics mine)

Humour, therefore, is not a way of making palatable the artist's intended didactic effect, for an artist should never aim at 'effect': this term is consistently associated with Dickens's unfortunate affinity for the cheap appeal of the theatre.[129] Dickens's selectiveness functions instead as a kind of synecdochic typology, in which the reader identifies a lifelike type by distinguishing exaggerated details: Dickens 'can sublimate the essentials of a marked type of character, exaggerate peculiarities in the boldest way, emphasize to the last degree points of mind or behaviour.'[130] The effect on the reader may be recognition of a more extensive truth, but such recognition must be only partial, or the effect would be neither humorous nor, perhaps, publishable. Dickens's use of caricature is a kind of literary charity; the omission of potentially shocking details, and correspondingly grotesque overemphasis on what remains will not alienate his readership: 'avoidance of the disagreeable, as a topic uncongenial to art – this is Dickens's principle.'[131]

Gissing is much harsher on Dickens's depiction of that which he did not behold in reality, such as social types with whom he had no actual contact, like the Cheerybles. There is no place either in Gissing's view of Dickens for an appreciation of the supernatural or the fantastic; even Dickens's use of coincidence is censured for violating rules of probability:

> In the fable of *Bleak House* there is much ingenuity, but an almost total disregard of probability; the fitting of incidents suggests a mechanical puzzle rather than the complications of human life; arbitrary coincidence takes the place of well-contrived motive.[132]

Twentieth-century critics have argued that the coincidences of *Bleak House* reinforce the mythic, powerful status of the Jarndyce will and the corruption at the heart of the novel; yet Gissing attributes this kind of plotting to loss of artistic control:[133]

> I have left it to this place to speak of the sin, most gross, most palpable, which Dickens everywhere commits in his abuse of "coincidence". *Bleak House* is the supreme example of his reckless-ness. It seems never to have occurred to him, thus far in his career, that novels and fairy tales (or his favourite *Arabian Nights*) should obey different laws in the matter of incident.[134]

A defender of Dickens might draw attention to Dickens's incorporation of fairy-tale motifs within realist fiction as an artistic strength rather than a weakness.[135] The imagining of what Dickens, in the Preface to *Bleak House*, famously called 'the romantic side of familiar things' allows the greater freedom of the romantic to contest the near-certainty of what Gissing determines as 'probable', fairy-tale motifs providing generic escapes from constrained 'realist' situations.[136] Under the heading 'Growth of Man and Writer', near the beginning of the *Critical Study*, Gissing gives a more judicious account of:

> that habit of mind which led him to discover infinite romance in the obscurer life of London. Where the ordinary man sees nothing but everyday habit, Dickens is filled with the perception of marvellous possibilities. Again and again he has put the spirit of the *Arabian Nights* into his pictures of life by the River Thames. [...] He sought for wonders amid the dreary life of common streets.[137]

'The dreary life of common streets' is a phrase more characteristic of Gissing's own work than Dickens's: GK Chesterton astutely remarked that the world described by the first chapter of the *Critical Study* 'seems infinitely less hard and cruel than the world described in Gissing's own novels.'[138]

Gissing is less than fair in censuring Dickens's seeming improbability, since when plotting a novel not even Gissing himself can avoid fiction's manipulation of apparent contingency; his rare happy endings in particular often feel rather contrived. For Gissing, Dickens's abuse of coincidence to bring about the consolation of a happy ending is plot's conspiracy with discourse to uphold the bourgeois values of Dickens's audience: 'to follow the path of the just is to ensure a certain amount of prosperity, and reward unlimited in buoyancy of heart.'[139] English fiction's master of the unhappy ending repeatedly expresses his discomfort with the contrivances of Dickens's plotting, and with his endings in particular: 'the art of adapting simple probabilities to the ends of a narrative he never mastered.'[140] (This is a also frequent complaint even from Victorian critics more favourable to Dickens). Unsurprisingly, Gissing finds the altered, happier ending of *Great Expectations* 'imbecile'.[141]

Just as his novels expose and collapse the weaknesses he perceives in Victorian literary convention, Gissing's critical revisions of Dickens late in his own career constitutes an assertion of his personal aesthetic of artistic 'sincerity'. Consequently, one of the most compelling aspects of Gissing's version of Dickens is the image of Dickens stories as rewritten by Gissing: Sam Weller 'deformed with no little coarseness'; the Cheerybles' casual benevolence doing more harm than good; *Dombey and Son* ending with the death of Paul; Mrs Gamp ill-treating and robbing her charges; Mrs Micawber 'worn out by anxieties' and 'her children growing up in squalor'; a calculating Little Em'ly 'acting with something like cold-blooded deliberation'; Mr Mell who 'sank from stage to stage of wretchedness, and died lamentably in the street or the workhouse'; Mr Micawber 'the terror of his acquaintances, [ending] in squalid misery'; Lizzie Hexam foul-mouthed and low-minded; Boffin 'a miser in reality'; *Edwin Drood* containing 'neither mystery nor murder'; most preposterously a Tiny Tim who '*did* die'.[142] Even the Autobiographical Fragment does not escape Gissing's revision:

> Dickens's biographer makes a fanciful suggestion that the fact of his having observed low life at so tender an age (from ten to twelve) accounts for the purity of tone with which that life is treated in the novelist's works. I shall take a different view of Dickens's method in this matter; it is not to be supposed for a moment that the boy, familiar with London on its grimiest side, working in cellars, inhabiting garrets, eating in cookshops, visiting a debtors' prison (his father was in detention for a time), escaped the contamination of his surroundings.[143]

Perhaps one lasting consequence of this early degradation is Dickens's apparent willingness to compromise for the sake of money. Gissing pays jaded tribute to Dickens's ability to combine 'the characteristics of true artist and man of business': as an embodiment of his class, the successful artist is also a 'brilliant example of the self-made man'.[144] After finishing the *Critical Study*, Gissing was also asked to write a volume on Thackeray, but he declined, feeling he should keep himself before the public gaze as a novelist and nothing else (although a letter to Edward Clodd suggests that the payment offered would not make the project worthwhile).[145] Gissing's view of Dickens's last years seems to be that his mentor ought to have done the same, instead of performing crowd-pleasing readings, 'shortening his life that he might be able to leave a fortune to his family.'[146] Forster confirms that Dickens left an estate worth £93,000.[147] The inheritance Gissing himself received from his literary parent was to prove continually troubling to him; his own novels repeatedly try to settle the account.

3

POVERTY AND IMAGINATION:
THE EARLY NOVELS

Was du ererbt von deinen Vätern hast,
Erwirb es, um es zu besitzen.
(What you have inherited from your forefathers you must first win
for yourself if you are to possess it.)
               Goethe, *Faust*, I, l. 682, quoted in Arthur Schopenhauer,
                                             Essays and Aphorisms

Revising Dickens: *Workers in the Dawn*

In 1897, Gissing stressed the historical distance between Dickens's novels and
present-day fiction; writing his first published novel *Workers in the Dawn* in
1880, he was still more directly preoccupied with, in Goode's words, not
being Dickens. 'One cannot of course compare my methods & aims with
those of Dickens', Gissing wrote to Algernon: he felt excluded from Dickens's
close identification with the values of his readership.[1] As the mouthpiece,
rather, of no class, excluded by his painful self-consciousness, his failure to
achieve substantial commercial success, his unhappy idealism, his periodic
avoidance of Society, his unsuitable marriages and his criminal record,
Gissing's writing articulates values that are openly antithetical to those of the
mass reading public, as the title of Gissing's lost novel *Mrs Grundy's Enemies*
suggests.[2] However, the genre in which such values are expressed are still in
some respects overtly Dickensian, albeit often negatively. Throughout the
early novels, the consolations of Dickens's fictive remedies of coincidence,
benevolence and the legacy are comprehensively refused. Even the day most
sacred to Dickens as potently symbolic of charity and all that is best in human
nature is mercilessly parodied in the description, irrelevant to the plot, of the
Pettindunds' bestial Christmas and the cheerless Christmases of Gissing's next
novel *The Unclassed*.[3]

    In *Workers in the Dawn*, Gissing may not be always fully in control of his
material, a complaint he would later make of Dickens; this early novel dramatizes the failure of Dickensian energy to overcome and contain the narratable.

Arthur Golding achieves nothing, either artistically or politically; Helen Norman's philanthropic schemes are terminated by her premature death from an inherited disease. The novel's structure refuses to reunite and resolve its disparate elements: Dickensianly named characters such as Mark Challenger or Lizzie Clinkscales disappear into the anonymous vortex of the metropolis, instead of being collected and narrated to a close within the final chapters.[4] Even Gissing's descriptive language shows the attrition of its energy by late nineteenth-century life:

> His countenance was decidedly grotesque, and, as he ate, which he did voraciously, he twisted it into such a variety of extraordinary shapes that, had it not been for the absence of spectators, one would have believed he was doing it to excite amusement.[5]

No amusement, however, is generated for the reader or imaginary spectator; a Dickensian effect is half-attempted and left deliberately incomplete. Orlando Whiffle is characterized, like many of Dickens's 'flat' characters, by a running joke, his inability to complete a pamphlet, but the joke is lifeless, and fails. Whiffle's large family evidently owes something to the Pocket household, but without the comic anaesthesia of Dickens's selective control of detail:

> The following was the tableau: in the centre stood Mr. Whiffle, his coat thrown off, his hair more stubbornly self-assertive than ever, in the act of administering corporal punishment to his first-born, Master Augustus Whiffle. With one arm he had secured the lithe youngster in that position which is technically known as "chancery," while the other hand, armed with a schoolmaster's cane, descended with alarming rapidity upon the most sensitive portion of the captive's frame. From every pore of Mr. Whiffle's body the perspiration streamed profusely, and, not content with the violence of his muscular exertion, he was engaged in the hopeless task of endeavouring to drown with his own voice the yells of his struggling victim. Poor Mrs. Whiffle, a very little, inoffensive-looking woman, from whose eyes the tears were streaming at the sight of young Augustus' sufferings, was doing her best with cries and entreaties to mitigate her husband's wrath, whilst at the same time it was all she could do to exercise surveillance over the other seven children.[6]

The reader senses Dickensian detail such as Whiffle's 'self-assertive' hair trying, and failing, to overcome the insistent physical realities of the boy's screams, the mother's tears and the kitchen laid waste. (*Bleak House* may also be echoed perhaps in the reference to 'chancery'.[7]) The reader sees later in this novel the consequences of Augustus's under-supervised upbringing in his gambling, debts, hypocrisy and fathering of Carrie's child; in *Great Expectations*, the careers of the young Pockets are an omitted detail.

The Dickens plot that Arthur Golding's narrative resembles most closely is that of *Oliver Twist*. Unlike Dickens's orphan, however, Arthur *is* corrupted by the poverty of his surroundings. He reacts with hostility to the kindness of this novel's Brownlow-figure, Mr Norman, and escapes back to a London that Gissing rewrites more 'realistically'. Like Oliver, he is helped by country-dwellers, and ruthlessly exploited in the city. The criminal who adopts Arthur, in Fagin's role of mock-benefactor, is a fraudster who exploits the public's charity by pretending to be blind, a perversion of the Christian meaning of the 'lilies of the field' that are the subject of his choice of song. Only Blatherwick's intoxication eventually allows escape: Arthur's earlier savage beating is a 'realistic' rewriting of Oliver's unlikely victory over Noah Claypole.[8] Like Oliver, Arthur hopes to become a bookseller; however, while Oliver is rescued from the need to labour by Brownlow's money, Arthur's narrative is suspended long enough for him to learn a trade. Lack of money constantly threatens to eliminate any process of *Bildung* from Arthur's narrative. His story is full of dead ends: it appears as though Arthur is to be allowed to develop by being educated first by the Normans and then by Lizzie Clinkscales; these possibilities are forestalled by Arthur's ungrateful if realistic reaction against benevolence and by Mrs Clinkscales's disapproval.[9]

Gissing does permit one happy coincidence to unite Arthur with Tollady, a benevolent Dickensian father-figure who houses and educates him.[10] This kind of good luck, which also reunites Arthur with his inheritance, rarely lasts in Gissing, however, and in this instance hostile circumstances are unable to overcome even money. Unlike Dickens's Cheerybles, Tollady is subjected to 'realistic' economic competition in business, and anxiety over a debt contracted to help an ungrateful family member brings about his premature death. Arthur has sufficient money to settle the debt, but bad timing and Gresham's sexual jealousy, incidentally unpunished by the book's ending, prevent him from doing so. The fact that the owner of Tollady's debt, John Waghorn, will later marry Maud Gresham, the daughter of Arthur's father's executor and the best friend of Helen Norman, the woman with whom Arthur will fall in love, is also structurally irrelevant, never reincorporated into the plot. In contrast to Dickens's (ab)use of coincidence, there is no providential ordering to bind the plot together: Arthur neither learns of nor confronts Carrie's connection with his childhood neighbour Augustus Whiffle, but only encounters its consequences. The connection is revealed to the reader, but unenforced by the plot: the deliberately unsatisfactory nature of the book's plotting shows Gissing's rejection of the controlled structuring of the classic Victorian novel.

In a pattern that is to be repeated throughout Gissing's career, characters such as Helen Norman argue convincingly in the dialogue for Art and social reform as authoritative moral values, while the plot ultimately conquers success in such aspirations, however noble or deserving they may be. (Henry James's *The Princess Casamassima*, published five years later, dramatizes a very similar situation, with a protagonist sensitive to both aesthetic beauty and social inequality, who fails to resolve his conflicting loyalties).[11] Gissing was appalled by social injustice, especially when younger, but argues as a condition of 'realism' that no wholesale political or utopian solution is feasible. Partial remedies, chief among them education, may be possible, but the inertia and selfishness of human nature forbid any social reorganization on a grand scale. The poor, for Gissing, should remain a separate class, but preferably be rather less brutish and degraded than they are at present: as Woolf, Orwell and David Grylls have all noted, Gissing is as sincere in his revulsion from the poor as in his sympathy for them.[12] Lacking Dickens's religious faith in moral perfectibility, or even Zola's positivist belief in the entire determination of character by environment, Gissing's politics are informed instead by a Schopenhauerian pessimism about the ability or even the willingness of the world to fulfil the desires of the self. According to Gabrielle Fleury, Gissing:

> always maintained that *Zola* is an *idealist* & an optimist as he believes in the possibility of amelioration & moral progress by social reforms, & I do not. To me moral progress & real changes wld be possible only by a thorough revolution in the heart of men. [13]

'We can only mark with regret how the philanthropist in [Dickens] so often overcame the artist', Gissing complained in his Preface to *Bleak House*.[14] Art and philanthropy frequently compete for the hero's attention in Gissing's earlier novels, but neither is viable in the world unless their intrinsic idealism is tempered with pragmatism. In *Thyrza* (1887), the heroine shares a surname and fate with Little Nell; however, the lives of the other characters are in practice made more productive and independent by the death of the idealized too-good-to-be-true heroine. In *A Life's Morning* (1888), art and politics must be subordinated to love in the happy ending on which Gissing's publisher insisted. In *Workers in the Dawn*, Helen argues persuasively that Arthur should give priority to his genius for Art over his urge for social reform, but neither value makes any effective difference to the novel's plot. *Workers in the Dawn*'s third volume does not transform the novel into a *Künstlerroman* that dramatizes Arthur's ultimate success; nor, for that matter, does it ever argue wholeheartedly for slum clearance and working-class education. (*The Unclassed* partially makes such a case, but the latter comprehensively fails in *Thyrza*.) The picture of 'The Palace of Art' never fulfils Golding's and Helen's ambitions for his genius, and even their love affair is forestalled by her discovery of his previous marriage. The plot seems to make generic promises to the reader, and then realistically refuse them, as if the fulfilment of such expectations would be insincere. As in the later *Born in Exile*, the hero's ultimate receipt of a legacy does not enable an immediately happy ending, but merely prolongs the epilogue before the protagonist's unhappy death abroad; Helen's premature death is a further irony given that Arthur would soon be a widower and free to marry her. All the elements for a happy ending are present: Gissing's antiprovidential, ironic ordering of circumstance deliberately brings them into the wrong conjunction. The novel's dialogic structure allows Gissing's ideological convictions to be articulated (this novel places particular emphasis on whether characters are speaking sincerely or not), but they are not redeemed or upheld by the pessimistic realism of his plot.

In Gissing's Schopenhauerian essay 'The Hope of Pessimism', written in 1882 but left unpublished in order not to offend Gissing's friend and employer, Frederic Harrison, Gissing rejects positivist meliorism in favour of a limited, unambitious ethics of altruism, and above all, mutual pity before the void as the only successful means of tolerating human existence.[15] The term 'idealism' in Gissing's early novels usually signifies something valuable but esteemed so little by the world that it is destined to fail: this is arguably the central theme of *Thyrza*.[16] Gissing's novels consistently dramatize the failure of idealism in the face of 'practicalities', while making the case that such ideals should nonetheless exist and be cherished. Gissing was an idealist both politically, in his cherishing of ideals of art and human happiness, and also philosophically in believing that the appearances of the perceptual world are not necessarily constitutive of reality. Treasured idealizations, such as the belief that art is in itself valuable or that love can survive in an essentially selfish social world, may be false, but existence in such a world is barely tolerable without them. However, at the same time, Gissing's materialism was robust enough to maintain that the perceptual world is the one that the self must live in all the same, and that therefore ideals have to negotiate with the actual business of existence.[17] In 1880, Gissing wrote to his sister Margaret:

> It will be a great part of my work through life to preach the fostering of *ideals*, in every sense of the word. It is because the vast majority of people have now no ideal at all, but live in mere gratification of tastes & appetites, that our social state is still so miserable, so far from that moderate perfection which the best natures are able to

conceive. Do your best to develop a clear ideal of what your life & thought should be, and then struggle to realise it. You never *will*, completely; but the mere struggle is everything.[18]

Forms of Development: *The Unclassed*

Gissing's next published novel, *The Unclassed* (1884), is less panoramic than its predecessor, but shows Gissing continuing to engage with Dickensian narrative conventions, especially in its deliberate use of the hackneyed plot-devices of an inheritance and a Family Romance. The twee benevolence of Ida's garden party and her cleaning of a slum tenement are also in a conspicuously Dickensian mode. However, Gissing again refuses to endorse the evaluative moral economy of the Dickens ending in which 'the good character must be good in spite of everything, or the Ruler of the universe seems dishonoured.'[19] The uncharacteristically happy ending of *The Unclassed* signals its own improbability, and indicates how easily hero and heroine might have ended differently. The narratable elements excluded from Dickens's confined moral closures remain visible at the close of this novel.

The plot which Gissing appears to rework in *The Unclassed* is that of *Bleak House*; but the transformation of this novel's Tom-all-alone's is so singular as to have little social impact beyond the individual case that it dramatizes. The symbolism of *Bleak House* connects Tom-all-alone's not only to the rest of the novel's London, but also to the Condition of England:

> But he has his revenge. Even the winds are his messengers, and they serve him in these hours of darkness. There is not a drop of Tom's corrupted blood but propagates infection and contagion somewhere. [...] There is not an atom of Tom's slime, not a cubic inch of any pestilential gas in which he lives, not one obscenity or degradation about him, not an ignorance, not a wickedness, not a brutality of his committing, but shall work its retribution through every order of society up to the proudest of the proud, and to the highest of the high. Verily, what with tainting, plundering, and spoiling, Tom has his revenge.[20]

For Gissing, however, the very isolation of the slum from the city which surrounds it, that which makes Jubilee Court a slum in the first place, insulates the upper worlds from such retribution; there is only small or no possibility of connection. In *Bleak House*, Richard Carstone may die, but only after he has morally compromised himself by pursuing the Jarndyce inheritance; Julian Casti's misery and death are more conspicuously unjust.

Dickens's philanthropic virgin Esther becomes Gissing's benevolent whore Ida; Waymark undergoes a far worse ordeal in Jubilee Court, near-crucifixion by the bestial Slimy, than any suffered by the virtuous in *Bleak House*. The most conspicuously unjust desert in *Bleak House*, Esther's disfigurement by smallpox (the physical details of which are elided by Dickens as they never would be by Gissing, who would also never permit its implausible reversal), is ironized into a just one in *The Unclassed*. 'The slums have avenged themselves,' declares the narrator when the same disease seeks out the slum-owner Abraham Woodstock in the chapter 'A Late Revenge'.[21]

The novel's hero is first seen working as a teacher at a school with the parodically Dickensian name, Tootle's. This job, as the fate of Egger proves, is no more remunerative than waiting on tables. (Gissing supported himself by private tutoring while writing *The Unclassed*.) Teaching is nonetheless a profession, thus maintaining Waymark's class-status of a gentleman: he may be seen to embody a parodic male version of the governess narrative (he gives Ida Starr a copy of *Jane Eyre*).[22] Like Nicholas Nickleby, Waymark morally objects to the exploitation of someone at the school (Smike/Maud Enderby); however, unlike Dotheboys Hall, the school is not improved by the manner of Waymark's leaving it, but remains just as bad.

Whereas in Dickens lack of money can generate the instability necessary to begin a narrative, in many of Gissing's novels poverty causes a functional inertia that retards further development of plot. Lack of money and plot development exist in mutual antagonism within *The Unclassed*: poverty, the novel's subject, threatens to overwhelm the form. Gissing wrote to his brother (perhaps rather pointedly, given Algernon's own restless changing of jobs): 'The grievously unhappy men are those who have no definite place in society, & in consequence no regularity of income, no social intercourse of the wholesome kind.'[23] A novelist himself, Waymark aestheticizes real lives into stories, but expects to have no narrative at all himself because of his own lack of money and temperamental inability to acquire it. His own story might be different from how it is; instead, for lack of money, it must fail to develop. At the beginning of the novel, Waymark claims that money strips the transactions that constitute realist narration of moral value:

"What is a fellow to do to get cash? […] I'm growing sick of this hand-to-mouth existence. Now if one had a bare competency, say two hundred and fifty a year, what glorious possibilities would open out. The vulgar saying has it that 'time is money'; like most vulgar sayings putting the thing just the wrong way about. 'Money is time', I prefer to say; it means leisure, and all that follows therefrom. Why don't you write a poem on Money, Casti? I almost feel capable of it myself. What can claim precedence, in all this world, over hard cash? It is the fruitful soil wherein is nourished the root of the tree of life; it is the vivifying principle of human activity. Upon it luxuriate art, letters, science; rob them of its sustenance, and they droop like withering leaves. Money means virtue, the lack of it is vice. [...] Give me a thousand pounds to-morrow, and I become the most virtuous man in England. Why? Because I shall satisfy all my instincts freely, openly, with no petty makeshifts and vile hypocrisies, which alone are the constituents of vicious habit. To scorn and revile wealth is the mere resource of splenetic poverty. What cannot be purchased with coin of the realm? First and foremost, freedom. The moneyed man [...] buys culture, he buys peace of mind, he buys love."[24]

The plot punishes Waymark for his sophistry, but the hero's recognition of the monetary basis of the best things in life, even love, is otherwise unopposed in the novel. Gissing problematizes the love affair between Waymark and Ida Starr, the novel's heroine, as far as the plot can bear, leaving a probably happy ending suspended in a moment of almost Jamesian irresolution. Earlier, Waymark had heartlessly digressed upon the theme of the prostitute in fiction:

"Love is the supreme in human life; and love brought to market, the temple of ecstatic worship degraded to a house of entertainment for the merest bodily need, the ideals of a young girl's heart little by little corroded and envenomed and blotted out by the reeking mists of debauched imagination, the fair bodily form corrupting with the degradation of the soul and metamorphosed to a horror, – what has earth to show more rich in artistic suggestion than this?"[25]

Gissing's own tone, however, is neither so melodramatic nor so unsympathetic as this; the crude allusion to Wordsworth's 'On Westminster Bridge' even makes Waymark sound rather a philistine. Gissing, after all, had himself fallen in love with and married a prostitute, albeit unhappily. The narration of Ida's early development shows far more understanding and sympathy than Waymark's heartless typology, exposing how much her status is the result of economic circumstances beyond her control. Society is unable to furnish Ida with a morally decent living, and she has nothing else to barter but the virtue automatically rewarded in Dickens's fiction. Compared to Dickens's sternness towards Nancy, Martha and the inhabitants of Urania cottage, Ida's representation by this (male) writer surpasses the 'tart with a heart' archetype to which she obviously appeals.[26]

Ida's and Waymark's initial meetings are dependent on Ida's income as a prostitute: she insists on being treated as economically independent and on paying her share of their expenditure. Waymark, however, feels himself to be feminized by this relation, especially when, in a mocking rewriting of Victorian certainties of virtue and closure, the prostitute becomes an heiress. The union between Ida and Waymark is prevented first by his lack of money, and then by her surplus of it. Waymark had previously seen Ida's narrative as resisting closure for lack of money:

> "Well, are you thinking how you can make a book out of my story?" [...]
> "I must wait for the end of it," he returned, holding out his hand, which she did not take.
> "The end? – Oh, you must invent one. Ends in real life are so commonplace and uninteresting."
> "Commonplace or not," said Waymark, with some lack of firmness in his voice, "the end of your story should not be an unhappy one, if I had the disposing of it. And I might have – but for one thing."
> "What's that?" she asked, with sudden interest.
> "My miserable poverty. If I only had money, – money," –
> "Money!" she exclaimed, turning away almost angrily. Then she added, with the coldness which she did not often use, but which, when she did, chilled and checked him, – "I don't understand you."[27]

Despite his pose of moral surrender to economic realities, Waymark is in fact still repelled by Ida's pollution by money. Even after she ceases to be a prostitute, Waymark feels trapped by the convention that a Victorian man may raise a woman's class with his money, but cannot accept money from a woman of a class lower than his own.[28] Waymark thus initially resists the happy ending that both he and Ida deserve:

> "You have every opportunity of making for yourself a good social position. You will soon have friends, if only you seek them. Your goodness will make you respected. Indeed I wonder at your remaining so isolated. It need not be; I am sure it need not. Your wealth – I have no thought of speaking cynically – your wealth must –"
> "My wealth! What is it to me? [...] I would give all I possess for one kind word from you. It will be a curse to me – unless you share it."[29]

Their union is also threatened by the characteristic 'two women' pattern of Gissing's fiction: Waymark has already become engaged to one of his own class. In the later *A Life's Morning*, Beatrice Redwing generously sacrifices her engagement to Wilfrid Athel so he can marry Emily Hood, whom he really loves. Waymark and Ida's union, however, is enabled more fortuitously by Maud's fear of hereditary insanity and her self-negating, religious piety. Gissing often genders religious fervour as feminine (like *Bleak House*, *The Unclassed* dramatizes the irrelevance of organized religion to dealing with the social problems it represents). But for Maud's change of heart, Waymark might have ended as unhappily married as his friend Casti.

Also, perhaps surprisingly, Gissing denies his hero a happy ending until Waymark alters some of his opinions about art. Like many couples in Gissing, Ida and Waymark, and Waymark and Maud as well, fall in love over books, music and landscape. Ida recognizes Waymark's allusion to *Twelfth Night* without knowing its origin; the initial pretext for continuing their intimacy is that he will lend her books. However, after Ida renounces prostitution to become, with evident symbolic resonance, a laundress, she finds, like Arthur Golding, that she has little energy for reading following a day's manual labour. The token of bourgeois culturation, the piano, vanishes from the interior of her home (catalogued with Gissing's characteristically Hogarthian precision); the only reminder of any culture is the fairy-tale name of her cat, Grim.

Without leisure that is funded either by prostitution or independent wealth, art cannot console, nor can beauty be 'the solace of life'. Waymark is a novelist, and Casti a poet, but neither are successful; the latter's classical epic is burnt by Harriet before even being published. The allusions to Keats around Casti function as ironic commentary on the historical distance between them, as great as that between Old and New Grub Street:

> "You'll laugh at me," Julian went on, "but isn't there a certain resemblance between my case and that of Keats? He too was a drug-pounder; he liked it as little as I do; and he died young of consumption. I suppose a dying man may speak the truth about himself. I too might have been a poet, if life had dealt more kindly with me."[30]

If Keats were alive today, the novel seems to hint, he would never even get into print. Casti echoes 'Ode to a Nightingale' when he asks Waymark to procure him an 'opiate', yet the drug will not provide him with the epiphany of a creative dream-state, but the illusory, poisonous gratification of the commercialized patent medicines on which his trade largely depends.[31]

Harriet justifies her destruction of Julian's poem by claiming that Art is worthless unless it has provable practical use or monetary value.[32] *The Unclassed* shows high cultural forms as repeatedly marginalized by baser economic realities. As for *Workers in the Dawn*, Gissing denies the reader's expectation of a *Künstlerroman*. Waymark's inheritance is spent on publishing his novel; its commercial failure is as predictable as that of Biffen's *Mr Bailey, Grocer* in *New Grub Street*, or even of *Workers in the Dawn*. For all its veracity, the effect of Waymark's novel in the real world will be negligible if no-one reads it. (Gissing himself was not to achieve a sizeable readership until *Demos* in 1886.) Waymark therefore rejects Dickensian popularity in valorizing an Art that exists only for itself, not for popular consumption:

> "This introduction to such phases of life will prove endlessly advantageous to me, artistically speaking. Let me get a little more experience, and I will write a novel such as no-one has yet ventured to write, at all events in England. I begin to see my way to magnificent effects; ye gods, such light and shade! The fact is, the novel of every-day life is getting worn out. We must dig deeper, get to untouched social strata. Dickens felt this, but he had not the courage to face his subjects; his monthly numbers had to lie on the family tea-table, which is emphatically *not* the place where you will find anything out of the common. Not *virginibus puerisque* will be my lay, I assure you, but for men and women who like to look beneath the surface, and who understand that only as artistic material has life any significance. Yes, that is the conclusion I am working round to. The artist is the only sane man. Life for its own sake? – no; I would drink a pint of laudanum tonight. But life as the source of splendid pictures, inexhaustible material for effects – *that* can reconcile me to existence, and that only."[33]

As Gissing's letters attest, this attitude has much in common with his own youthful aesthetic beliefs.[34] Yet Waymark's declarations lack Gissing's sense of social responsibility. Waymark's voice, Gissing suggested in a letter to Algernon, is not the same as the author's:

> You evidently take Waymark's decl[aration] of faith as my own. Now this is by no means the case. Waymark is a *study of character*, and he alone is responsible for his sentiments. Do you not perceive this in the very fact of that *contradiction* in the book of which you speak? If my own ideas are to be found anywhere, it is in the practical course of events in the story.[35]

The reader is as shocked as Woodstock by Waymark's bad taste when he heartlessly aestheticizes Ida's 'whole story [as being] a rather uncommon one, full of good situations'; the actual events of the novel's plot undercut Waymark's aesthetic detachment, and the happy ending ultimately proves him mistaken.[36] Waymark's credo is tested when he supplies his art with both subject matter and money by rent-collecting, a union of artistic vocation and immoral occupation. Such a form of labour is dependent on accumulated capital and social inequality, and therefore morally obnoxious. In fact, Waymark conspicuously fails to live by his professed creed. He foregoes his own commission and, like Dickens's Pancks, allows poor tenants to postpone payment. Waymark's actual practice in life, as opposed to his theories of art, resembles conventional human sympathy more closely than his declared naturalist detachment.

Getting too close to his subject matter, the artist is dragged into and imprisoned within his material by 'one of the chief characters', Slimy.[37] In a singular display of eloquence, Slimy justifies his actions with ethics effectively equivalent to Waymark's. The horrific ordeal is not even the outcome of malice: Slimy wishes to end his life with a single enjoyable experience, and only bad luck, the loss of a key through a hole in a trouser-pocket, prevents the rent-collector's release.

> "Fifty year [...] an' not one 'appy day. I was a-thinkin' of it over to myself, and, says I, 'What's the reason on it?' The reason is, 'cos I ain't never 'ad money. Money means 'appiness, an' them as never 'as money, 'll never be 'appy, live as long as they may."[38]

Only after physical torture does Waymark reject pure aestheticism, realize that he is in love with Ida, and conclude that while art might exist for art's sake, life should be lived for its own sake, not art's. Artist or not, Waymark's egotism must be punished (later in Gissing's career, the humbling of egotism becomes arguably the predominant theme of his short stories.) The plot of *The Unclassed* does therefore seem to dramatize a more conventional moral economy of reward and punishment. Virtues are articulated in the discourse and for once are only threatened, rather than defeated, by the plot. Gissing hated social evils such as landlordism; for all his revulsion from the poor and pessimistic despair at the power of politics or philanthropy to effect significant change, he felt sufficiently passionate about this theme to allow the plot of this novel to advertise against this abuse of accumulated capital. As late as the 1898 *Critical Study*, he wrote:

When, in the end, Mr. Casby has his impressive locks ruthlessly shorn by the agent risen in revolt against such a mass of lies and cruelty and unclean selfishness, we feel that the punishment is inadequate. This question of landlordism should have been treated by Dickens on a larger scale; it remains one of the curses of English life, and is likely to do so until the victims of house-owners see their way to cut, not the hair, but the throats, of a few selected specimens.[39]

The ending of *The Unclassed* negotiates an uncomfortable truce between Gissing's representations of society, money and virtue, as perhaps he recognized in an uneasy disclaimer in the Preface to the revised 1895 edition: 'The narrative [...] should be read as narrative pure and simple. Romance has no moral.'[40] Although the relationship between Ida and Waymark was initiated by one uneconomic, selfless act, Waymark's gift to the starving prostitute, it is ultimately underwritten by Woodstock's money, whose origin, narrated in the chapter 'Antecedents', is money-lending, gambling and pawnshops. In Dickens, such dirty money would have to be lost or morally cleansed by the likes of a Boffin before becoming an acceptable reward. In Gissing, nearly every legacy has a comparably tarnished pedigree, reminding the reader that inherited money must still have been gained somewhere. Waymark and Ida's happy ending is paid for by another's unscrupulous conduct. Waymark's sophistry is overturned, but it remains the case that virtue is dependent on financial comfort: as O'Gree puts it, ' "There's no behaving like a gentleman on twenty-five pounds a year." '[41] The negotiation for a happy ending here is successful, but problematized, and the numerous obstacles that Gissing places in the way of his protagonists emphasize the singularity, the mere contingency, of this particular ending. There remain in London unreformed slums, unfulfilled gentlemen and unhappy prostitutes outside the specific events of this narrative: 'chance alone had thus raised [Ida] out of misery'.[42]

You Can't Take it With You: *Demos*

At the beginning of *The Unclassed*, Waymark appears to endorse Karl Marx's famous conception, in 'The Power of Money in Bourgeois Society', of money as the sole agent in a capitalist society that is capable of fulfilling the imagination's desires:

If I long for a particular dish or want to take the mail-coach because I am not strong enough to go by foot, money fetches me the dish and the mail-coach: that is, [money] converts my wishes from something in the realm of imagination, translates them from their mediated, imagined or willed existence into their *sensuou*s, *actual* existence – from imagination to life, from imagined being into real being. In effecting this mediation, it is the *truly creative* power.[43]

Many of the imaginations in Gissing's early novels, however, are too limited by the determining effects of an upbringing in poverty for such creative desire. Lack of imagination prevents a better self being developed: for instance, even after Jane Snowdon gains money and leisure, she finds that her upbringing has deprived her permanently of the concentration necessary for her to learn how to read.[44] *Demos* (1886), according to the author 'a savage satire on working-class aims and capacities', written 'from a very Conservative point of view', dramatizes the consequences of imaginations stunted by poverty being given the money to fulfil their limited desires.[45] The narrator rules that:

> The fatal defect in working people is absence of imagination, the power which may be solely a gift of nature and irrespective of circumstances, but which in most of us owes so much to intellectual training. Half the brutal qualities perpetrated by uneducated men and women are directly traceable to lack of the imaginative spirit, which comes to mean lack of kindly sympathy.[46]

Even with servants and money, Mrs Mutimer suffers from the lack of activity that Orwell notices in families who inherit in Dickens; she stubbornly retains her class identity, even to the extent of doing her own housework. The narrator's George Eliot-like direct address to the reader masks the exclusion of 'working people' from 'us': imaginative sympathy is only possible between human beings with a minimum standard of education and culture, which are both, of course, partly dependent on money. The reader is not to expect human sympathy between characters who are unlikely to have developed it because of the determining effects of their environment.

While Gissing's novels of the 1880s are populated mostly by working-class characters, both narrator and implied reader are always the class above. The narrator's voice is distinct enough for him to constitute an autonomous character in the novel; yet although Gissing allows the narrator to express opinions, he is not automatically privileged beyond the viewpoint of the many other characters who contribute dialogue to the text. (The free-floating, de-authorized discourses of gossip and rumour are crucial narrative devices in *Demos*.) In spite of the narrator's *ad hominem* attacks on Richard's political speeches, the reader is nonetheless capable of evaluating them independently of such interventions. The speech of the characters in *Demos* can articulate political truths such as Richard's eloquent description of the working-class's lack of freedom, and how the minimum standard of leisure and culture enjoyed by the Walthams, and by the implied reader, is dependent on exploitation: 'everyone who lives at ease and without a thought of changing the present state of society is tyrannizing over the people. Every article of clothing you put on means a life worn out somewhere in a factory.'[47] The Reverend Wyvern seems to occupy a position of authorial commentary, but as with Waymark, his Schopenhauerian detachment can seem like pitiless solipsism in the face of the human suffering that surrounds him, and thus his voice may not be reliable either.

In *Thyrza*, Gissing's next novel, Walter Egremont's literary lectures fail to affect the lives of his proletarian audience; the real social good in the novel is achieved by the morally tarnished Dalmaine.[48] Politics for Gissing have to function pragmatically, rather than idealistically; several characters in *Demos*, such as Alfred Waltham, eventually moderate their political beliefs out of self-interest. Daniel Dabbs turns from socialism to capitalism after inheriting a public house: 'in very fact he concerned himself as little with economic reforms as with the principles of high art, and had as little genuine belief in the promised revolution as in the immortality of his own soul.'[49] High art, politics and religion are ideals that claim to satisfy desire; none is capable of fulfilling the promises they make. Gissing was knowledgeable about socialism without being especially sympathetic; his pessimism about human nature, and about class identity especially, makes him sceptical about the power of mass movements to effect social change. He approvingly copied into his commonplace book Herbert Spencer's maxim that 'there is no political alchemy by which you can get golden conduct out of leaden instincts.'[50]

The Mutimer children lack the self-awareness to see the legacy as anything other than romance come true, especially Richard, who, like Pip, wrongly imagines the money to be his just reward. Their suspiciously fortuitous inheritance proves not to be fairy gold, but a monkey's paw that destroys a family by fulfilling its wishes.[51] Money does not lead to a happy ending for any of the three siblings, but instead to a failed, unprofitable utopian community and death, a bigamous, unhappy marriage and dissipation and crime. The novel itself is critical throughout of stories which merely offer a delusive image of desire fulfilled. The narrator says of the physically dissipated, self-indulgent Hubert, 'the romance which most young men are content to enjoy in printed pages he had acted out in his life.'[52] 'Romance' is usually a pejorative term in Gissing, the antonym of the 'realism' towards which sincere art should strive. Eldon's story is indeed that of a conventional romance: after being wrongfully disinherited and enjoying adventures abroad, he is finally restored to his estate and the woman he loves. However, for Gissing to tell the story from

Eldon's point of view would be insincere: the artist must portray the world he actually perceives around him. The plot of *Demos* is dominated by the manufacture of delusive fictions: Eldon's attempt to live his life as if he were the hero of a bad French novel, the too-good-to-be-true speculative narrative of the 'butterene' investment, Richard's self-glorifying and unsuccessful published account of his life, even socialism's illusory master-narrative of working-class liberation, the production of which is, as Richard's audience grumble, ' "as easy as tellin' lies." '[53] The novel's most productive manufacturer of fictions is the speculator, fraudster and bigamist Rodman; the most eager consumer of both his fictions and the printed kind his credulous wife Alice. 'Poor Princess!' comments the narrator. 'She had had her own romance, in its way brilliant and strange enough, but only the rags of it were left.'[54] The novel suggests that had Alice been better educated, perhaps her imaginative desires might be of a more elevated kind, but her appetite for romances is an artless, uniformed, feminnine kind of consumption, like her visits to pastry shops:

> Her reading had hitherto been confined to the fiction of the penny papers; to procure her pleasure in three gaily-bound volumes was another evidence of rise in the social scale; it was like ordering your wine by the dozen after being accustomed to a poor chance bottle now and then. At present Alice spent the greater part of her day floating on the gentle milky stream of English romance. [55]

Ultimately, Alice, 'only a subordinate heroine', renounces fictions by marrying the prosperous but humble journalist, and thus writer of, perhaps, comparative truths, Keene.[56] (One might think by comparison of the satisfactory union of the antihero's sister Dora Milvain and the magazine editor Whelpdale in *New Grub Street*.).

The producer of the only valid fictions in this text is the idealized working-class girl Emma Vine, neglected, like Biddy in *Great Expectations*, following Richard's rise to fortune. Like a virtuous Dickens character, Emma resists corruption by the desire for money – ' "I never thought about money [...] It was quite enough to be your wife" ' – and even refuses to marry for money when the proposal would provide her family with a route out of destitution.[57] Emma's lack of self-interest makes her a more reliable storyteller:

> Emma had two classes of story: the one concerned itself with rich children, the other with poor; the one highly fanciful, the other full of a touching actuality, the very essence of a life such as that led by the listeners themselves. Unlike the novel which commends itself to

the world's grown children, these narratives had by no means necessarily a happy ending; for one thing Emma saw too deeply into the facts of life, and was herself too sad, to cease her music on a merry chord; and, moreover, it was half a matter of principle with her to make the little ones thoughtful and sympathetic; she believed that they would grow up kinder and more self-reliant if they were in the habit of thinking that we are ever dependent on each other for solace and strengthening under the burden of life.[58]

As in his later writing on Dickens, Gissing suggests that the desire for happy endings is an immature habit that should be overcome by the better sort of reader. Like Gissing, Emma ends her realistic stories unhappily in order to make her audience reflect on the true nature of the material conditions that have generated them.

While material poverty produces in Emma clear-sighted artistic sincerity, poverty of culture stunts Mutimer's imagination. The narrator notes that his lack of sympathy and self-deception is attributable to Mutimer's possessing only practical books, and to his 'profound distrust of culture, which was inseparable from his mental narrowness, however ambition might lead him to disguise it'.[59] Culture in *Demos* does at least bring superior vision: the novel's language is preoccupied throughout with vision as knowledge, particularly in the keen, penetrating eyes of Mr Wyvern. Even the bourgeois Mrs Eldon translates class difference into the medium of sight: ' "What does [class] mean, if not that our opportunities lead us to see truths to which the eyes of the poor and ignorant are blind?" '.[60] Lacking Hubert's and Wyvern's culturally acquired ability to see 'beneath the surfaces of things', Richard is easily misled by false appearances, especially by money's power to dissolve, confuse or defer signification. ' "Money seems always to bring long words with it somehow," ' observes Dabbs.[61] ' "Them figures frighten me; I don't know what they mean," ' complains Mrs Mutimer, adding when Richard breaks his engagement to Emma, ' "It's the money as prevents you from seeing it." '[62]

Like Pip, Richard misreads his own plot.[63] Like *Great Expectations*, *Demos* punishes its central character for the crime of using money to purchase the false appearance of a higher class. Like Pip, Richard acts the part of a gentleman, and indulges in needless consumption; he even goes one better than Pip by succeeding in the aim of marrying a lady:

He was suffering, too from the *malaise* peculiar to men who suddenly acquire riches; secret impulses drove him to gratifications which would not otherwise have troubled his thoughts. Of late he had been yielding to several such caprices. One morning the idea

possessed him that he must have a horse for riding, and he could
not rest till the horse was purchased and in his stable. It occurred to
him once at dinner time that there were sundry delicacies which he
knew by name but had never tasted; forthwith he gave orders that
these delicacies should be supplied to him, and so there appeared
upon his breakfast table a *pâté de foie gras*. Very similar in kind was
his desire to possess Adela Waltham. [...] To have a 'lady' for his
wife was now an essential in his plans for the future, and he knew
that the desired possession was purchasable for coin of the realm.[64]

Demos's narrator is less forgiving, however, than the older, wiser Pip who
narrates *Great Expectations*. The narrator is particularly severe on the violation
of Mutimer's political idealism by his personal vanity. Mutimer repeatedly
asks the public world to judge him fit for a happy ending, but the reader's
privileged view of Mutimer ironizes this declared desire. Mutimer desires,
impossibly, to be both a gentleman and 'the glorified representative of his
class. He would show the world how a self-taught working man conceived the
duties and privileges of wealth.'[65] Before the legacy, the narrator is more
sympathetic towards Richard, admitting his possession of such virtues as
sincerity and 'strong domestic affections.'[66] Richard's political dreams are
harmless enough until he is granted the money to fulfil them. However, the
desire to establish a capitalist enterprise on socialist principles, altering the
semantics of political economy by trying to 'do away with distinctions
between capital and labour' is as romantically impossible a fantasy as Alice's
of being a Princess, or 'Arry of being anything other than a 'hopeless black-
guard'.[67] Once the money is lost, these false appearances fall away to reveal
the true meanings beneath, with immediate consequences for Mutimer's
marriage:

> What was the meaning now first revealed to her in that
> countenance? [...] It was the face of a man by birth and breeding
> altogether beneath her. [...] He was not of her class, not of her
> world; only by violent wrenching of the laws of nature had they
> come together. [...] 'I go back to London a mechanical engineer in
> search of employment.' They were the truest words he had ever
> uttered; they characterised him, classed him.[68]

Like the unreformed Bella Wilfer, Adela was prepared to marry Richard
openly for money: explaining how she found the hidden will, she impulsively
substitutes a metonymic 'piece of money' for her wedding-ring.[69] Lacking
either money or the shared interest in culture that is the basis of the cross-class

unions in *Workers in the Dawn* and *The Unclassed*, the Mutimers' essentially mercenary marriage must collapse.

In the classic English *Bildungsroman*, the hero must reconcile his desires with reality and with the values the author wishes to promote. *Demos* promises in its middle volume to be a kind of anti-*Bildungsroman*, with Richard degenerating instead of developing, and being ultimately punished with an unhappy ending. Adela describes her melodramatic discovery of the will as 'the crucial test of her husband's nature': it is a test that he fails, and she passes.[70] Adela recognizes Hubert's aristocratic claim to his property over Richard's right to make better use of it, and her eventual marriage to the man she loved first is the just reward for her successful moral development. However, towards the end of the third volume, Gissing subverts such expectations of punishment and reward. Adela has been as ready as the narrator to condemn Richard's faults, but in London her judgement begins to alter:

> She could never forget that he toiled first and foremost for his own advancement to a very cheap reputation; he would not allow her to lose sight of it had she wished. But during the present winter she had discerned in him a genuine zeal to help the suffering, a fervour in kindly works of which she had not believed him capable. Very slowly the conviction had come to her, but in the end she could not resist it. One evening, in telling her of the hideous misery he had been amongst, his voice failed and she saw moisture in his eyes. Was his character changing? Had she wronged him in attaching too much importance to a fault which was merely on the surface? Oh, but there were too many indisputable charges against him. Yet a man's moral nature may sometimes be strengthened by experience of the evil he has wrought.[71]

The use of free indirect discourse earlier in the novel has allowed the reader to ironize characters' mistaken judgements; here, however, it dramatizes Adela's self-interrogation, and permits her revised judgement of her husband to be presented free from the narrator's intervention. The narrator repeatedly indicates that the contradictions of Mutimer's character make it difficult to classify him accurately: 'the world would be a terrible place if the men of individual energy were at all times consistent', 'clearly there was some element of his nature which eluded grasp and definition', 'how complex a matter is the mind of a strong man with whom circumstances have dealt so strangely.'[72] Such statements are only half-ironic, since, for all Mutimer's faults, Gissing's novels show society's classification of men such as him to be indeed inadequate. Deprived of the enabling and corrupting power of money, Mutimer's contradictory elements finally coalesce into something more admirable, an ironic parallel of Gissing's later middle-class characters' moral decline as a result of degrading poverty. The shift into using Adela as a means of judging Richard permits his unhappy ending to be seen as undeserved: 'Could not his faults be atoned for otherwise than by this ghastly end?' she pleads.[73] Adela's repayment of the scheme's debts and accurate posthumous narration of Richard's story confer on her the deferred status of the novel's virtuous central character. Even more than *Vanity Fair*, a novel much admired by Gissing, *Demos* is 'a novel without a hero', the mantle passing from Mutimer to Adela to Eldon, without fitting any of them comfortably. For all of the narrator's special pleading on his behalf at the beginning of Chapter 13, the little of Eldon the reader in fact sees does not permit Hubert to be interpreted as the deserving hero of the novel: in fact, he resembles more closely the repellent Paterian dilettantes Vincent Lacour in *Isabel Clarendon* or Reuben Elgar in *The Emancipated*. It is easy for the reader to be disgusted by the reactionary sentiments Eldon expresses at the end of the novel, but surely such unattractiveness cannot be an artistic misjudgement on Gissing's part.[74] Despite Eldon's strong association with culture – Arnold-like, he refers to giving his 'instincts free play' – the reader is encouraged to distrust him for his duplicitous past and his willingness to sack all the workers in New Wanley.[75] Hubert's pastoral reversion of Wanley is an even more impossibly utopian dream than his predecessor's aim of working-class liberation.[76] Gissing ambiguously described the ending to James Payn thus: 'The novel will certainly end cheerfully. Mutimer is killed, but that is mere justice.'[77] The reader's expectation is problematized: Richard's hubris should be punished, but not by an angry mob stoning him to death; Adela deserves to be happy, but not perhaps with the dissipated aesthete that she eventually marries.

Such political truths as are articulated by this novel, even compared to those in *Workers in the Dawn* and *The Unclassed*, thus have a muted ideological impact. Gladstone, thought at one time to be the author of the anonymously published *Demos*, described *The Unclassed* as 'a novel of the speculative and didactic' class, a judgement that Gissing thought 'the only just word anyone has yet uttered concerning it in public.'[78] Yet no novel can be wholly either didactic or speculative, and *Demos*'s speculation makes its didacticism contradictory and confusing. Although it appears to be a political novel, *Demos* is purposely too irresolute and incoherent to bear any effective political message; the political theme is subordinated to Gissing's grand theme of the power of money. "It's my belief as money's the curse o' this world; I never knew a trouble yet as didn't somehow come of it, either 'cause there was too little or else too much"', bewails Mrs Mutimer.[79] 'Yes', the reader might respond, 'but so what?', since in Gissing's fictional world one can hardly choose to live without money.

The Pathology of Labour: *The Nether World*

John Goode and Fredric Jameson have both described the rigid 'zoning' of the city in Gissing, where the city's juxtaposition of separate classes serves to reinforce not the possibility of mobility, as in Dickens's fiction, but the strength of class barriers.[80] Within a specific, topographically limited, fictive environment, Gissing narrates downward circular trajectories of exploitation, misery and labour. *The Nether World*, in particular, refuses the symbolic coincidences of the Dickensian city and the assertions of One Nation made by the Industrial Novel, the nineteenth century's earlier incarnation of the novel of labour.[81] The only connection between classes in Gissing's final working-class novel is through the market: jewellery, for instance, is a commodity manufactured in the nether world for the conspicuous consumption of the class that is entirely absent from it. The industry that manufactures appearances frequently comes under Gissing's eye: Sally Fisher makes ulsters, Margaret Barnes jackets and Carrie Golding mantles, Pennyloaf Candy shirts, the reformed Ida becomes a laundress, the Trent sisters are seamstresses: 'Every stitch at the lining of a hat meant a fraction of a coin.'[82] Yet the stream of material wealth between upper and nether worlds is never diverted into the Augean slum:

> Wealth inestimable is ever flowing through these workshops, and the hands that have been stained with gold-dust may, as likely as not, some day extend themselves in petition for a crust. In this house, as the announcement tells you, business is carried on by a trader in diamonds, and next door is a den full of children who wait for their day's one meal until their mother has come home with her chance earnings.[83]

In Charles Kingsley's *Alton Locke* (1850), a novel to which Gissing's early works had been compared by his reviewers, Jemmy Downes makes a coat, which he uses to cover the corpses of his family; having become infected, the coat eventually kills George Locke.[84] As in Dickens's threat of contagion by Tom-all-alone's, the mutual economic dependence of worlds ensures some retributive justice. Gissing habitually rejects the consolation of such a moral economy: the impersonality of the market ensures not the connection of separate classes, but their separation.

Carlyle had complained in *Past and Present* that the cash nexus enforced such impersonality, but throughout his work recommends devotion to labour as a self-sufficient moral remedy. Labour, as I have suggested, is a value that the Victorian novel promotes but cannot directly represent; in Dickens, labour can serve as a means of moral redemption towards a happy ending for sinning but repentant characters. Gissing demonstrates a limited loyalty to the Carlylean virtue of hard work, especially in his own self-image as a toiling artist; however, he shows the physical reality of labour more 'sincerely' than any of his contemporaries.[85] Reversing Welsh's formulation, for Gissing, work is present as an experience, but not as a value in itself. 'Work in itself is *not an end; only a means*', he wrote emphatically to his sister Margaret.[86] In contrast to the valorization of labour's redemptive quality by most Victorian fiction, for Gissing the debilitating effects of labour, 'the curse of curses', are such that it is only undertaken resentfully in order to continue existence, even intellectual labour, as *New Grub Street* shows.[87] Gissing only seems to value labour where it is the best of a limited number of possibilities, as in *The Unclassed, Isabel Clarendon, The Odd Women, The Crown of Life* and *Will Warburton*.

Bernard Bergonzi argues in his introduction to *New Grub Street* that Gissing is the first English novelist to represent labour sincerely.[88] Yet, as I have suggested, labour's inherent resistance to narratability, its essential dullness, makes its sincere depiction a constant threat to the plot, threatening to retard, forestall or cancel its progression. Of a character like Stephen Candy, who works a sixteen-hour day and who will soon die of heart disease, there is little more for the novelist to tell. Carlylean virtues are opposed by Gissing's insistence on a 'sincere' presentation of the debilitating effects of labour on the self; this novel narrates not the rewarding of correct moral values with money and love, but a far more basic plot of the struggle to continue biological existence. HG Wells categorized Gissing's novels as 'the genre of nervous exhaustion'; Eduard Bertz described them as 'social pathology'; Irving Howe dubbed Gissing 'the poet of fatigue'.[89] The virtual qualification of a Gissing protagonist is tiredness. The body's needs propel the self into the market but, should failure result, the body visibly wastes and ultimately disappears. 'Money & health,' Gissing wrote to Algernon, 'nothing can be done without them, yet to obtain & *re*tain them you must have a good measure of both.'[90]

Consumption is thus an antagonistic process between the self and the world, in 'the battle for the day's food of which society does its best to rob each individual'.[91] No-one in Gissing actually starves to death, although several come close (Gabrielle Fleury translated *New Grub Street* as *La Rue des Meurt-de-Faim*). Although necessary to acquire food to enable the body to continue functioning, the conditions of labour itself are hostile to the body, as shown in the chapter 'Pathological', which narrates Clara Hewett's first day at her new job:

> The hours were insufferably long; by nine o'clock each evening
> Clara was so outworn that with difficulty she remained standing,

yet not until midnight was she released. The unchanging odours of
the place sickened her, made her head ache, and robbed her of all
appetite.[92]

Labour itself may be too repetitive to be narratable – the reader never sees
John Hewett making cabinets, and first sees Sidney after his day's work –
but its effects can be shown. Tiredness represents the absence of the valued
qualities (energy, physical capital) that the market has claimed in return for
continued existence, translated through the cash nexus.

Waymark claims in *The Unclassed* that morality is essentially superstructural
to the material reality of economic need; the plot punishes him for his
sophistry. The denizens of *The Nether World*, closer in status to Woodstock's
tenants than to his rent-collector, could make such a claim with more justice.
For most of this novel's characters, ethics, obedience to the law and even love
are subordinate to the struggle to eat and find shelter. Morality is not a higher
truth existing autonomously from the text asserted by the novel's discourse
and confirmed by its ending, but a social construction supererogatory to the
economic realities in which the plot takes place. Oliver Twist is rewarded by
Dickens for his pure resistance to the market; in the nether world such resistance, or failure to negotiate with the market through virtue or incompetence,
will be punished by the implacably hostile environment. For any values to
exist in this novel at all, they can only be articulated by the virtuous characters
after the day's work has been completed, or by Gissing's middle-class narrator. It is easier for the narrator to sustain values such as consistency and
sincerity, for he is the only character not subject to historical time. The other
characters, however, must obey biological imperatives to eat, sleep and mate;
under the compulsions of 'circumstances', moral values may have to be compromised.

The fierceness of the struggle for existence in the nether world ensures the
death of imaginative sympathy. The articles Gissing wrote for *The Pall Mall
Gazette* and the Russian newspaper *Vestnik Evropy* demonstrate the extent of
Gissing's knowledge of politics, in particular socialism, but his individualistic
conception of class was less influenced by Marx than by Herbert Spencer,
'perhaps our greatest living philosopher.'[93] For Gissing, it is not classes, but
individuals within a class who struggle to gain economic advantage over
each other. Emotions are subordinate to this economic struggle, and even
mediated through it. "Me an' you'll settle accounts to-night, see if we don't.
Mother told me as she owed you a lickin', and I'll pay it off, with a little on my
own account, too."[94] Monetary metaphors are never 'dead metaphors' for
Gissing: they articulate the hold of financial relations on social life.

The most effective way of increasing one's economic status in the nether world is through deceit or criminality. As usual, Gissing provides a semi-criminal pedigree for the story's inherited wealth, in this case land-grabbing and horse-trading. In the commodified universe of this novel, appearance takes priority over reality; the narrator warns that, 'whatever you touch is at once found to be sham.'[95] Joseph James Snowdon makes money from the specious production of signs: advertising, canvassing, fraud and nickel-plating; Bob's artistic interest in die-casting leads to his becoming a forger and to his death. Even the honest John Hewett is forced to dye his hair black in an attempt to get work; Clara is not wholly selfish, but has to act inauthentically to ensure her continued survival. Conversely, once the villains Joseph James Snowdon and Scawthorne become rich, they are able to be more generous.

The fraudster-cum-solicitor Scawthorne is the unlikely success story of *The Nether World*. In the lengthy narrative of his origins, Gissing even attributes to him the bookish and sensitive characteristics of many Gissing heroes:

> His father had a small business as a dyer in Islington, and the boy, leaving school at fourteen, was sent to become a copying-clerk in a solicitor's office; his tastes were so strongly intellectual that it seemed a pity to put him to work he hated, and the clerkship was the best opening that could be procured for him. Two years after, Mr Scawthorne died; his wife tried to keep on the business, but soon failed, and thenceforth her son had to support her as well as himself. From sixteen to three-and-twenty was the period of young Scawthorne's life which assured his future advancement – and his moral ruin. A grave, gentle, somewhat effeminate boy, with a great love of books and a wonderful power of application to study, he suffered so much during those years of early maturity, that, as in almost all such cases, his nature was corrupted. Pity that some self-made intellectual man of our time has not flung in the world's teeth a truthful autobiography. Scawthorne worked himself up to a position which had at first seemed unattainable; what he paid for the success was loss of all his pure ideals, of his sincerity, of his dis-interestedness, of the fine perceptions to which he was born. Probably no one who is half-starved and overworked during those critical years comes out of the trial with his moral nature uninjured; to certain characters it is a wrong irreparable. To stab the root of a young tree, to hang crushing burdens upon it, to rend off its early branches – that is not the treatment likely to result in growth such as nature purposed.[96]

It is a repeated topos in Gissing that a certain individual might have turned out better had they received an education equal to their temperament and capabilities.[97] Unable to resist or to change the nature of his environment, Scawthorne succeeds by adapting to it, presenting a more advantageous front than if he remained true to his natural 'disinterestedness.' Gissing's narrator does not approve of the choices made by Scawthorne; nor will he for Godwin Peak and Jasper Milvain, but he acknowledges sincerely the nature of what is ranged against such 'original natures frustrated by circumstance'.[98]

Scawthorne's family do not protect him from the market, but compel his participation. The Dickensian value most strikingly overturned in this novel is that of the family as an inviolable refuge from the market. Clem Peckover and her mother scheme first together and then separately for their own economic advantage; Joseph James Snowdon swindles his own daughter out of her inheritance; Bob Hewett abandons his wife and children. Gissing experiments with the speculative investment of Dickensian energy in the Byasses, but as in *Workers in the Dawn*, such energy is unrecuperated.[99] The Byasses are left estranged, perhaps permanently, revealing such energy to be a poor investment. One might also compare Nicholas Nickleby's triumphant ascent through the ranks of the Crummles' theatre company with the jealous consequences of Clara Hewett's Spencerian rise.

Characters who turn against their own family are punished by the plot; but so are the loyal, virtuous characters, Sidney Kirkwood and Jane Snowdon, who remain unfulfilled and poor. A family can survive in the nether world not by transcending the nature of the market, as in Dickens's endings, but by recognizing its realities. The reconstructed unhappy family at the novel's ending is a parodic rewriting of Dickens's oddly shaped reconstructed families:

> A noteworthy difference between children of this standing and such as pass their years of play-time in homes unshadowed by poverty. For these, life had no illusions. Of every mouthful that they ate, the price was known to them. The roof over their heads was there by no grace of Providence, but solely because such-and-such a sum was paid weekly in hard cash, when the collector came; let the payment fail, and they knew perfectly well what the result would be.[100]

As Gill notes, the ending of *The Nether World* also constitutes a pessimistic rewriting of the muted optimism of the epilogue to *Middlemarch*.[101] Virtuous acts such as John Hewett's 'rescue into love' of Margaret Barnes, or Sidney's care for Hewett's children, are ultimately so 'unhistoric' as to be almost insignificant, barely above the horizon of possible representation.[102] Although Michael Snowdon's philanthropic scheme attempts to transcend purely economic motives, Gissing's deployment of the word 'idealist' to describe Snowdon himself signals that, like nearly all such projects in Gissing, it is too 'impractical' to succeed. Jane feels, correctly in the world she inhabits, that accepting her grandfather's money and his intentions for it will place her under obligations that she can never discharge, and attract fortune-hunters such as the Peckovers and even her own father. The economic conditions of the nether world mean that only a pessimistic conclusion is possible:

> In each life little for congratulation. He with the ambitions of his youth frustrated; neither an artist, nor a leader of men in the battle for justice. She, no saviour of society by the force of a superb example; no daughter of the people, holding wealth in trust for the people's needs. Yet to both was their work given. Unmarked, unencouraged save by their love of uprightness and mercy, they stood by the side of those more hapless, brought some comfort to hearts less courageous than their own. Where they abode it was not all dark. Sorrow certainly awaited them, perchance defeat in even the humble aims that they had set themselves; but at least their lives would remain a protest against those brute forces of society which fill with wreck the abysses of the nether world.[103]

The 'battle for justice' is rarely won at all in Gissing's fiction; the narrated defeat of the virtuous is at best only a 'protest.' The discourse can articulate values, but they are contained or defeated by the plot: if the reader is to draw any moral conclusion from the novel, he must do so almost in defiance of the events that it narrates. The illiterate working class of this novel are excluded from the terms of their own representation (with especially heavy irony in the classical allusions of the chapter 'Io Saturnalia'); the subjects of the novel are in turn equally alien to Gissing's implied reader. Gissing suggests that it is the failure of his readership to perceive the truths he accurately represents that calls the novel into existence:

> The children of the upper world could not even by chance give a thought to the sources whence their needs are supplied; speech on such a subject in their presence would be held indecent. In John Hewett's position, the indecency, the crime, would have been to keep silence and pretend that the needs of existence are ministered to as a matter of course.[104]

The real conditions of middle-class life, as enjoyed by Gissing's readership and desired by his later heroes, are exposed by his portrayal of the world that underlies it. Sincere representation of the nether world can escape beyond the boundaries of the text into the careful reader's perception of the real.

Gissing would later complain that Dickens's 'sympathy with the poor a little outweighs his judgement'.[105] Gissing was rarely guilty of such an error: his refusal of inappropriate Dickensian sentiment dramatizes the realistic limits of sympathy. After the defeat of his idealistic project in *Thyrza*, Walter Egremont confesses, ' "I can no longer rave on the subject; the injustice is a *fact*, and only other facts will replace it; I concern myself only with facts" ', adding cynically, ' "And the great fact of all is the contemptibleness of average humanity." '[106] Gissing's earlier novels show a conviction of human nature so pessimistic that it makes any wide-ranging remedy for the diseased body politic ludicrously utopian:

> Well, as every one must needs have his panacea for the ills of society, let me inform you of mine. To humanise the multitude, two things are necessary – two things of the simplest kind conceivable. In the first place, you must effect an entire change of economic conditions: a preliminary step of which every tyro will recognize the easiness; then you must bring to bear on the new order of things the constant influence of music. Does not the prescription recommend itself? It is jesting in earnest. For, work as you will, there is no chance of a new and better world until the old be utterly destroyed.[107]

Utopias are yet another imaginative, romantic desire of the imagination that the world is incapable of fulfilling. *Demos* shows successively Cullen, whose incendiary speeches are a substitute for political action instead of a spur to it, an unknown speaker whose vision of political reform is undercut by the debility of his body and Kitshaw, whose cod *News from Nowhere* utopia is merely degraded entertainment like his impressions of music-hall singers.[108] In *The Nether World*, Eagles calculates utopian national economies that are futile on his own wage of two pounds a week. ' "It used to be a favourite mental exercise with me" ', says Heatherley in *Workers in the Dawn*, ' "to originate schemes of future Utopias. But I fear I now see only too clearly the futility of all such dreams. The powers of Government are slight, Miss Norman, when weighed in the balance against human passions." '[109] Even the same novel's radical Will Noble, surprisingly, is 'convinced there *must* be a rich class and a poor class', albeit organized by merit rather than the accident of birth.[110]

One of Gissing's relatively few references to politics, in an open letter to

Wakefield friends of Algernon's who had misinterpreted *Workers in the Dawn*, is characteristically ambiguous:

> First & foremost, I attack the criminal negligence of governments which spend their time over matters of relatively no importance, to the neglect of the terrible social evils which should have been long since sternly grappled with. Herein I am a mouthpiece of the advanced Radical party. [...] If readers can put faith in the desperate sincerity of the author, they will not be disgusted with the book.[111]

'Herein' – yet no further: let the inhabitants of the nether world be adequately fed, clothed, housed, and its most singular individuals, such as *Thyrza*'s Gilbert Grail, educated; otherwise, let existing social structures remain.[112] Gissing's early reading of Shelley did not allow him to subjugate the autonomy of art to any narrow political purpose, hence the disagreement with Morris dramatized in *Demos*.[113] Gissing's Schopenhauerian pessimism and conception of a complex model of human psychology forestall any totalizing answer to social problems, just as they forbid simple endings to his fiction.

4

THE PRICE OF CULTURE:
GISSING'S MAJOR PHASE

Life is a terrific struggle for all who begin it with no endowment
save their brains.

Born in Exile

"But I have vast faith in the extra pound a week. […] What was it
Beatrice called me yesterday? A materialist; yes, a materialist. […]
We can't get out of the world of material; how long will the mind
support itself on an insufficient supply of dry bread?"

Mrs Baxendale, A Life's Morning

In the novels of Gissing's middle period, his 'major phase' beginning with
1890's *The Emancipated*, the novelist generally permits his characters a higher
level of income and consequently a greater freedom of action than is afforded
to the earlier protagonists. Since bodily needs are usually 'accounted for' by
this income, the later novels are concerned instead with the defence of
forms of high culture against an increasingly vulgar external world that is
hostile to 'the best that has been thought and known' if it cannot be turned to
a profit.

Although allusions to the value of culture are common in Gissing's work,
including Shakespeare, Dr Johnson, Sir Thomas Browne and, pre-eminently,
Greek and Latin literature, Gissing's belief that the cultural residuum should
be cherished does not overpower his perception that in reality it is not. In an
excellent essay, Diana Maltz has recently written of Gissing's 'reluctance to
relinquish the "impractical" Ruskinian values of aesthetic and moral cultivation, even as he admits their futility in the face of commercial competition and
a widespread cheapening of ethical values.'[1] Culture is a value that is
cherished, like love and virtue, but like them it cannot survive without money.
The nature of money-getting in the world as Gissing saw it is hostile to the
creation and the preservation of high culture. Early reviewers of Gissing
tended to notice the insistence of this theme in his work: the *Guardian* reviewer
of *A Life's Morning* observed that Gissing's moral is that 'life is a hopeless and

degrading coil for all who have not the means of culture; and that the means of culture are wealth, power, and worldly position'.[2]

After being released from prison in 1876, Gissing read Matthew Arnold's *Culture and Anarchy* (1867) and also, apparently, the Preface to the 1874 edition of *Higher Schools and Universities in Germany*. His American notebook records Arnold's recommendation of 'fresh and free play of the best thoughts upon our stock notions and habits', and Gissing also copied the following passages:

> The thing [culture] call it by what name we will, is simply the enabling of ourselves, whether by reading, observing or thinking, to come to as near as we can to the firm, intelligible law of things, and thus to get a basis for a less confused action and a more complete perfection than we have at present.
>
> The functions of a disinterested literary class – a class of non-political writers, having no organized and embodied set of supporters to please, simply setting to observe and report faithfully, and looking for favor to those isolated persons only […] are of incalculable importance.[3]

Matthew Arnold's exhortation to discover the 'firm, intelligible, law of things' through culture is crucial in Gissing's idealist exposure of the economic inequalities that underwrite late-Victorian Philistine life.[4] Arnold's regenerative project provided Gissing with an ideology for valorizing and defending culture for its own sake. However, Arnold's exhortation to discover 'the firm, intelligible law of things' entails the perception of the economic injustice seemingly necessary for the enjoyment of culture. In his mock-utopia *Erewhon* (1872), Samuel Butler also exposes the dependence of culture on accumulated wealth:

> People oppose money to culture, and imply that if a man has spent his time in making money he will not be cultivated – fallacy of fallacies! As though there could be a greater aid to culture than the having earned an honourable independence, and as though any amount of culture will do much for the man who is penniless, except make him feel his position more deeply. The young man who was told to sell all his goods and give to the poor, must have been an entirely exceptional person if the advice was given wisely, either for him or for the poor; how much more often does it happen that we perceive a man to have all sorts of good qualities except money, and feel that his real duty lies in getting every half-penny

that he can persuade others to pay him for his services, and becoming rich. It is only in so far as the love of money implies the *want* of money, that it is the root of all evil.[5]

For Gissing's early working-class protagonists, culture can provide a means, albeit a precarious one, to transcending the crudely material. Arthur Golding paints scenes from Tennyson and Shakespeare; Waymark and Ida exchange books and lines of poetry; Gilbert Grail studies; when able to, Sidney Kirkwood draws. Even the appreciation of nature is a high-cultural practice: Carrie Golding and the working man in Gissing's early essay 'On Battersea Bridge' seem unable to appreciate scenery properly because of their ignorance of Wordsworth. Jasper and Marian are drawn together on their walk as much by their shared love of Tennyson as by the rural surroundings; Ryecroft enjoys his breakfast honey more for its literary associations.[6] Unless financially endorsed, however, cultural aspirations ultimately fail to provide an escape from the slums: Arthur paints no more after 'The Palace of Love', and fails to become a famous artist; allusions draw Ida and Waymark closer together but are insufficient alone to guarantee their union; Sidney abandons drawing, having to labour to support two families. As HG Wells noted, Gissing's simultaneous valorization of culture and the cataloguing of 'the insufficiency of the cultivated life and its necessary insincerities' are the main theme of Gissing's work in the 1890s.[7] In Gissing's 1890s fiction, one can perceive the beginnings of the modern sensibility of culture as autonomous high art, and culture as civilization, as society, existing in hostile opposition to each other. The position is articulated thus by Lionel Trilling in *Beyond Culture*:

> We cannot mention the name of any great writer of the modern period whose work has not in some way [...] expressed the bitterness of his discontent with civilization, who has not said that the self made greater legitimate claims than any culture could hope to satisfy.[8]

Gissing also shows an awareness of further meanings of 'culture', especially its Hegelian meaning of 'development'.[9] Disappointed in her marriage, Amy's character changes as she undergoes 'the culture of circumstances'.[10] As noted in the previous chapter, working-class protagonists are unable to develop because they have been limited by the circumstances of their birth and upbringing. Golding is born middle-class, but raised as an artisan, and so has too much cultural 'catching-up' to do during the narrative to progress effectively. Richard Mutimer is born proletarian, and is unable to develop because of his lack of culture, leaving a gap in *Demos*'s thematic structure filled by the cultured bourgeois Hubert Eldon. 'Culture' as development for Gissing is identified explicitly with high culture, and implicitly with the leisure required to study it: culture's separate meanings overlap to become almost the same thing. Gissing is careful, however, to discriminate between culture as true development and as the merely superficial acquisition of accomplishments. In *The Emancipated*, Cecily Doran acquires first the vulgar show of culture, and after her mortification by the failure of her marriage, sets herself to acquiring true culture through a course of strenuous reading. Miriam Baske is liberated into the correct cultural course in the opposite direction, from the narrow 'Hebraism' of her Puritan upbringing into genuine 'Hellenistic' development supervised by Mallard.

Such a process of enculturation must be only ever personal and private, rather than wholesale, such as Egremont's failed literary lectures; inevitably this process is of marginal importance to society at large. Just as in Gissing's fictive universe the world's rejection of a hero can perversely establish his real value, so the value of culture is proved by its low esteem by the vulgar, shallow world. Where high culture is adapted to the values of the commercialized world, the result is condemned as vulgar and cheapening. In *Workers in the Dawn* and *The Unclassed*, the works of art valorized in the discourse go unrecognized by the world, and the plot renders them irrelevant. In *New Grub Street*, literature has become a commodity for the day's market only, of no lasting value. In *The Emancipated*, *Sleeping Fires* (1895) and *By the Ionian Sea* (1901), classical history and culture are only barely perceptible to the sharp-eyed protagonist or the narrator. In *Workers in the Dawn*, *New Grub Street*, *The Whirlpool*, *The Crown of Life* and *Will Warburton*, art is so debased by the market that it can have no lasting value. *In the Year of Jubilee* and *The Crown in Life* show culture being co-opted entirely by the market, commodified into advertisement and spectacular display.

Art and the Marketplace: *New Grub Street*

Although literature is the cornerstone of culture for Gissing and for his bookish heroes, the valorized texts are writing from the past, especially the classical past. With the single exception of Meredith, the Victorian writers whom Gissing esteemed most were already dead by the time he began his own literary career.[11] Gissing shared with many *fin de siècle* literary writers the conviction that, under present conditions, the commercial success of a novel with the newly literate reading public, far from being a measure of literary value, proved its worthlessness. Robert Louis Stevenson famously wrote to Edmund Gosse:

> That is the hard part of literature. You aim high, and you take

longer over your work; and it will not be so successful as if you had
aimed low and rushed it. What the public likes is work (of any kind)
a little loosely executed; so long as it is a little wordy, a little slack, a
little dim and knotless, the dear public likes it: it should (if possible)
be a little dull into the bargain. I know that good work sometimes
hits; but with my hand on my heart, I declare I think it by an accident.[12]

Like one of Henry James's writer-heroes, and indeed James himself,
Gissing longed for commercial success while trying at the same time to maintain high artistic standards. (*New Grub Street* is echoed in particular in James's
'The Lesson of the Master' and 'The Next Time'.) Repeatedly, Gissing read
successful novels of his day constantly while complaining of their worthlessness in his diary and letters. Like James, Gissing consciously aimed at artistic
value above popularity, but was baffled by the 'mushroom reputations' of
authors such as Hall Caine, JM Barrie, Marie Corelli and others who had far
greater commercial success with books inferior to his own.[13] (Gissing's lack of
an independent income brings a bitterer edge to his bewilderment than
James's.) Gissing's own literary reputation was comparatively minor until the
mid-1890s, yet he evidently took his own writing with Jamesian seriousness;
the buying public's disdain of his novels thus provided Gissing with further
proof of the separation between the values of the world and true value.[14] ' "If
one goes on the assumption that the ill word of the mob is equivalent to high
praise," ' claims the disillusioned Egremont, ' "one will not, as a rule, be far
wrong, in matters of literature." '[15]

The place of the novel as a secure form of high culture can therefore be
only equivocal at best, and at times Gissing seems to feel that his own writing
is inherently compromised by its economic association with the present-day
reading public.[16] I have suggested that in *The Nether World*, Gissing represents
labour as an activity that violates the integrity of the self. Without either the
independent wealth of Henry Ryecroft or a benefactor such as Coleridge's
patron Gillman, longed for by Reardon in *New Grub Street*, writing becomes by
necessity a form of labour.[17] Literary labour is thus only undertaken resentfully in response to the demands of immediate circumstances; therefore for
Gissing its product, fiction, is especially selfconscious about its own nature.
Gissing's greatest novel, *New Grub Street* (1891), satirizes the very modes of production that have called it into being, a three-volume novel that protests at the
deadening artistic consequences of the three-volume system; Brantlinger
suggests that the novel is 'a manifesto against itself', that nineteenth-century
realism is 'materialism as critique of materialism.'[18] Gissing wrote in his
preface to the Autograph edition of *David Copperfield*:

Not only were our great novelists well aware that English readers would turn away from a picture of literary life on its unsuccessful side, but they themselves had no inclination to deal with so depressing a subject. To their minds, an unhappy novel was a contradiction in terms; they saw in fiction the solace of life.[19]

Unlike the consoling images of literary life offered by *David Copperfield* and *Pendennis*, *New Grub Street* seems to be a novel intended by its author to make the reader feel uncomfortable about reading novels.

As manual labour drains the resources of the body in *The Nether World*, enforced literary labour leads to illness and death in *New Grub Street*, as if a book can only be produced at physical cost to the self. According to Morley Roberts, Gissing was fond of exclaiming of successful writers ' "How can such an one write? He has never starved." '[20] Gissing wrote to EL Allhusen, a book collector, 'To purchase books at the cost of dinners is assuredly a sign of the true spirit – the real love of letters.'[21] Writing, the body, clothing are all translated through the cash nexus; buying a book means going without a meal; writing a book can mean prolonged starvation.[22] As he writes *Margaret Home*, Reardon is plagued by lumbago, faintness, colds, aches and sleeplessness; when Carter gives him a clerkship, he is so weak he can barely walk home. Amy describes Reardon's artistic conscientiousness as 'morbid'; the philistine John Yule suggests that Reardon's ills might be cured by 'a couple of antibilious pills before bed-time'.[23] Alfred Yule prematurely ages, suffers from dyspepsia, and finally loses his sight. Jasper worries that Marian's health is not very robust and distastefully notes her breathlessness and ink-stained fingers, visible signs of exertion and labour; eventually he prefers the more attractive spectacle of leisure presented by the heiress Amy Reardon. Even Jasper is not immune: by the final chapter: he has become successful, but at the expense of bodily capital:

> Jasper had changed considerably in appearance since that last holiday that he spent in his mother's house at Finden. At present he would have been taken for five-and-thirty, though only in his twenty-ninth year; his hair was noticeably thinning; his moustache had grown heavier; a wrinkle or two showed beneath his eyes; his voice was softer, yet firmer.[24]

Selling writing for money puts the self at the mercy of external circumstances: the economic, the pathological and the industrial. Marian Yule dreams of the technological advance of the 'Literary Machine' that will free the human race from this form of labour, but the machine is Marian herself, 'exhausting herself in the manufacture of printed stuff which no one even pre-tended to be more than a commodity for the day's market.'[25] Circumstances and temperament – 'her submissive and timid nature kept her at home' – make Marian, although she is a working woman, hardly more independent from Yule than her oppressed proletarian mother.[26]

Gissing's representation of mechanized literary production knowingly reverses Arnold's conception of the relation between culture and its pro-duction. Arnold dismisses commercial life as mere 'machinery'. Gissing's commitment to realism obliges him to expose high culture's very dependence on the commercial values its role supposedly counteracts. Literature in *New Grub Street*, Biffen and Reardon's Arnoldian 'free play among the classic ghosts' notwithstanding, has become part of the machinery for generating Philistine wealth; old John Yule accuses mass literacy of being 'Machinery for ruining the country'.[27] Post-Romantic virtues of culture – inspiration, the uniqueness of each work of art, the appeal to Man's better nature and, most importantly, autonomy from industrial capitalism – are altogether reversed by the conditions of commodity culture: production according to demand, the homogeneity of manufactured consumer products, vulgarism and mass pro-duction. As Walter Benjamin later averred, the individual work of art loses its 'aura' when made subject to the multiple reproductions of high capitalism.[28] Milvain accepts and celebrates these new conditions of literary production:

> "But just understand the difference between a man like Reardon and a man like me. He is the old type of unpractical artist; I am the literary man of 1882. He won't make concessions, or rather, he can't make them; he can't supply the market. [...] I am learning my business. Literature nowadays is a trade. Putting aside men of genius, who may succeed by mere cosmic force, your successful man of letters is your skilful tradesman. He thinks first and foremost of the markets; when one kind of goods begins to go off slackly, he is ready with something new and appetising. He knows perfectly all the possible sources of income."[29]

However, the literary market lambasted in the dialogue of *New Grub Street* is not strictly, as John Sloan notes, a sincere representation of the actual con-ditions under which the novel was produced.[30] Like the majority of Gissing's novels, *New Grub Street* is set some seven or eight years earlier than when it was written; by 1891, the three-volume novel was already declining as a com-mercially viable form.[31] The system portrayed in the novel in fact enabled a number of authors with mediocre sales, such as Reardon, or, before this novel – his first to go to a second edition – Gissing himself, to make a better living

than if paid strictly on royalties alone.[32] Gissing's own commercial practice
does not suggest wholesale resistance to the conditions of the literary world of
the novel – although of course, as a professional writer, he could hardly
choose to live outside of the literary market. In the six years following 1890,
Gissing produced the lengthy, ideologically engaged novels *Born in Exile*, *The
Odd Women* and *In the Year of Jubilee*. However, he also manufactured four one-
volume novels of arguably inferior quality (*Denzil Quarrier*, *Sleeping Fires*, *The
Paying Guest* and *Eve's Ransom*, the best of the four), as well as some thirty-five
short stories, a form financially lucrative but which Gissing had previously
considered beneath his artistic dignity.[33] These were followed, in 1896, by the
writing of *The Whirlpool* – as Bertz noted, a three-volume novel in all but its
binding. 'So I am entered upon the commercial path, alas! But I shall try not
to write rubbish,' Gissing wrote to Bertz in 1893.[34]

The younger Gissing chafed at the restrictions imposed by Mudie's and
Mrs Grundy and was disturbed by Britain's revilement of Zola. After Zola
had been improbably rehabilitated in Britain, however, and Hardy had
further tested the limits of the permissible by producing *Tess of the D'Urbervilles*,
Gissing was not tempted to excess by the 'new wine of liberty'.[35] Rather, with
the passage of time, he seemed to show an increasing willingness to compromise with the market, garnering more widespread and favourable critical
response. *The Town Traveller*, for instance, includes Dickensian Cockney stereo-
types, coincidence, humour and even a happy ending.[36] While still shrinking
from 'conscious insincerity of workmanship' after the writing of *New Grub
Street*, Gissing periodically seems to display as much of Milvain as of
Reardon.[37] Even as early as 1884, Gissing can be found advising his brother
to avoid the 'disagreeable' in his writing, and warning him that 'moral indignation is simply not marketable'; later, he would sensibly side with HG
Wells's publisher 'from the commercial point of view' against Wells in a
dispute over price and packaging.[38]

Although the nature of the literary market is heavily criticized in *New Grub
Street*, Gissing was too naturally conservative, and too much a realist, to propose a utopian solution to this specific social problem. In the characteristic
pattern of Gissing's fiction, the intransigence of the characters is as much to
blame as the nature of the world they inhabit. In Gissing's earlier novels,
poverty can disable the imagination and forestall the progression of narrative,
but even with the slightly higher income available to the characters of later
novels, their temperament can also prevent development:

> "Milvain's temperament is very different from mine. He is naturally
> light-hearted and hopeful; I am naturally the opposite. What you
> and he say is true enough; the misfortune is that I *can't* act upon it. I

am no uncompromising artistic pedant; I am quite willing to try and do the kind of work that will sell; under the circumstances, it would be a kind of insanity if I refused. But power doesn't answer to the will. My efforts are utterly vain; I suppose the prospect of pennilessness is itself a hindrance; the fear haunts me. With such terrible real things pressing upon me, my imagination can shape nothing substantial."[39]

New Grub Street does not dramatize Reardon's choice between success at the cost of writing productions as facile as those of Milvain, and the noble failure of remaining true to his artistic nature. All of the novel's cast, including even the impractical Biffen, who remains dignified and sincere despite being ridiculed by the narrator, recognize without self-delusion the nature of the hostile economic system in which they struggle to survive.

"I didn't think so much of money when we were married," Amy continued. "I had never seriously felt the want of it, you know. I did think – there's no harm in confessing it – that you were sure to be rich some day; but I should have married you all the same if I had known that you would win only reputation.'
"You are sure of that?"
"Well, I think so. But I know the value of money better now. I know it is the most powerful thing in the world. If I had to choose between a glorious reputation with poverty and a contemptible popularity with wealth, I should choose the latter."[40]

Reardon is prevented from being successful by the combination of his temperament with the peculiar pathology of literary labour. Needing money to survive, Reardon writes a one-volume sensational novel so beneath the notice of the narrator that its title is not even recorded; this insincere production is rejected by his publisher. Because of his temperament, Reardon is unsuited to the writing of sensational fiction, or even to writing when under financial pressure. More frequently than in any of Gissing's novels since *Workers in the Dawn*, the narrator intercedes on behalf of the hero (a special pleading that was reduced when the author later revised the novel for the French edition):[41]

But try to imagine a personality wholly unfitted for the rough and tumble of the world's labour-market. From the familiar point of view these men were worthless; view them in possible relation to a humane order of society, and they are admirable citizens. Nothing is easier than to condemn a type of character which is unequal to the coarse demands of life as it suits the average man. These two were richly endowed with the kindly and the imaginative values; if fate threw them amid incongruous circumstances, is their endowment of less value? You scorn their passivity; but it was their nature and their merit to be passive. Gifted with independent means, each of them would have taken quite a different aspect in your eyes. The sum of their faults was their inability to earn money; but, indeed, that inability does not call for unmingled disdain.[42]

' "The world has no pity on a man who can't do or produce something it thinks worth money" ', complains Reardon.[43] The novel enforces the reader's acquiescence in both Reardon's complaint at the world's commodification of literary value but also in Amy and Jasper's frustration at Reardon's inability to better his situation.[44] For Gissing, virtuous poverty is a convenient fiction for novelists who wish to establish moral values apparently, if deceptively, separate from those of the market. As shown by the early novels, Gissing rejects such a notion, especially for those who by temperament or upbringing are particularly ill-suited to deprivation. ' "Some great and noble sorrow may have the effect of drawing hearts together, but to struggle against destitution, to be crushed by care about shillings and sixpences – that must always degrade" ', writes the gentle-natured Reardon to Amy, turned savage and antisocial in penury.[45] ' "Poverty will make the best people bad" ', agrees Mrs Yule, later adding that if Yule ' "became rich, he would be a very much kinder man, a better man in every way. It is poverty that has made him worse than he naturally is; it has that effect on almost everybody." '[46] What Gissing means by 'money' is once more instantly translateable into commodities: food, clothing, comfortable surroundings. Gissing makes little distinction between essentials and luxury objects, since with enough money, one would naturally purchase both. Jasper persuasively argues that it is not personal culture but luxuries that make for a genteel standard of living:

> "You shall be my wife, and you shall have as many luxuries as if you had brought me a fortune."
> "Luxuries! Oh how childish you seem to think me!"
> "Not a bit of it. Luxuries are a most important part of life. […] If ever I seem to you to flag, just remind me of the difference between these lodgings and a richly furnished house."[47]

Jasper cynically outlines to Marian the impossibility of the ideal of 'love in a hut': fashionable bohemianism in Gissing can never be more than an affectation, since if comfort can be afforded, one would naturally prefer it.[48] The true enjoyment of high culture requires genteel surroundings: as Jacob Korg writes of *A Life's Morning*, 'only in a leisured environment [can] the potentialities of mind and spirit be fulfilled.'[49] Neither Marian nor Reardon has an adequate response for the economic logic of preferring to live with luxuries than without. Godwin Peak and Emily Hood, in *Born in Exile* and *A Life's Morning* respectively, are prepared to make considerable sacrifices for the sake of bourgeois comfort, and the material details and the moral effects of poverty are both so exhaustively described in Gissing's fiction that it is made difficult for the reader wholly to disapprove:

> "Look at those houses; every detail, within and without, luxurious. To have such a home as that!"
>
> "And they are empty creatures who live there."
>
> "They do *live*, Amy, at all events. Whatever may be their faculties, they all have free scope. [...] The power of money is so hard to realise; one who has never had it marvels at the completeness with which it transforms every detail of life. [...] I have no sympathy with the stoical point of view; between wealth and poverty is just the difference between the whole man and the maimed. [...] As a poor devil I may live nobly; but one happens to be made with faculties of enjoyment, and those have to fall into atrophy. [...]
>
> "Can I think of a single subject in all of the sphere of my experience without the consciousness that I see it through the medium of poverty? I have no enjoyment which isn't tainted by that thought, and I can suffer no pain which it doesn't increase. The curse of poverty is to the modern world just what that of slavery was to the ancient. Rich and destitute stand to each other as free man and bond. You remember the line of Homer I have often quoted about the demoralising effect of enslavement; poverty degrades in the same way."[50]

It is interesting that Reardon, as enthusiastic a classicist as his creator, should note the unjust economic basis of the cultural utopia of Ancient Greece: once again, anything of value can only exist if it is financially supported. Reardon also puns on 'realize': the immensity of money's power is difficult both to comprehend, and to represent fully in art.

Amy inwardly notes that Reardon lacks tact in discoursing thus upon the degrading effects of poverty, since poverty has such a harmful effect on their own marriage.[51] The close relationship between environment and development dramatized in the earlier novels is more sophisticated but no less powerful in Gissing's fiction of the middle class, especially for middle-class women. Women are closer to the nexuses of economic exchange: they manage the domestic economy and do the shopping; the more sheltered upbringing of middle-class women makes them less able to endure deprivation.[52] Although the novel satirizes the naivety of Amy's expectations of wealth and comfort when she marries a writer, at the same time Gissing implies a middle-class reader who expects no less of a minimum standard of civilized cleanliness. (In *The Town Traveller*, Parish wins money by correctly guessing that, according to a newspaper competition, 'as nations grow civilized they give more and more attention to […] hyjene'.)[53] When Amy returns to the bourgeois comfort of her mother's house, the novel's double-voiced discourse is strained between rhetoric and irony:

> How clean and sweet everything was! It is often said, by people who are exquisitely ignorant of the matter, that cleanliness is a luxury within reach even of the poorest. Very far from that; only with the utmost difficulty, with wearisome exertion, with harassing sacrifice, can people who are pinched for money preserve a moderate purity in their persons and their surroundings. By painful degrees Amy had accustomed herself to compromises in this particular which in the early days of her married life would have seemed intensely disagreeable, if not revolting. […] When Amy began to cut down on her laundress's bill, she did it with a sense of degradation. One grows accustomed, however, to such unpleasant necessities, and already she had learnt what was the minimum of expenditure for one who is troubled with a lady's instincts.
>
> No, no; cleanliness is a costly thing, and a troublesome thing when appliances and means have to be improvised. It was, in part, the understanding she had gained of this side of the life of poverty that made Amy shrink in dread from the still narrower lodgings to which Reardon invited her. She knew how subtly one's self-respect can be undermined by sordid conditions. The difference between the life of well-to-do educated people and that of the uneducated poor is not greater in visible details than in the minutiae of privacy, and Amy must have submitted to an extraordinary change before it would have been possible for her to live at ease in the circumstances which satisfy a decent working-class woman. She was prepared for final parting from her husband rather than to try to effect that change in herself.
>
> She undressed at leisure, and stretched her limbs in the cold, soft, fragrant bed.[54]

Amy has received a rather bad press from critics including Orwell, Robert L Selig and Patricia Stubbs, but Gissing notes very carefully that the smug hostess of the ending is the visible result of the processes narrated by the novel.[55] Amy was raised by a snobbish mother who lives 'only in the opinions of other people', an inauthentic existence 'based on bold denial of actualities.'[56] Learning subsequently that economic and biological conditions determine life, Amy adapts to become more knowledgeable about them. Ignorant at first of the economic truths possessed by the other characters, Amy educates herself by reading literary gossip, publishers' agreements, copyright law and articles about Darwin and Spencer. Very early in the novel, she already sounds like her future second husband: "Art must be practised as a trade, at all events in our time. This is the age of trade. Of course if one refuses to be of one's time, and yet hasn't the means to live independently, what can result but break-down and wretchedness?"[57] Amy is the keeper not only of Reardon's house but also, perhaps surprisingly, his artistic conscience. Although, in preferring to be the wife of a literary man than that of a clerk, she may be motivated more by class-consciousness than by an ideal of romantic artistic autonomy, the compromises she attempts to force on Reardon are not Mephistophelean bargains for his artistic soul, but efforts to ensure that the family can survive on the proceeds of his writing, even that Reardon might eventually produce superior artistic work again.

Amy, like many of Gissing's middle-class women, relishes the publicity that results from commercially successful artistic production; Reardon's temperament makes him shrink from it. Jasper's ultimately successful speculation is founded on the principle that literary success and social success are inseparable. Partway through her marriage to Reardon, Amy becomes conscious that 'her tastes were social', and the precarious nature of the Reardons' friendship with the Carters shows that even the most basic level of intercourse is dependent on a minimum level of income. Social 'circulation' is a form of financial speculation: Jasper will spend his available capital in the expectation of its generating a higher income in the future. "Marian's money is to be spent in obtaining a position for myself", he declares; Marian is under no illusions that her inheritance is an essential precondition of her marriage to Jasper.[58] Amy's inheritance is eventually spent on promoting Jasper himself. Milvain is conscious of the status of his work as a renewable commodity with no permanent value, whose price thus depends, like a worthless consumer product, on novelty appeal and spectacular display: "The question is: How can I get the eyes of men fixed upon me?"[59] A prominent characteristic of the consumer economy of the late nineteenth century was the huge growth in advertising, and the literary market was no exception.[60] The Jedwoods provide a very literal example of the marriage of commerce and Art: Jedwood 'advertises hugely', while his wife entertains lavishly.[61] Alfred Yule, by contrast, has been forced into a disastrous marriage by the biological urge, explicitly identified as such, that requires him to keep a wife.

> His brothers, John and Edmund, cried out that he had made an unpardonable fool of himself in marrying so much beneath him; that he might well have waited until his income improved. This was all very well, but they might just as reasonably have bidden him reject plain food because a few years hence he would be able to purchase luxuries.'[62]

The unappealing spectacle presented by Mrs Yule disqualifies him from entertaining powerful editors; his failure to socialize is his failure to succeed. (Gissing later complained that his marriage to Edith similarly prevented him from receiving company).[63] Conspicuousness is both the means of success and the measure of it; the invisible writer is thus a failure.

The shape of *New Grub Street*'s plot enforces the reader's acquiescence with Jasper's claim that 'success has nothing whatever to do with moral deserts'; that rather, as Marian puts it with justifiable bitterness, 'There's no such thing as deserving. Happiness or misery come to us by fate.'[64] John Goode notes correctly, however, that 'it is crucial to our understanding of the novel that we shouldn't just think of Milvain as an appalling cynic. [...] Reardon's whole story depends on his tacit acquiescence in Milvain's world view.'[65] Yet Goode perhaps overstates the extent to which Milvain's rationality is unopposed in the novel. In Jasper's own Social Darwinist terms, his hard work, intellect and willingness to compromise with public taste should assure him of the most conspicuous success. However, he is out-negotiated by several other characters.

Jasper's own sister Maud exposes his own failure to resolve what John Sloan terms the 'cultural challenge' in Gissing's work. Jasper takes to disposable literary work because it suits his temperament, yet even he is taken aback by Maud's exploitation of her temperamental ability for society. As an attractive woman with no other resources, marrying for money is perhaps an even better option for the emotionally cold Maud than it was for Isabel Clarendon:

> Her attire was still simple, but of quality which would have signified recklessness, but for the outlook whereof Jasper spoke to Whelp-dale. The girl looked very beautiful. There was a flush of health and happiness on her cheek, and when she spoke it was in a voice that rang quite differently from her tones of a year ago; she moved and uttered herself in queenly fashion.[66]

Jasper is concerned by Maud's increased expenditure on clothes after moving to London, but her promiscuous investment in externals to secure a higher return later is only a more successful version of his own literary and social speculations. (One meaning given in the *OED* for 'utter' is to put a piece of currency, perhaps counterfeit currency, into circulation.)[67] Jasper is intimidated by the richer, more successful Dollomore: although he sourly suggests that her marriage proves unhappy, Maud's alternatives are hardly more attractive.

Jasper's more appealing sister Dora (who resembles *David Copperfield's* Agnes Wickfield more closely than she does Dora Spenlow) achieves almost the impossible in *New Grub Street*: happiness, marriage and a form of literary success, without compromising her moral nature. Although minor characters, both sisters share some common attributes of the Gissing protagonist:

> The truth was that nature had endowed them with a larger share of brains than was common in their circle, and had added that touch of pride which harmonised so ill with the restrictions of poverty. Their life had a tone of melancholy, the painful reserve which characterises a certain clearly defined class in the present day [...] Wattleborough saw fit to establish a Girls' High School, and the moderateness of the fees enabled these sisters to receive an intellectual training wholly incompatible with the material conditions of their life.[68]

As intelligent and clear-sighted as her brother, Dora comprehends his arguments, for which she is the most frequent *ficelle* (to use Henry James's term), without accepting them. Dora can endure limited privation, and sets moral limits on what she will do to escape it: ' "Who ever disputed the value of money? But there are things one mustn't sacrifice to gain it." '[69] The possibility of the reader concurring both with this, and with Amy's desire for bourgeois cleanliness, is characteristic of Gissing's disturbing technique of contradictory, multiple, dialogic assertions. The novel appeals to the reader's moral sensibility, while also exposing the financial basis of the bourgeois comfort that permits the possession of such a sensibility.

Dora's self-reliance is achieved in part by her ability to renounce sex if necessary, an option only open in Gissing to women and the most exceptional men.[70] Her reward is a husband who overcomes the other characters' mockery to win the reader's respect. Whelpdale is not a mere literary tradesman, having tried, and failed, to be an authentic literary artist first. His subsequent ventures, even the possibility of his selling sewing-machines on commission, can thus be seen as rational efforts to survive in a hostile, competitive world. (Whelpdale's effervescent vigour may also owe something to Gissing's pot-boiling friend Morley Roberts, who produced not only novels, short stories and poetry, but also advertising copy.)[71] *Chit-Chat* and the literary agency are concessions to the market, but they are dependent on Whelpdale's possessing at least a certain amount of literary integrity and culture in the first place. John Sloan (although for a different purpose) demonstrates the surprisingly high educative content of *Tit-Bits*, the model for *Chit-Chat*. *Chit-Chat* is worthless, but harmless; Dora's children's books, like those produced by Mary Vincy in the epilogue of *Middlemarch* or illustrated by Bertha Cross in *Will Warburton*, comfortably evade the categories of the novel's debate about cultural value. Milvain may be 'the literary man of 1882', but the far-sighted Whelpdale is more like the literary man of 1891, especially in his founding of a literary agency. (Gissing himself began using an agent in 1891.[72]) Had his novels succeeded too, one might view him as a kind of prototype Arnold Bennett, who also edited a magazine and wrote literary 'how-to' manuals.

New Grub Street's ending is thus discomfiting, manifesting something like the revenge of the discourse on the plot. The economic logic dramatized by the plot leads us to expect Jasper's editorship, comfortable home and practical wife as, in this novel's universe, his earned reward. Yet, as Grylls observes, 'what Gissing shows contradicts what he asserts.'[73] The ending cannot be satisfactorily resolved, for the novel is structured on paradox. In Adrian Poole's terms, 'if the pursuit of money degrades, it is even more certain that the lack of money will degrade even further. [...] This, then, is the paradox about money, that the *pursuit* of money must degrade, but the *possession* of it is necessary for the sustenance of all moral and personal good.'[74] Grylls agrees: 'poverty demoralizes; the best escape from poverty is commercialism; but commercialism also demoralizes.'[75] The fates of Reardon, Biffen and the Yules have dissociated the concepts of reward and justice, a dissociation reinforced by the narrator's heavy sarcasm towards the Milvains' comfortable surroundings, hitherto recommended as the essentials of civilized life. Chapter titles such as 'Jasper's Magnanimity', 'Reardon becomes Practical', 'Jasper's Delicate Case' and 'Rewards', also show the discourse's ironizing of the plot. Gissing's perception of the contradictions between the values promoted by late-Victorian British literary culture and the realities of literature's production are voiced in the contradictory assertions made by this novel.

Can't Buy Me Love: *Born In Exile*

In her study of *Born in Exile* and *Jude the Obscure*, Patricia Alden classifies both novels as anti-*Bildungsromanen*.[76] As I have suggested, Gissing's fiction systematically affronts the expectations generated by conventions of Victorian fiction, and *Born in Exile* satirizes those of the *Bildungsroman* in particular. Unlike the usual narrative pattern of a social and sexual apprenticeship, followed by useful accommodation into the social structure, the plot of *Born in Exile* is centred on an individual that society is incapable of accommodating. A traditional structure of reward and punishment, of the accommodation of the self's desire into a useful social role, is visible within the text, but with the relations between them purposely skewed; this novel seems to wish to disavow the shape of its own plot.

Although Godwin Peak's inner thoughts are narrated in greater detail than those of any other Gissing protagonist since Arthur Golding, such narration is not always reliable. This novel is the story of a fraud; at times the reader is not certain whether they, too, are being defrauded by the hero's presentation of a false appearance, having nothing more to interpret than Peak's own unreliable dialogue, or thoughts related in free indirect style. In *Demos*, Gissing's use of free indirect style allows the reader to contest the narrator's harsh judgement of the novel's characters. *Born in Exile* deploys this technique both to allow the hero to incriminate himself morally but at the same time to try independently to justify himself. The hero of this novel, even more than Richard Mutimer, repeatedly compels the reader's judgement of his actions. In the following passage, for example, the narrator's ironic condemnation of Peak's ambitions and the justice of Peak's arraignment of society are simultaneously voiced:

> He was now playing the conscious hypocrite; not a pleasant thing to face and accept, but the fault was not his – fate had brought it about. At all events, he aimed at no vulgar profit; his one desire was for human fellowship; he sought nothing but that solace which every code of morals has deemed legitimate. Let the society which compelled to such an expedient bear the burden of its shame.[77]

Peak's nature is noble; his actions are not. The reader may agree with Marcella Moxey's surprise that ' "Surely there was never a man who united such capacity for great things with so mean an ideal" ', but might also concur with Mrs Moorehouse's simple claim that ' "It's better to be in a comfortable room." '[78] An idyllic bourgeois home and a middle-class wife to manage it may seem to the novel's implied reader a lowly aim for such a singular individual as Peak; but, as in *New Grub Street*, the narrator is careful to emphasize the desirability of such an environment. Gissing may ironize Peak's means of achieving his desires, but not their object. The idealized rural haven of the Warricombes' home contains all that Peak desires: picturesque, comfortable surroundings, an attractive mate and a leisured environment in which to pursue disinterested cultural activities. In the polyphony of Gissing's fiction, two contradictory views are freely asserted; the narrative's tone is ironic, but since both levels of meaning are ironized, the result is a kind of ambiguity:

> This English home, was it not surely the best result of civilisation in an age devoted to material progress? Here was peace, here was scope for the kindliest emotions. Upon him – the born rebel, the scorner of average mankind, the consummate egoist – this atmosphere exercised an influence more tranquillising, more beneficent, than even the mood of disinterested study. In the world to which sincerity would condemn him, only the worst elements of his character found nourishment and range; here he was humanised, made receptive of all gentle sympathies. [...] Nothing easier than to contemn the mode of life represented by this wealthy middle class; but compare it with other existences conceivable by a thinking man, and it was emphatically good. It aimed at placidity, at benevolence, at supreme cleanliness, – things which more than compensated for the absence of a higher spirituality.[79]

William Empson's seventh type of ambiguity 'is that of full contradiction, marking a division in the author's mind.' One instance that he cites of this type is:

> the Freudian use of opposites, where two things thought of as incompatible, but desired intensely by different systems of judgements, are spoken of simultaneously by words applying to both; both desires are given a transient and exhausting satisfaction, and the two systems of judgement are forced into open conflict before the reader.[80]

Gissing's narrator acknowledges both the hollowness and attractiveness of Peak's vision; the vagueness of 'a higher spirituality' confesses the discourse's inability to provide an attractive alternative to the image of bourgeois comfort.

Gissing's work consistently dramatizes the influence of environment on the self, thus in this context Godwin's desire for '"the atmosphere of a – of a comfortable home"' is at least partly intelligible.[81] Peak feels such an environment to be his destiny, the ending that his singular narrative deserves. However, in this instance, he is prevented from achieving it not by lack of money, but by his working-class birth. Although nothing that Peak wants is attainable without money, class is a still greater obstacle to his fulfilment of his desires, since even money cannot erase permanently the traces of his proletarian origin. Like his creator, Peak has been educated out of his class by a society that has failed to think of what it might do with a generation of learned working-class scholarship boys exiled from their families.[82] Such an education cannot be forgotten (it would almost be a blessing to characters such as Kingcote, Reardon, Biffen, the Milvain sisters, Peak, Lashmar and Warburton if it were). In this instance, education generates the narrative, by separating Peak not from his patrimony, but from his class, from the non-narratable world of anonymous labour that would otherwise be ordained by his proletarian birth:

> What is to be done with the boy?
> All very well, if the question signified, in what way to provide for the healthy development of his manhood. Of course it meant nothing of the sort, but merely: What work can be found for him where he may earn his daily bread? We – his kinsfolk even, not to think of the world at large – can have no concern with his growth as an intellectual being; we are hard pressed to supply our own mouths with food. […] Obviously he cannot heave coals or sell dogs' meat, but with negative certainty not much else can be resolved, seeing how desperate is the competition for minimum salaries. He has been born, and he must eat. By what licensed channel may he procure the necessary viands?[83]

The unstable, narratable elements of this story are constituted less by the waywardness of the hero's inappropriate desires, as in the classic *Bildungsroman*, than by the plot's own teleological uncertainty, as it seeks to provide a 'licensed channel' among only 'negative certainties'. Peak feels that his imposture is legitimized by society's failure to provide a suitable place for one of his education: since society has educated Peak for a destiny neither it nor he is capable of fulfilling, he is entitled to violate its laws to secure an appropriate destiny for himself. VS Pritchett's diagnosis of Gissing and Reardon could be applied to Peak equally well:

> The grudge is concerned with education and opportunity. It has two aspects. Why pass an Education Act, giving clever Board School boys the chance to become cultivated men when they will only find themselves in stultifying and unseemly surroundings and without the means to live in some accord with their minds; and why educate ordinary boys so that they can become the customers for everything that is vulgar and trivial in popular, commercial culture?[84]

Peak's scornful attitude to his class is nonetheless ironized by the narrator; as *Demos* shows, no amount of novelistic wish-fulfilment can alter the rigidity of the Victorian class system. Whatever society's limited possibilities for social mobility, one cannot be born 'an aristocrat of Nature's own making' to a plebeian family.[85] Like Pip, Peak never outgrows the Family Romance. In his essay on this topic, Freud writes:

> At about the period I have mentioned, then, the child's imagination becomes engaged in the task of getting free from the parents of whom he now has a low opinion and of replacing them by others, who, as a rule, are of higher social standing. He will make use in this connection of any opportune coincidences from his actual experience, such as his becoming acquainted with the Lord of the Manor or some landed proprietor if he lives in the country or with some member of the aristocracy if he lives in town. Chance occurrences of this kind arouse the child's envy, which finds expression in a phantasy in which both of his parents are replaced by others of better birth.[86]

As with many heroes of English nineteenth-century *Bildungsromanen*, Peak's destiny takes him to London. In the city's enforced mixing of classes, Peak feels his desire for distinction still more fiercely:

> He chanced once to be in Hyde Park on the occasion of some public ceremony, and was brought to pause at the edge of a gaping plebeian crowd, drawn up to witness the passing of aristocratic vehicles. Close in front of him an open carriage came to a stop; in it sat, or rather reclined, two ladies, old and young. Upon this picture Godwin fixed his eyes with the intensity of fascination; his memory never lost the impress of those ladies' faces. Nothing very noteworthy about them; but to Godwin they conveyed a passionate perception of all that is implied in social superiority. Here he stood, one of the multitude, of the herd; shoulder to shoulder with boors and pick-pockets; and within reach of his hand reposed those two ladies, in Olympian calm, seeming unaware even of the existence of the throng. Now they exchanged a word; now they smiled to each other. How delicate was the moving of their lips! How fine must be their enunciation! On the box sat an old coachman and a young footman; they too were splendidly impassive, scornful of the multitudinous gaze. – The block was relieved, and on the carriage rolled.

They were his equals, those ladies; merely his equals. With such as they he should by right of nature associate.

In his rebellion, he could not hate them. He hated the malodorous rabble who stared insolently at them and who envied their immeasurable remoteness. Of mere wealth he thought not; might he only be recognised by the gentle of birth and breeding for what he really was, and be rescued from the promiscuity of the vulgar![87]

The spectacle presented by the aristocratic carriage has the same enduring effect on Peak as Eve Madeley's photograph on Maurice Hilliard in *Eve's Ransom* (1895), or the engravings of society women on Piers Otway in *The Crown of Life*. Desire becomes reified in a visual image that the libido imagines to be perfect; the image's meaning is 'implied' because the true content of the spectacle is not instantly legible to the 'gaping plebeians' but latent, requiring imaginative investment from the singular hero to lift him from his obscurity within the crowd. At the same time, the over-inflated idealism of Peak's language allows the reader to ironize the hero's libidinal over-investment in this delusive vision of aristocratic refinement.

Peter Brooks has identified the theme in the nineteenth-century novel of the rediscovery of the self's own origins, with the plot being a paradoxical recapitulation of the circumstances of its own genesis.[88] In *Born in Exile*, however, the pattern is reversed, since education makes the narrative of the return to origins impossible. Andrew Peak's effective termination of Godwin's Whitelaw career shows that in this case reunion with familial origins cannot reaffirm the line of development of the self, as for the reconstructed families of Dickens's endings, but retards it.

He, it was true, belonged to no class whatever, acknowledged no subordination save that of the hierarchy of intelligence; but this could not obscure the fact that his brother sold seeds across a counter, that his sister had married a haberdasher, that his uncle (notoriously) was somewhere or other supplying the public with cheap repasts.[89]

Great Expectations's Pip, who has an uncle that sells seeds, resolves his equivocal status by escaping to the colonies, an option considered by Peak.[90] Like Pip, Peak has felt that 'it is a most miserable thing to feel ashamed of home', that 'he is no longer a companion for his kindred'; for Gissing, however, this is a much smaller sin than for Dickens.[91] Peak's family and Twybridge classmates embody the alternative to his narrative of self-determination, lapsing into class-ordained labour too ordinary to be narrated: 'The dominion of the commonplace had absorbed them, all and sundry; they were the stuff which destiny uses for its every-day purposes, to keep the world a-rolling.'[92] (When Peak works as a mining engineer for eight years between parts one and two of the novel, this is not narrated.) The children of Peak's sister are 'already born into the world of draperdom'; the narrator is careful to note, however, how much happier the other Peaks are in their allotted place in the world.[93] Peak's notions of aristocracy and exile are ultimately self-romanticizing, as is suggested by the near-oxymoron of the novel's title. While he may have a legitimate grievance against the rigidity of the late-Victorian class system, Peak's desire to rise is driven mostly by an egoistic sense of his own singularity, the wish to be, in Adrian Poole's words, 'an autonomous subject, the sole originator of desire':[94]

> "You and I are different," said Oliver impatiently. "I am content to be like other people."
> "And I would poison myself with vermin-killer if I felt any risk of such contentment! Like other people? […] Oh what a noble ambition!"[95]

Since Peak's separation from his class is enforced by his education, *Born in Exile* opens with his last day at school. The novel's first scene puns on 'class': not only educational and social classes, but taxonomic classes as well. The prizegiving ceremony at Whitelaw College thus dramatizes a version of natural selection in which Peak's birth and inherited poverty will count against him in his struggle for existence before it has even really begun.

> He was a young man of spare figure and unhealthy complexion. […] Under any circumstances, he must have appeared ungainly, for his long arms and legs had outgrown their garments, which were no fashionable specimens of tailoring. The nervous gravity of his countenance had a peculiar sternness; one might have imagined that he was fortifying his self-control with scorn of the elegantly clad people through whom he passed.[96]

In this scene, Peak's failure to achieve overambitious goals, awkwardness with women, and harsh judgement by the bourgeois observatrix Mrs Warricombe hint already at the likely future course of his narrative:

> "Such a very unprepossessing young man I never met! He seems to have no breeding whatever."
> "Overweighted with brains," replied her husband; adding to himself, "and by no means so with money, I fear."[97]

The outward appearance of the Warricombes, by contrast, confirms the pre-determination of their success: Mr Warricombe has 'a countenance suggestive of engaging qualities'; the female members of his family are dressed 'with taste which proclaimed their social standing'; his son's 'countenance [...] told of a boyhood passed amid free and joyous circumstances.'[98]

As is so often the case in Gissing's portrayal of social life, the premium placed by society on attractive surfaces inevitably generates false appearances. Middle-class society for Gissing is constituted by an oppressive network of disciplinary gazes: the bourgeoisie affect to despise the deliberate cultivation of appearances for the sake of success, but judge harshly those who fail to conform to its expected conventions of dress and behaviour. Since the labour he is capable of performing is insufficiently well paid to purchase what he desires, Peak must trade in the commodity of his appearance. 'Always an observer', the aptly named hero Peak obsessively scrutinizes and judges his own appearances by the codes of the class to which he aspires.[99] Like every upwardly mobile proletarian who suffers 'pangs of complex origin', he takes scrupulous pains over his dress and his accent; better-dressed once he is salaried, Peak 'defied inspection'.[100] His posing as a would-be clergyman is a direct consequence of the attention to appearances that society insists upon for worldly success.

In distinguishing between sincerity and authenticity, Lionel Trilling writes that:

> The English novelists of the nineteenth century [...] appear to be in agreement that the person who accepts his class situation, whatever it may be, as a given and necessary condition of his life, will be sincere beyond question. He will be sincere *and* authentic, sincere *because* authentic.[101]

By contrast:

> The villain in plays or novels is characteristically a person who seeks to rise above the station to which he was born. He is not what he is: this can be said of him both because by his intention he denies and violates his social identity and because he can achieve his unnatural purpose only by covert acts, by guile.[102]

Trilling also suggests, however, that the condition of covert acting is forced to a greater or lesser degree on everyone:

> Society requires of us that we present ourselves as being sincere,

and the most efficacious way of satisfying this demand is to see to it that we really are sincere, that we actually are what we want our community to know we are. In short, we play the role of being ourselves, we sincerely act the part of the sincere person, with the result that a judgement may be passed upon our sincerity that is not authentic.[103]

Peak's imposture is legitimate when judged under a conception of society that is resigned to the division between the internal, authentic self and the public, performative self demanded by social convention. Lucy Crispin suggests that Peak 'has to distort himself to become himself'; Charles Swann that 'being and seeming are terms called into doubt by the narrative'.[104] The narrator rules feelingly that 'intelligent young men in society' may only survive by cultivation of a 'double consciousness [...] one must learn to act a part, to control the facial mechanism, to observe and anticipate'.[105] Under the pressure of scrutiny both from within and from the outside world, Peak's identity fractures:

> Peak had been talking for more than a quarter of an hour. Under stress of shame and intellectual self-criticism (for he could not help confuting every position as he stated it) his mind often wandered. When he ceased speaking there came upon him an uncomfortable dreaminess which he had already once or twice experienced when in colloquy with Mr. Warricombe; a tormenting metaphysical doubt of his own identity strangely beset him. With involuntary attempt to recover the familiar self he grasped his own wrist, and then, before he was aware, a laugh escaped him, an all but mocking laugh.[106]

Peak's relentless self-scrutiny produces a divided consciousness even before the imposture, which begins 'under the marvelling regard of his conscious self'.[107] (In a peculiar episode which the narrative does not explain, Malkin sees Peak's *doppelgänger* in America, as if such self-division in the hero of the novel cannot help but produce further *fin de siècle* doublings.)

When Gissing dramatizes sexual relationships, especially those across class divides, his concern with vision intensifies still further. His love scenes record gazes met and avoided, falling eyes and frank stares, facial expressions successfully interpreted or only guessed at. The issue of marriage is so closely associated with that of class in this novel that the erotic and the classificatory/disciplinary gaze are conflated into one.[108] The love scene that finally occurs in *Born in Exile* (Part the Fifth, Chapter II) is dominated by 'mutual scrutiny':

under the pressure of extreme emotion neither Sidwell nor Peak are able to control their bodies' visible manifestations.[109] Charles Darwin writes in the section on 'Blushing' in *The Expression of Emotions in Man and Animals* (1872):

> Men and women, and especially the young, have always valued, in a high degree, their personal appearance; and have likewise regarded the appearance of others. The face has been the chief object of attention, though, when man aboriginally went naked, the whole surface of his body would have been attended to. Our self-attention is excited almost exclusively by the opinion of others, for no person living in absolute solitude would care about his appearance. Every one feels blame more acutely than praise. Now, whenever we know, or suppose, that others are depreciating our personal appearance, our attention is strongly drawn to ourselves, more especially to our faces.[110]

As Grylls observes, Darwin provides both subject and form in *Born In Exile*.[111] Gissing read Darwin's *On the Origin of Species by Means of Natural Selection, or the Preservation of Favoured Races in the Struggle for Life* in 1889, pronouncing it 'a queer jumble of thoughts.'[112] *The Origin of Species* narrates how Darwin's investigations into classification led him to formulate his theory of evolution.[113] Peak's fantasy of aristocracy is constructed to resist the accuracy of his classification as a proletarian, which would threaten to contain and limit the potentialities of his identity. He desires singularity over being a common, representative type: 'By birth, by station, he was of no account [...] Godwin Peak must make his own career. [...] Was he in any respect extraordinary? were his powers noteworthy?'[114] ' "I am glad nothing much depends on my successfully defining you" ', replies Earwaker, another risen proletarian, when the dispenser's son defends ' "hereditary social standing" ' against the brutish masses who can nonetheless ' "send forth fine individuals" ' such as himself.[115] Yet the very quality rewarded by Darwinian evolutionary narrative is not the stubborn inflexibility of Gissing heroes such as Peak, but its reverse, the ability to adapt. Gissing's imagination used the theory of evolution to justify his preconceptions of the hostility of the exterior world to the better self: natural selection proves that success is proof of something other than virtuous conduct. The hero 'laugh[s] his approval' when Earwaker quotes Sir Thomas Browne's claim that ' "a man should be something that all men are not, and individual in somewhat beside his proper name," '[116] but Peak's desire for distinction is one that will make him extinct. As Gillian Beer expresses it:

> The survival of the fittest means simply the survival of those most

fitted to survive; this implies not distinction, nor fullest development, but aptness to the current demands of their environment –
and these demands may be for deviousness, blueness, aggression,
passivity, long arms, or some other random quality.[117]

"You have been trying to adapt yourself," admonishes Marcella Moxey "to
a world by which you are by nature unfitted."[118] As with the central figures of
classical tragedy, the obduracy of a Gissing hero can be at the same time his
most admirable trait and the quality that will ensure his failure. A new species
that evades classification must have some evolutionary advantage in the
environment it inhabits, or it will become extinct. Peak's initially authentic
but ultimately impractical, inflexible temperament puts him at a disadvantage
in the modern world. 'Heroes of passion are for the most part primitive
natures, nobly tempered,' adjudges the narrator, 'in our time they tend to
extinction.'[119] Peak craves the stability of a happy ending to his story; however, Beer has argued that Darwinian theory ultimately overthrows traditional nineteenth-century models of closure, positing instead an ateleological
narrative that stubbornly resists a definitive moral perspective:

> Darwinian theory [...] has no place for *stasis*. It debars return. It
> does not countenance absolute replication (cloning is its contrary),
> pure invariant cycle, or constant equilibrium. Nor – except for the
> extinction of particular species – does it allow either interruption or
> conclusion.[120]

The new temporal perspective of Darwinism undercuts Godwin's schemes of
self-determination, leaving him isolated within historical time:

> He knew enough of the geology of the county to recognise the
> rocks and reflect with understanding upon their position; a
> fragment in his hand, he sat down to rest for a moment. Then a
> strange fit of brooding came over him. Escaping from the influences
> of personality, his imagination wrought back through eras of geo-
> logic time, held him in a vision of the infinitely remote, shrivelled
> into insignificance all but the one fact of inconceivable duration.[121]

Peak cannot return to the past through science, nor by returning to his
origins nor by imagining himself an early nineteenth-century country parson.
He even admits that his deception will be found out sooner or later; although
the course of Peak's narrative is self-willed, he knows it to be self-destruc-
tive.[122] He is finally exiled from the Warricombe household not for being an

impostor, but for being a proletarian. Even the sympathetic Marcella, who loves Peak, flinches when noticing the resemblance between him and his uncle Andrew. It is as if physiognomy confirms that no matter what Peak's actions, heredity must finally catch up with and classify him. The authorship of 'The New Sophistry' confirms for Peak's prospective brother-in-law Buckland Warricombe his prejudices about Peak's class:

> "He has somehow got the exterior of a gentleman; you could not believe that one who behaved so agreeably and talked so well was concealing an essentially base nature. But I must remind you that Peak belongs by origin to the lower classes, which is as much to say that he lacks the sense of honour generally inherited by men of our world. A powerful intellect by no means implies a corresponding development of the moral sense."[123]

Buckland's snobbery is ultimately undercut by his later marriage to the daughter of a wealthy dealer in tallow and hides; by then, however, Peak has already been exposed and exiled.

In one of Gissing's characteristic reversals of expectation, even after Sidwell becomes intellectually independent through losing her faith, and Godwin financially independent following Marcella's death, a happy ending still does not take place. Although Sidwell loves Peak, the barriers of class are too strong for the success of their union, and the possibility of forgiveness by the Warricombes can be no more than 'an idea out of old-fashioned romances.'[124] ('Romance' and 'romantic' never appear in this novel without ironic shading.) Peak desires Sidwell for her class and family, and thus can hardly ask her to renounce these for his sake. Such a fantasy is unrealistic, and Sidwell is not, as Peak dryly notes, 'the heroine of a romance.'[125] Perhaps, given Gissing's typical portrayal of 'exogamous' marriages, it is better that they should never marry.[126] Peak finally reverts to novelistic type and like Arthur Golding, Pip, Alton Locke and other nineteenth-century heroes of equivocal class, goes abroad, where he dies.

Characteristically for Gissing, the failure of this individual to find an appropriate place within society condemns both individual and society. The novel allows Peak to voice his critique of society but also shows that his failure is partly his own fault; Gissing is never wholly a determinist. As for Vincent Lacour in *Isabel Clarendon*, Peak's fatalist pleading that he has been determined by circumstances is not sufficient to relieve him of moral responsibility.[127] 'Character is fate, but of necessity we attribute to mortals a share in the shaping of their own ends', the narrator rules in the short story 'A Song of Sixpence'.[128] Even the most repressed of Gissing's central characters possess

some measure of free will; his unhappy endings always hint at an alternate
ending had different actions been taken. In an excellent essay on Gissing
published in 1908, Paul Elmer More suggests that:

> The knot of fate and free-will is not always disentangled, there is no
> conventional apportioning of rewards and penalties such as Dickens
> indulged in at the end of his novels; but always, through all the
> workings of heredity and environment, he leaves the reader con-
> scious of that last inviolable mystery of man's nature, the sense of
> personal responsibility.[129]

The success of a number of Peak's contemporaries shows that by desiring
social mobility, independence and love, Peak's error is to ask too much from a
hostile universe; success, once more, requires compromise. Early in the novel,
the narrator cynically suggests that:

> The perfectly graceful man will always be he who has no strong
> apprehension either of his own personality or of that of others,
> who lives on the surface of things, who can be interested without
> emotion, and surprised without contemplative impulse.[130]

Bruno Chilvers is burdened with neither proletarian origins nor scruples.
'One type of the successful man of our day,' he represents the modern type of
the wholly inauthentic man, living entirely on the surface, as a 'marketable' if
oxymoronic Darwinian clergyman.[131] At Whitelaw, Bruno Chilvers takes first
prize in the subjects in which Peak comes second; finally he acquires a wife of
even higher standing than Sidwell (who had, to her credit, rejected him).

Another of Peak's contemporaries, 'naturally marked for survival among
the fittest', stays happily integrated with his proletarian roots, acts sincerely
even against his own economic advantage, but is still successful in his career,
and eventually comes to enjoy a high standard of living, as symbolized, typically, by the improved decor of his lodgings.[132] Godwin finds himself envying
the less ambitious, more principled Earwaker:

> Earwaker had his place in the social system, his growing circle of
> friends, his congenial labour; perhaps – notwithstanding the tone in
> which he spoke of marriage – his hopes of domestic happiness. All
> this with no sacrifice of principle. He was fortunate in his temper,
> moral and intellectual; partly directing circumstances, partly guided
> by their pressure, he advanced on the way of harmonious develop-
> ment. Nothing great would come of his endeavours, but what he

aimed at he steadily perfected. And this in spite of the adverse conditions under which he began his course.[133]

Earwaker's ability to set aside the desire for a mate distinguishes him from Peak: his lack of 'preposterous sexual spectacles' allows his negotiations with the world to take place more clear-sightedly (although as Swann points out, in Darwinian terms he is a failure if he does not reproduce).[134] Able neither wholly to renounce authenticity like Chilvers, nor sex like Earwaker, Peak's self-creation must therefore fail.

Although not included in Whitelaw's initial natural selection, Malkin provides a comic subplot to Peak's tragic fall. A man who, according to the narrator, 'has never been humiliated by circumstances, never restricted in his natural needs of body and mind', Malkin rebounds from each check to his desires with Dickensian energy.[135] Parodying Peak's narrative, the object of Malkin's desire is exactly the same: ' "For these next three years I shall live as becomes a man who has his eyes constantly on a high ideal – the pure and beautiful girl whom he humbly hopes to win for a wife." '[136] Malkin's Pickwickian resilience, tonally at odds with the rest of the novel, undercuts the seriousness of Peak's narrative: he even finally returns from temporary exile abroad to marry the girl whose education he has directed to this purpose.

Born in Exile, perhaps the most perplexing of all Gissing's novels, shows his portrayal of the world at its most epistemologically incoherent. The novel tells the story of a hero who attempts to achieve very little by means that will ensure his failure: as the narrator of *The Emancipated* opines, 'Religious hypocrisy is in our day a very rare thing; so little is to be gained by it.'[137] The text's own mode of discourse, the languages of social appearance and Social Darwinism, construct a scrutability of the narrative of origins; consequently Peak cannot possibly succeed. The central viewpoints of both the central character and the narrator seem wayward, even arbitrary, oscillating between 'desire' and 'fate'. Authorial privilege is invoked to expose Peak but partly to forgive him; the aspirations of the hero are satirized while his grievance is admitted to be just. The novel's conception of identity vacillates between agency and determinism, between free will and inherited characteristics, enabling the reader to undercut Peak's schemes of self-determination. Too much flexibility or pragmatism is condemned as an inauthentic violation of authenticity; too little becomes a stubborn impracticality that results in failure and death. Gissing's most fiercely independent protagonist aims at the 'reward of successful artifice'; transcendentally homeless (in Lukàcs's terms), Peak sacrifices his future in order to gain a nostalgic, atavistic environment.[138] The hero's alienated consciousness seeks a regressive accommodation. The free-thinking, evolutionist atheist, trained as a scientist, becomes in appearance the most orthodox of Anglicans; the dispenser's son aims at aristocracy. Conversely, the novel's most eloquent defender of scientific progress is the charlatan cleric Bruno Chilvers. Peak wishes for middle-class society to be democratized just enough to allow him to enter, but for it to remain exclusive enough to separate him from the masses. He vacillates between the exertion of his individual will and resignation to circumstances: sometimes vocally asserting his right to self-determination; at others 'essentially a negativist, guided by the mere relations of phenomena.'[139]

Peak is not 'cast in heroic mould'; unlike the European heroes cited in Jacob Korg's influential article 'The Spiritual Theme of *Born in Exile*', Peak neither murders nor duels, but pretends to be studying to enter the Anglican church.[140] 'The moralist and the realist were always at odds in Gissing,' states Korg. 'Like most of Gissing's novels, *Born in Exile* ends by heightening our awareness of moral questions without providing answers to them.'[141] Gissing's plots can appear to imply an ideology that is wholly conservative, yet the direction of the narrative and the discourse's fluctuations in tone question the validity of the realistically represented existing power structures within which the plot occurs, yet do not provide alternatives to them.[142]

5

GISSING'S CITY OF WOMEN: THE LATER NOVELS

.

If you want to earn the gratitude of your own age you must keep in step with it. But if you do that you will produce nothing great. If you have something great in view you must address yourself to posterity: only then, to be sure, you will probably remain unknown to your contemporaries; you will be like a man compelled to spend his life on a desert island and there toiling to erect a memorial so that future seafarers shall know he once existed.

Arthur Schopenhauer, *Essays and Aphorisms*

Economies of Knowledge: *In the Year of Jubilee* and *The Odd Women*

Gissing reproved Dickens for idealizing the poor; like Dickens, though, Gissing can be guilty in his earlier novels of idealizing female characters such as Thyrza and Emily Hood. Gissing's work of the 1890s, however, begins to interrogate society's construction of sexual difference more closely.[1] The development of Gissing's male heroes is inhibited by lack of money and temperament; his heroines are limited further still by their gender. Godwin Peak's antiquated notions of gender are satirized in *Born in Exile*, a novel which also shows sympathetically that the torments inflicted by society on Peak are greater still for Marcella:

> The emancipated woman has fewer opportunities of relieving her mind than a man in corresponding position [...] for Marcella, frustrate in the desire with which every impulse of her being had identified itself, what future could be imagined?[2]

As one might expect from a writer who nominates Ruth Pinch as his favourite female character in Dickens, Gissing seems to share with many of his male characters the belief that, ideally, a woman's place lies in the patriarchal, Dickensian sphere of motherhood and domestic management.[3]

Nonetheless he is capable of sympathy – if not consistently – towards those women for whom such a role is not possible. Gissing's conception of gender is not so rigidly essentialist that he cannot imagine alternatives to marriage and child-rearing, however important such roles may be. He is severe, however, on female characters who adopt such a role only to abandon it, such as Alma Rolfe. The dialogic, self-interrogating structure of Gissing's novels allows his exceptional female characters to protest at societal restrictions, since the frustration they experience is even greater than that of the male protagonists. Although female emancipation may seem inimical to the novelist's own libidinal needs for sexual fulfilment and domestic comfort, Gissing is nonetheless able to perceive the justice of desiring it.

Whereas many male protagonists are disabled by an education that makes them superfluous in the world they inhabit, lack of practical education can disable Gissing's heroines still further. In an often-quoted letter to Bertz, Gissing claimed that 'there will be no social peace until women are intellectually trained very much as men are. More than half the misery of life is due to the ignorance & childishness of women.'[4] The female education that Gissing envisages is more pragmatic than the ideal of independent broad culture cherished by his heroes, and in *The Odd Women* (1893), Gissing's political instincts are too conservative and his expectations too pessimistic to suggest anything more radical than typewriting wage-slavery as a route to female independence, the same labour that is joyfully escaped by Widdowson when he inherits his legacy.[5] Once again, the artist must present a vision of the world as he sees it, however unpalatable such a vision may be.

In *Demos*, Alice Mutimer's expectations of married life are artificially raised by her uneducated taste in reading. After Virginia Madden becomes an alcoholic, her taste in reading degenerates from the study of serious works to unthinking consumption of library novels. The severity of *Demos*'s judgement on Alice's weakness is echoed by *The Odd Women*'s radical feminist Rhoda Nunn:

> "Miss Royston had a certain cleverness, I grant, but do you think I didn't know that she would never become what you hoped? All her spare time was given to novel-reading. If every novelist could be strangled and thrown into the sea, we should have some chance of reforming women. The girl's nature was corrupted with sentimentality, like that of all but every woman who is intelligent enough to read what is called the best fiction, but not intelligent enough to understand its vice. Love – love – love; a sickening sameness of vulgarity. What is more vulgar than the ideal of novelists? They won't represent the actual world; it would be too dull for their

readers. In real life, how many men and women *fall in love*? Not one in every ten thousand, I am convinced. Not one married pair in ten thousand have felt for each other as two or three couples do in every novel. There is the sexual instinct, of course, but that is quite a different thing; the novelists daren't talk about that. The paltry creatures daren't tell the one truth that would be profitable. The result is that women imagine themselves noble and glorious when they are most near the animals. This Miss Royston—when she rushed off to perdition, ten to one she had in mind some idiot heroine of a book."[6]

The desire to 'represent the actual world' is of course a principle of Gissing's fiction; his representation of the unsatisfactory nature of the world for educated middle-class women is at least sincere, if uncomfortable to read. Gissing's failure in what is now his most frequently discussed novel to represent a utopian, and hence insincere, solution has provoked widely differing interpretations of Gissing's sexual politics. Susan Colón has drawn attention to the novel's apparent self-negations:

> *The Odd Women* is itself an odd contradiction: it promises to differ from the usual romance plot by being about singleness, but by far most of its content is devoted to the stories of couples; it promises to be about women's professionalism, but it has next to nothing concrete to say about the characters' workaday lives and jobs; it promises to be about women's emancipation, but (in the view of many) it does more to reinscribe patriarchal norms than otherwise.[7]

For Kathleen Blake, *The Odd Women* is 'lucidly feminist'; Patricia Stubbs finds it marred by the author's inability to moderate his own misogyny; for Katherine Bailey Linehan, this novel is uniquely free from the imaginative limitations of the author's own prejudices. There is more agreement on the openness of the novel: Ann L Ardis reads the text as a detached Zolaesque naturalist experiment; according to Wendy Lesser, 'Fairness [...] is the weakness of *The Odd Women* as well as its strength'; Karen Chase suggests that 'Gissing possessed nothing so determinate as a precise attitude'.[8] Consequently, *The Odd Women* is a particularly unsatisfying book to read. Patricia Comitini concludes in a perceptive essay on *The Odd Women* that 'the only resolution this novel can come to is non-resolution'.[9] Gissing's novel characteristically fails to achieve a resolution of the issues that it raises: the refusal of a simple ending in this novel, and also *In the Year of Jubilee*, is an attempt to represent the complexity of the issues that the novels dramatize.[10]

Once again, Gissing comprehensively fails to provide any generic utopian or romantic contingencies that might alleviate the plight of his heroines, especially in respect of their possession of money. In the event which precipitates the plot into narratable financial disequilibrium, the Madden sisters' father is killed the day before he had planned to insure his life and provide for them. ' "Women" ', Dr Madden opines, ' "should never have to think about money" ', but of course his daughters are subsequently forced into negotiation with the market.[11] "What a blessed thing it is for a woman to have money of her own!" exclaims *In the Year of Jubilee*'s Nancy. "It's because most women haven't, that they're such poor, wretched slaves."[12] Money is again the means by which desire is thwarted more than it is fulfilled. The money inherited by the Madden sisters is only sufficient for Virginia, Alice and Monica to live on because of the deaths of the other three. They possess the capital to open a school, but are prevented from doing so by Virginia's nervous temperament; Alice is finally able to take the risk only after the death of one remaining sister and the institutionalization of the other. Micklethwaite is prevented by lack of money from marrying for seventeen years, during which he and his fiancée physically decay. Widdowson inherits money and, in effect, uses it to purchase and then imprison Monica.

Gissing's sexual politics are instinctively conservative, but he dramatizes in Widdowson the repressiveness of the Ruskinian ideal of woman.[13] His writing seems at its most contradictory on the subject of gender: Deirdre David argues that 'in articulating the feminist challenge to patriarchy, [Gissing] himself was subject to contradiction; that is to say, the novel's subversion of patriarchy is determined by what it seeks to subvert'; Gail Cunningham observes that 'No constant view of woman appears in his work [...] he is opinionated without having consistent views; aggressive without always identifying his target.'[14] Everard Barfoot and Rhoda Nunn want to marry each other but fail to do so because in effect, as Cunningham observes, one pretends to want a free union in order to achieve marriage, and the other asks for marriage as a pretext for establishing a free union.[15] The Widdowsons' marriage also exposes the mis-signification and paradox that underlie late-Victorian sexual politics:

> The first falsehood she had ever told him, and yet uttered with such perfect assumption of sincerity as would have deceived the acutest observer. He nodded, discontented as usual, but entertaining no doubt.
>
> And from that moment she hated him. If he had plied her with interrogations, if he had seemed to suspect anything, the burden of untruth would have been more endurable. His simple acceptance of her word was the sternest rebuke she could have received. She

despised herself, and hated him for the degradation which resulted from his lordship over her.[16]

In The Year of Jubilee (1894) condemns its female characters' craving for the excitement of public spaces, but is sympathetic to their need to escape their imprisonment by gender and class. Nancy Lord's restless boredom, Fanny French's sexual commerce, Beatrice French's defeminizing entry into business, Jessica Morgan's decline from student to flirt to religious enthusiast, even Ada's violent hysteria can all be read as reactions against the limitations of the role to which their gender confines them.[17] Gissing appears especially sympathetic to the constraints under which Nancy, the heroine, finds herself, even if he is critical of the steps she initially takes to escape them. Nancy is degraded by her egoistic contact with the public spectacle of the Jubilee, but the anonymity offered by her temporary escape into the crowd permits at least imaginary release from the real boundaries of her social identity.

Nancy suffers for her desire for independence but overcomes the narrator's initial scorn of her superficial education and naive self-deceptions to gain the reader's respect. She realistically reverses the progress of *Our Mutual Friend's* Bella Wilfer, beginning in domestic isolation from the market and moving to hard-nosed economic pragmatism. After the superficial culture of her schooling, Nancy's true 'education' is into economic realities. Initially, she rejects the commercial man Luckworth Crewe in favour of Lionel Tarrant's apparent distance from the market:

> "I suppose that's the view you take of everything? You rate everything at market price."
>
> "Marketable things, of course. But you know me well enough to understand that I'm not always thinking of the shop. Wait till I've made money."
>
> "Silly boy, don't I love you just because you are *not* one of the money-making men? If you hadn't a penny in the world, I should love you just the same; and I couldn't love you more if you had millions."[18]

Tarrant's appearance of untainted gentility is an affected one, however: his pedigree leads back not to old money, but to the brand of black-lead that bears his surname.[19] Nancy's story dramatizes again Gissing's grand theme that while having money is not the same thing as having freedom, freedom is nonetheless unattainable without money: 'she saw as never yet the blessedness of having money and a secure home.'[20]

After a sexual awakening treated very sympathetically by Gissing, Nancy

finally attains independence and regains the man she loves; however, she is
made to surrender one in order to keep the other. (The difficulty of 'New
Women' characters retaining both love and autonomy is a recurrent topos of
1890s fiction.)[21] Of all of Gissing's many reversals of narrative expectation,
the ending of *In the Year of Jubilee* is perhaps the most baffling: even Gissing
himself admitted that 'the last volume is not of a piece with what comes
before.'[22] Two successive inheritances might have provided for the Tarrants
but, as so often in Gissing, each brings frustration rather than fulfilment.
Tarrant's aunt has fallen prey to, significantly, an advertising-broker, and has
speculated her fortune away. Lord's will tries to prevent Nancy from marrying before she is twenty-six, but she learns of this after she is already married.
All but the very least alert of Gissing's readers must detect the Lords' family
romance far in advance of its revelation. However, Nancy and Horace's
re-established connection with their mother does not bring them a fortune:
rather, Mrs Damerel is after their money. Even after Nancy and Lionel
inherit a third, substantial legacy from her dissipated, conveniently consumptive brother, they still live apart, against her apparent wishes. The ending
could thus be read as the author enacting misogynist revenge on his mould-
breaking heroine, but for Gissing to grant Nancy the utopian ending she both
desires and deserves would violate his own conditions of realism. One of the
plot's several ironies is that, while Nancy overcomes the societal limitations of
her gender to be elevated by her ordeal, the over-conventionally masculine
Tarrant is degraded by his. As Nancy learns to negotiate while maintaining
her moral integrity, Tarrant retreats into the vulgar solipsism that ' "There's
no villainy, no scoundrelism, no baseness conceivable, that isn't excused by
want of money." '[23] The narrator opines that 'he must be a strong man whom
the sudden stare of Penury does not daunt and, in some measure, debase.'[24]
Tarrant proves a weak man, and, in the train of thought that follows this
statement, narrated in free indirect discourse, he spuriously rationalizes temporary abandonment of Nancy. In a characteristic Gissing irony, while Nancy
proves herself worthy of a happy ending that includes regaining her husband,
Lionel himself does not.[25] (In a letter to Roberts that protests against a reviewer's complaint that the novel contains no attractive characters, Gissing lists
Nancy, Arthur Peachey and, perhaps surprisingly, Mr Lord, as admirable,
but not Tarrant.)[26]

Gissing even refuses the improbability of a *Künstlerroman*-ending to *In the
Year of Jubilee* by allowing Tarrant to shut Nancy's novel in a drawer instead of
letting it be published (like that of Herminia Barton in *The Woman Who Did*):

> "It isn't literature, but a little bit of Nancy's mind and heart, not to
> be profaned by vulgar handling. To sell it for hard cash would be

horrible. Leave that to the poor creatures who have no choice. You
are not obliged to go into the market."[27]

Nancy opts to perform the role of Victorian housewife for the man to whom
she is bound by the law: reconciling herself to their partial separation, she
'commanded her features to the expression which makes whatever woman
lovely – that of rational acquiescence.'[28] Although the narrator spitefully adds
that 'on the faces of most women such look is never seen', Nancy's need to
command her features into a false appearance suggests that, although
sacrificing sincerity in the surface she presents to her husband, she may
manage to retain a form of authenticity underneath; if her real thoughts are
different, the novel censors them.[29] The much-criticized ending of this novel
is thus another deliberately unappealing Gissing resolution, but, like Gissing's
less equivocally unhappy endings, it dramatizes again the failure of society to
reward exceptional individuals.

Late-Victorian constructions of gender must not, for Gissing, be represented as other than they are; nor can the transformations of the consumer
economy, however repellent the author evidently finds them.[30] *In the Year
of Jubilee* is also notable for Gissing's most sustained investigation of the
spectacular, commodified, unreal economy that for him is epitomized by the
Jubilee.[31] Gissing was appalled by the victory of misleading signifiers over true
referents in the age of 'shams gigantic & innumerable'.[32] One meaning of a
'year of jubilee' is a time of restitution, when property reverts to its rightful
owners, but in this novel, Gissing warns that the spectacular society might
never be able to make good on its hollow promises of gratified desire, again
emphasizing that the pursuit and spending of money entails the generation of
false appearances.[33] Even the appearances of education, clothing and houses,
sign-systems favoured by the discourse of Gissing's own novels, can prove mis-
leading. Facility of reproduction in a highly industrialized age generates a
more complex semantics of visual meanings:

> Though the furniture was less than a year old, and by no means of
> the cheapest description, slovenly housekeeping had dulled the
> brightness of every surface. On a chair lay a broken toy, one of
> those elaborate and costly playthings which serve no purpose but to
> stunt a child's imagination. Though the time was midsummer, not a
> flower appeared among the pretentious ornaments. The pictures
> were a strange medley – autotypes of some artistic value hanging
> side by side with hideous oleographs framed in ponderous gilding.[34]

Gissing's narration feels the need to correct its own representations: for instance, as if addressing the surprising fact that the speech of the vulgar French sisters is not written in phonetic cockney, the narrator adds that their accent 'signified only that they had grown up amid falsities, and were enabled, by the help of money, to dwell above-stairs, instead of with their spiritual kindred below.'[35] In these new metropolitan conditions, signifiers of class are especially misleading: Barmby, the French sisters and even Nancy are of a lower class and education than they appear to be, a 'veneer' of education thinly covering the appearance they present to the outside world.[36]

The successful counterpart to Nancy's unpublished novel is Crewe's highly successful manual of advertising, which, in an ironic inversion of the unprofit-able literature produced in *New Grub Street*, pays for itself by carrying advertise-ments. Fraud, advertisement and misrepresentation predominate in Gissing's vision of social life in this novel.[37] Crewe sells untruthful advertisements; Lord makes his money from selling pianos on hire-purchases to families who wish to present the false appearance of gentility; Peachey's employer makes sham disinfectant; the Frenches' father was a builder, a trade associated in this novel with fraud and unsightly urban sprawl. Beatrice, 'an observant young woman, with a head for figures', brilliantly reads the conditions of the market in founding a business that combines human greed, female vanity and mis-leading surfaces:[38]

> This winter saw the establishment of the South London Fashion-able Dress Supply Association – the name finally selected by Beatrice French and her advisers. It was an undertaking shrewdly conceived, skilfully planned, and energetically set going. Beatrice knew the public to which her advertisements appealed; she under-stood exactly the baits that would prove irresistible to its folly and greed. In respect that it was a public of average mortals, it would believe that business might be conducted to the sole advantage of the customer. In respect that it consisted of women, it would give eager attention to a scheme that permitted each customer to spend her money, and yet to have it. In respect that it consisted of ignorant and pretentious women, this public could be counted upon to deceive itself in the service of its own vanity, and maintain against all opposition that the garments obtained on this soothing system were supremely good and fashionable.
>
> On a basis of assumptions such as these, there was every possi-bility of profitable commerce without any approach to technical fraud.[39]

Nancy's labour in the business consists of the renting-out of her genteel appearance to the surface of the business. As in *Born in Exile*, appearances are a commodity to be traded, and in this novel even consumed: Nancy and Horace amuse themselves by looking in shop-windows; at Teignmouth, Nancy 'found amusement enough in watching the people – most of whom were here simply to look at each other'.[40] Information, especially secrets both commercial and sexual, is a commodity that is traded several times in this novel. Signification itself, whether truthful or not, becomes part of economic relations:

> High and low, on every available yard of wall, advertisements clamoured to the eye: theatres, journals, soaps, medicines, concerts, furniture, wines, prayer-meetings – all the produce and refuse of civilisation announced in staring letters, in daubed effigies, base, paltry, grotesque. A battle-ground of advertisements, fitly chosen amid subterranean din and reek; a symbol to the gaze of that relentless warfare which ceases not, night and day, in the world above.[41]

Economic competition is not merely an image of evolutionary competition, but evidence of it, the struggle for pounds, shillings and pence modernity's version of the struggle for existence. Beatrice's shop, 'with its windows cunningly laid out to allure the female eye, spread a brilliant frontage between two much duller places of business', is like a male animal in Darwin's account of sexual selection.[42] As no species is ever secure in Darwinian theory, no class is secure in this commercialized economy, and Gissing fears that the lower classes, untroubled by culture's refinement of instinct, are better adapted for this kind of commercial struggle than the higher: 'to fill his pockets [Crewe] would no more hesitate about destroying the loveliest spot on earth, than the starving hunter would stay his hand out of admiration for bird or beast.'[43] The novel's most conspicuous successes are thus the aspirant modern types Beatrice French and Luckworth Crewe, who may even eventually marry each other, thus producing offspring that will be superbly adapted to their vulgar environment. Aside from their vulgarity, however, neither character is wholly unsympathetic; both are simply well adapted to their environment, not immoral in themselves, but true representatives of their immoral age.

Negotiating *The Whirlpool*

Towards the end of *In the Year of Jubilee*, Tarrant promises his wife (perhaps not altogether sincerely) that once he has become more successful in his profession, they might abandon the scheme of living in separate establishments:

"I don't aim at a house in London; everything there is intolerable,
except the fine old houses which have a history, and which I could
never afford. For my home, I want to find some rambling old place
among hills and woods, – some house where generations have lived
and died, – where my boy, as he grows up, may learn to love the old
and beautiful things about him. I myself never had a home; most
London children don't know what is meant by home; their houses
are only more or less comfortable lodgings, perpetual change within
and without."[44]

For Gissing, as for Dickens, a connection to an authentic self can be redis-
covered in a relationship with a rural landscape, especially one associated
with childhood. The alternative in Gissing to the dangerous sexualized
'whirlpool' of London is usually a nostalgic Wordsworthian communion with
the countryside. Gissing's own father wrote three volumes of Wordsworthian
poetry and was married in the chapel at Grasmere; Wordsworth, along with
Dickens, was the author most closely associated in Gissing's own mind with
childhood and paternity. Although the rural sequences are frequently the
weakest part of Gissing's fiction – I would agree with James Joyce's judgement
on *The Crown of Life* that Gissing is at his least convincing when writing about
nature – these associations are a crucial part of Gissing's mental landscape.[45]

Routledge's Jubilee Guide to London and its Suburbs (1887) claims that suburbia's
existence between city and country allows the Londoner the possibility of
escape from urban to rural landscape:

> The visitor has only to mount the roof of any omnibus going
> towards the suburbs, and in less than an hour he will not only have
> got away from the crowded streets, but [...] he will presently find
> himself in the midst of as pure an atmosphere and as rural and
> pleasant a scene as can be found in any town of England.[46]

Gissing, however, reads London suburbia as a spectacle both of the English
bourgeois cultural yearning for retirement to the countryside, and of its
failure, portraying suburbia in a condition of grotesque Dickensian squalor
stripped of its fantastic elements:[47]

> Her place of abode favoured neither health nor mental tranquillity.
> It was one of a row of new houses in a new quarter. A year or two
> ago the site had been an enclosed meadow, portion of the land
> attached to what was once a country mansion; London, devourer of
> rural limits, of a sudden made hideous encroachment upon the old

estate, now held by a speculative builder; of many streets to be constructed, three or four had already come into being, and others were mapped out, in mud and inchoate masonry, athwart the ravaged field. Great elms, the pride of generations passed away, fell before the speculative axe, or were left standing in mournful isolation to please a speculative architect; bits of wayside hedge still shivered in fog and wind, amid hoardings variegated with placards and scaffolding black against the sky. The very earth had lost its wholesome odour; trampled into mire, fouled with builders' refuse and the noisome drift from adjacent streets, it sent forth, under the sooty rain, a smell of corruption, of all the town's uncleanliness. On this rising locality had been bestowed the title of 'Park.'[48]

Until the late 1890s, Gissing nonetheless seems to find London indispensable for the production of his fiction. 'There grows in the North Country,' wrote Arnold Bennett in 1897, 'a certain kind of youth of whom it may be said that he was born to be a Londoner.'[49] Coming to London from the provinces was for hundreds of *fin de siècle* writers, including Bennett and Gissing, a virtual precondition of literary success. 'As "all roads led to Rome," when she was mistress of the world,' wrote Herbert Fry in 1880, 'now every thinker and worker, every artist, every inventor, seems to turn to London and find his best home or market here, where the multitudinous transactions of mankind are concentrated and carried on.'[50] 'London', Bennett adds, 'is the place where newspapers are issued, books written, and plays performed.'[51] Reardon and Biffen complain of having been seduced into poverty in London by the perception that successful writers must live there: ' "Because I was conscious of brains, I thought that the only place for me was London. [...] London is only a huge shop, with an hotel on the upper storeys." '[52] Gissing wrote *Born In Exile* after moving to Devon with his second wife, whom he had met in a London music-hall.[53] Within two years, however, Gissing had tired of both Edith and Devon, and returned to London. The whirlpool had drawn the author in once more; he wrote to Clara Collet in 1897: 'I need London for my work; in very truth, I can do very little away from it'.[54]

As HG Wells, among others, has noted, Gissing tends to group the characters of his novels around a particular 'structural theme': the subject of *The Whirlpool* (1897) is 'the fatal excitement and extravagance of the social life of London.'[55] Nearly all Gissing's protagonists must learn how to negotiate with London, how to preserve the self in an environment where the financial preconditions of life are still more strongly visible. For Gissing, London was a metonym for the commodification of human relations. A reviewer of *The Whirlpool* noted: 'All London speaks to him in the language of money; streets, clubs, theatres, lodgings, restaurants, suggest to him the human fight and fret and fume over money, its conventional tyranny and exigence'.[56] Bennett's protagonist, Richard Larch, is tempted into the moneyed heart of the metropolis on his first night in London, meeting enforced urban exchange in its most blatantly conspicuous forms: the shop window, the newspaper advertisement, the music hall and the prostitute. Commodification, modernity, femininity and publicity also combine to threaten the autonomy of the male protagonist of *The Whirlpool* (1897), the last of Gissing's novels in which the protagonist attempts to escape the condition of enforced negotiation with the hostile market. Subsequently, this condition is accepted, and even celebrated, by more resigned or less scrupulous protagonists such as the businessman-hero Piers Otway, the charlatan Dyce Lashmar or the successful grocer Will Warburton.

The identification of London with the market in this novel allows Gissing literally to map the characters' distance from it; in no other Gissing novel is the hero so preoccupied with the location of his home. London is more than just a setting; like the whirlpool that figuratively represents it, and also like money, the metropolis seems to have a power of its own. It takes strength greater than that usually possessed by the passive Gissing hero to resist the capital's pull towards its centre and steer clear. Charles Booth wrote in the ninth volume of *The Life and Labour of the People in London*, in the section 'London as a Centre of Trade and Industry':

> London maintains and develops a comprehensiveness that is almost magnificent in its catholicity and range. [...] These varied changes lead to an altered relationship between many parts of the industrial whole, and the fresh adaptations necessary, even though they be signs of growth, not infrequently involve dislocation.[57]

Modern living dislocates the self both literally and figuratively: drawn further into the heart of the symbolic whirlpool of urban life, and literally towards the geographical centre of London, Rolfe becomes subject to the disturbing fragmentation and estrangement of urban existence: 'In returning to Gunnersbury he felt hardly more sense of vital connection with this suburb than with the murky and roaring street in which he sat at business.'[58]

Initially, Rolfe barely participates at all in the social and economic life of the capital. In spite of his age, Rolfe is an ingénu within the urban social community into which he is gradually drawn (like Longdon in the 1899 London novel *The Awkward Age* by Henry James, an early and by no means complimentary reviewer of *The Whirlpool*).[59] Rolfe is able to live within his means, possessing sufficient income to travel and freely purchase books, although he is too indolent to move to the more comfortable lodgings his income could allow. Rolfe errs in believing that such a position of static compromise can be maintained as long as he lives within London. In this novel, the city is repeatedly described in terms of restless movement, change, excitement, spectacle; the market is hungry for new consumers, and draws the passive Rolfe into enforced negotiation through the medium of sexual desire. The whirlpool is also an image for the nexus of sexual relations, themselves heavily associated with money, appearances, speculation and London. The word 'engage' recurs in the novel in its meanings of marriage, employment and spending leisure-time, as if, beneath the level of perception, these meanings might overlap.[60] Through gazing at the reified body of the woman to whom he becomes 'engaged', Rolfe is forced into the public negotiation of desire that is the marriage contract.

The narrator notes disapprovingly that when Alma plays music, she does not enjoy it for its own sake, but for the pleasure of being looked at. Rolfe's eroticized gaze transforms her into another spectacular commodity on offer in the metropolis, and she becomes affordable once her price drops following her father's ruin and suicide. Once the price of Alma decreases, she is left vulnerable to a commercial transaction (hostile takeover? speculative deposit?) from the characters closest to the workings of the economy, the vulgar self-advertiser Dymes and the self-made millionaire Redgrave. Although his proposal 'must not read like a commercial overture', Rolfe's marriage still has to be paid for.[61] He admits earlier that ' "the educated man who marries on less than a thousand is either mad or a criminal." '[62] Rolfe has nine hundred; the difference, as Mr Micawber might have warned him, will prove crucial.

The financial preconditions of marriage are made still more conspicuous in the case of Rolfe's friend Morphew. When Morphew's income matches the price that her father has set on his *fiancée* Henrietta Winter, he will be able to marry. When Winter dies before this happens, his widow sanctions the match out of indignation at the small amount left to her in his will. In a typical Gissing twist, however, Henrietta herself cancels the engagement after learning of Morphew's illegitimate child from an affair with an unemployed servant-girl. This earlier union had begun in the London streets, the public spaces of the capital holding the illusory satisfaction of unfulfilled desires.[63] ' "This beastly town is the ruin of me, in every way" ', Morphew complains.[64]

Morphew's only recourse for increasing his income is speculation, an activity to which Gissing, like Dickens, is persistently hostile. 'The Britannia Loan, &c., &c., &c., had run its pestilent course; exciting avarice, perturbing quiet industry with the passion of the gamester, inflating vulgar ambition, now at length scattering wreck and ruin,' fumes Rolfe.[65] (The name of Frothingham's business suggests both sham, as in 'Britannia metal', and

national bankruptcy.) The speculative economy of *The Whirlpool* functions on
a principle of entropy: while accepting that participation of some kind with
the market is inevitable, the novel still warns that speculators never get out as
much as they put in. Morphew gains a couple of hundred pounds, and loses
three; Mrs Frothingham attempts to repay the wrong done by her husband to
'worthy recipients of her bounty', but the payment from the wreck will be no
more than ' "eighteenpence in the pound" '.[66] As time passes, Harvey's stock
decreases in value: the one character unaffected by the Britannia crash in the
first chapter now has to learn the language of speculation. Earlier, Harvey
suggests that (typically of a Gissing protagonist) his purchases of books provide
a legible narrative of the development of his life; his reading is now 'the
money article in his daily paper' and 'financial newspapers'.[67] Friction with
the market must wear away capital: the more Harvey attempts to realize, the
more he loses; by the ending of the book, the unstable fluctuations of the plot
have decreased his capital.

Midway through the novel, a long discussion of the hero's finances is
prefixed by the narrator's observation that, 'Alma took it for granted that
Harvey would not allow *their* expenditure to outrun *his* income' (my italics).[68]
Consumption is female; income, except from prostitution, male: attempting
to resist the lure of speculation, Rolfe calls upon himself for 'moderate manliness'.[69] Harvey's labour in the money markets is pathologized as a violation of
his masculine identity, not fertile production but onanistic speculation:

> He felt like one who meddles with something forbidden – who pries,
> shamefaced, into the secrets of an odious vice. To study the money-
> market gave him a headache. He had to go for a country walk, to
> bathe and change his clothes, before he was at ease again.[70]

Marriage to an urban woman makes static compromise with the demands
of the market impossible. The solicitor Leach is worked to death by the consumption of his womenfolk; Hugh Carnaby has to go into business to pay for
Sibyl's neverending consumption. For the Rolfes, ' "The choice between
vulgar display with worry, and a simple, refined life with perfect comfort" ', is
no choice at all, since the economic conditions of middle-class life in London
do not allow the 'perfection' of the latter to exist.[71] 'Comfort' has been reified
into commodities that must be paid for. Even in their first home in rural
Wales, Mrs Frothingham notices that the 'simple life' in Wales is in fact very
close to the normal standard of bourgeois luxury. ' "There's no middle way,
with peace" ', Harvey admits later in the book. ' "Living nowadays means
keeping up appearances." '[72]

Like the Carters and Mrs Reardon in *New Grub Street* and the Mumfords in

The Paying Guest, the Carnabys continually live slightly beyond their means. The Rolfes and the narrator both note fastidiously the conspicuousness of Sibyl's consumption:

> Mrs. Carnaby's requirements were one or two expensive trifles, which she chose with leisurely gratification of her taste. It surprised Alma to see this extravagance; one would have thought the purchaser had never known restricted means, and dreamt of no such thing; she bought what she happened to desire, as a matter of course. And this was no ostentation for Alma's benefit. Evidently Sibyl had indulged herself with the same freedom throughout her travels; for she had brought back a museum of beautiful and curious things, which must have cost a good deal. Perhaps for the first time in her life Alma experienced a sense of indignation at the waste of money. She was envious withal, which possibly helped to explain the other impulse.[73]

A more adept version of Zola's *Nana* – Hugh's brother notes how well Sibyl has looked after their business affairs during Hugh's stay in prison – Sibyl apparently sells her own body to pay for her spending, exchanging a virtue worth far more than the fripperies she buys with the proceeds. ('Spend' can also mean both to exhaust by using up wastefully, and, in nineteenth-century slang, to orgasm.[74]) Her speculation also costs Sibyl's exhausted husband most of his physical capital during his prison sentence, as if his body too becomes 'spent'.

As Rachel Bowlby has suggested, the new public spaces created by the department store and similar changes in the practice of shopping, placed commerce and femininity into new, and often uneasy, relations.[75] The increasingly popular practice of shopping as a leisure activity by middle-class women makes them subject to spectacular gaze in urban public spaces.[76] In such liminal environments, the figure of the prostitute, both consumer object and saleswoman for her own commodified body, underlies the typology of the modern urban woman.[77] Minnie, the servant-cum-prostitute of 'Raw Material' in *Human Odds and Ends* is categorized as 'no longer raw material, but a finished article of commerce.'[78] In *The Whirlpool*, Mrs Strangeways acts as a procuress for Redgrave. The novel pivots on a virtual act of prostitution by Sibyl Carnaby: Mrs Lant suggests to Carnaby that Sibyl has slept with Redgrave to ensure his investment in her husband's company. 'Such a woman might surely have sold herself to great advantage', notes the narrator sardonically of Sibyl's marriage; in language that connects prostitution to urban topography, Alma indignantly accuses Sibyl of being 'a woman who had sold herself for money, whose dishonour differed in no respect from that of the woman of the pavement.'[79] Carnaby himself recounts the story of 'a woman in London who keeps up a big house and entertains all sorts of people': the story exposes the economically and sexually corrupt economic basis of Society's supposedly respectable façade.[80]

The first Mrs Frothingham (Alma's biological mother), Mrs Bunscombe (the music-hall singer divorced by Rolfe's landlord as Rolfe marries Alma) and Mrs Abbott prior to her desertion all provide examples of the alternate urban type of the neglectful mother. Alma tries to be a good rural wife like the over-idealized Mrs Morton but, drawn once more into the whirlpool of the city, she reverts to type and the domestic experiment fails: ' "Art and house-keeping won't go together." '[81] When Alma becomes a professional musician, she yields the meaning of her name to the vulgar publicity of newspapers and advertisements. In the commodified environment of this novel, an attempt at artistic success cannot succeed without the sacrifice of both capital and sincerity. Alma negotiates again with the hostile, consuming economy in the persons of her former would-be purchasers, Dymes and Redgrave. As with *In the Year of Jubilee*, Gissing's muted, heavily qualified feminism permits the reader to identify in Sibyl's consumption, Alma's artistic ambitions and the excessive socializing of the Leach sisters a wish to escape the limitations of prescribed gender roles; but such aspirations are as stunted by economic reality as the laudable desires of Gissing's earlier male characters to travel, produce art or read classical literature. The novel holds that there are values, particularly parenthood, which should not be sacrificed to satisfy such desires; consequently, Alma's neglect of motherhood in pursuing her career is to be deplored.[82]

Heredity – duplicity inherited from her father, and nervous excitability from her mother – and (urban) environment combine to propel Alma into the manufacture of fraudulent appearances. This labour costs Alma valuable reserves of physical capital.[83] William Greenslade locates Alma's degenera-tion within late nineteenth-century discourses of female hysteria, in particular Herbert Spencer's calculation of the 'taxation' exacted on the female body by roles other than motherhood.[84] Physically and financially, she must get out less than she put in: although the concert appears to be a success, the amount of money spent on the inflated signification of advertisements means it makes a loss. Alma is subsequently eliminated by the whirlpool's Spencerian unwill-ingness to support any authentic or artistic project which does not conform to the commercial values of the market. In this novel, not only has art become commercialized, but art that is not commercialized cannot survive. Culture has become mere display, shopping and advertising: 'Advertising is a work of art,' proclaims Dymes; Alma's Vuillaume violin is replaced by an inferior, probably shop-bought, model.[85] Mrs Strangeways's first husband painted, and 'died in a garret or a workhouse'.[86] Thistlewood tries to be an artist, but exchanges a finger for 'the honour of working himself to death to support a very expensive young woman, who cared no more for him than for her cast-off shoes', before he realizes the fatal nature of artistic life, and reduces his ambitions to become a teacher.[87] Successful culture is either debased, like Dymes's catchy pop tunes, or imitative, like the photography shop, which along with Carnaby's bicycle factory provides new, democratic technology for 'the better kind of clerk'.[88]

At the height of her urge to re-enter society, Alma claims that as the 'wife of a gentleman of independent means; in theory, all circles should be open to her.'[89] Such circles are not merely social circles, but also the downward spiral of those caught in the whirlpool. Also open to Alma, therefore, are the infernal circles of the 'ghastly whirlpool which roars over the bottomless pit.'[90] In 1885, and subsequently throughout his life, Gissing read Dante, who was according to Michael Wheeler 'the presiding genius of nineteenth century social criticism'. Gissing revives in this novel the image from his working-class novel of London as a hell on earth.[91] He also refers to an earlier version of Hell:[92]

> "The whirlpool!" muttered Carnaby, with a broken laugh. "It's got hold of *me*, and I'm going down, old man – and it looks black as hell."
> "We shall see the sunlight again together," replied Rolfe, with forced cheerfulness."[93]

The musician Orpheus escapes Hell but accidentally leaves his wife Eurydice behind; Sibyl keeps her explorer husband in the whirlpool, making bicycles.[94] The exposure of Alma's part in Redgrave's death exhausts her remaining physical capital, and she dies (not through suicide, as has been claimed) following an accidental overdose of a patent medicine remedy for 'fashionable disorder of the nerves.'[95]

As a widower, Rolfe can at last escape to Basil Morton's house in idyllic Greystone. (Finally leaving his wife in 1897, Gissing also left the whirlpool of London for Italy and then Dorking, determined that his son 'shall grow up away from London'.[96]) Morton's existence depends on contradictions: "It was in the town, yet nothing town-like [...] He lived by trade, but trade did not affect his life.'[97] Although Patrick Parrinder notes that Morton's old-fashioned form of economic existence is doomed, supported in this 'sincere' way, for the moment Morton's course in life steers clear of the whirlpool, with the result that he hardly appears in the novel at all.[98] The novel's closing rural setting is the only possible location for the kind of education Rolfe plans for his son, away from the dangerous influences narrated in the novel. The endings of *The Odd Women*, *In the Year of Jubilee* and *The Whirlpool* all involve a child, its presence providing the hope of a better future existence, but also a warning that better futures cannot be achieved without sacrifice.

The Businessman as Hero: *The Crown of Life*

It is characteristic of Gissing's later work that the hero of *The Whirlpool* eventually finds some economic equilibrium by investing in a shop; his later heroes tend to accept a greater accommodation to economic realities. The minor characters Sally and O'Keefe in the early *The Unclassed* open a shop, but as the only route out of prostitution and penury. Compared to Kingcote's wrench into labour in *Isabel Clarendon* (1886), Will Warburton becomes a grocer relatively cheerfully; as in *The Unclassed*, at least such a means of income is secure, since it relies on basic biological need. For a gentleman with an education but no independent means, shopkeeping may be the least degrading of the available options; as Morphew and, rather less ingenuously, Alexander Otway suggest:

> "A fellow like myself – decent family, public school, and that kind of thing – naturally fights shy of shopkeeping. But I've got to the point that I don't care what I do, if only it'll bring me a steady income in an honest way. I ought to be able to make several hundreds a year, even at starting, out of that business."[99]

> "I would apply myself to the science and art of money-making in the only hopeful way – honest buying and selling. There's something so satisfying about it. I envy even the little shopkeeper, who reckons up his profits every Saturday night, and sees his business growing. But you must begin early; you must learn money-making like anything else. If I had made money, Piers, I should be at this moment the most virtuous and meritorious citizen of the British Empire!"[100]

As I have argued, in the 1890s Gissing showed a greater willingness to cooperate with the literary market, and his representation of commerce also alters, notably in his last completed novel *Will Warburton*. Luisa Villa has recently suggested that 'The predicament of [Gissing's] hero-grocer somehow reflects that of the fiction-writer *vis-à-vis* the literary market-place, and the happy ending of his "romance of real life" seems to foreshadow a degree of reconciliation with the economics of democratic modernity.'[101] Gissing's late novels do not articulate a critique of market values to the same degree as his earlier work, and have received less critical attention since his death. Yet comparatively slighter, if enjoyable, works such as *The Paying Guest* (1896) and *The Town Traveller* received more attention and praise in Gissing's own lifetime than the works more valued by present-day critics.[102] As Gissing became more successful as a novelist, his protagonists, too, generally become more successful, leading ultimately to Henry Ryecroft's perfect escape. The success of the businessman-hero Piers Otway even secures success in love as well: Gissing's treatment of the erotic notably softens after he fell in love with Gabrielle Fleury in 1898.[103] This relationship and his greater commercial success in the late 1890s mark a watershed in his work as important as Nell's death and Gissing's European travels in 1888–9.

In *The Crown of Life*, Gissing's familiar preoccupations nonetheless remain in place: money and its lack, education and intellectual development, high culture, the material conditions under which love might flourish or die. Gissing also continues to ironize Victorian narrative conventions. Piers's narrative begins when he is told of an inheritance that is due to him. The multiple legacies in this novel, like nearly every inheritance in Gissing, fail to provide the escape into Marxian freedom ostensibly available to those with an 'independence'. Jerome Otway's unhappy first wife inherits two thousand pounds after she marries, when it is too late to raise her value in the marriage market. Mrs Hannaford uses her inheritance to escape her appalling husband: 'The money is my own and I will be free' – but the possession of wealth makes her a target for the fortune hunter Daniel Otway.[104] The resulting fear of scandal costs Mrs Hannaford her life; in this kind of economy, it is perhaps as well that her daughter Olga will not inherit so dangerous a legacy. Jerome Otway dies intestate, depriving Piers of the capital that he deserves and needs in order to make his fortune in Russia. The sophist aesthete Kite, another of Gissing's impoverished artists, subsists on a tiny inherited annuity of £45 4s. 4d., barely sufficient to keep him alive; 'also, no doubt, it kept him from doing what he might have done, in art or anything else.'[105] For those with a certain temperament, such as Kite or *Our Mutual Friend*'s Mortimer Lightwood, a tiny amount of wealth can be even more disabling than poverty.

Piers Otway gives away most of the inheritance he receives from his mother to his speculating, inauthentic, market-driven brothers Alexander and Daniel. (Surprisingly, given Gissing's tendency to incorporate auto-biographical material and the fact that he himself had two brothers, Algernon, also a novelist, and William, who died at the age of twenty, this late novel is the first since *Demos* to deal at length with the brother/brother relationship. Gissing also had two sisters – perhaps he found sibling conflict across gender boundaries more dramatic: the Baskes, the Lords, the Milvains, the Warricombes). The capital that remains to Piers is invested in business. Late in his career, Gissing evolves a taxonomy of labour that allows different moral returns on different kinds of employment; the novel forces the reader's concurrence with Irene's contention that ' "A useful life isn't to be despised." '[106] Piers rejects dishonest, inauthentic or exploitative labour in London for 'steady, dogged toil' abroad.[107] Surprisingly, in this novel (and also *A Life's Morning*), academic, not physical, labour is pathologized into the language of physical capital:

> "You are injuring your health," said Mrs Hannaford gravely, "and it is unkind to those who care for you."
> "Wait a few weeks," he replied cheerily, "and I'll make up the health account."[108]

Like Wilfrid Athel, Piers exhausts himself by attempting to enter a career for which he is temperamentally unsuited. Culture is best enjoyed not in competitive examination, but privately and disinterestedly, like Jerome Otway's enthusiasm for Dante (whose associations here are more positive than in *The Whirlpool*).

Like Rolfe, Piers is propelled into economic negotiation by sexual desire. He is first seen gazing at engravings in a shop window. The novel's opening conflates female beauty (the idealized subject of the photographs) with money, consumption and social mobility. 'He could not satisfy himself with looking and musing; he could not pluck himself away.'[109] In an ironic inversion of the narcissistic flawless self-image that, according to Rachel Bowlby, modern commercialism offers the self, Piers is made overly self-conscious by his sudden awareness of the financial realities that underlie social and sexual life, and of his own low value according to them: 'Every shop-mirror which reflected him seemed to present a malicious caricature'.[110]

'Satisfaction' can only be achieved from purchase, which requires money. After falling in love with Irene Derwent, the real embodiment of his idealistic sexual desire, Piers resolves to earn money. His early desire for singular, disinterested literary work is immediately displaced by the narrative of needing money: 'He had dreamt of distinction; that also must be patiently awaited. In the meantime, labour. He enjoyed intellectual effort; he gloried in the amassing of mental riches.'[111] The meaning of 'mental riches' must shift from the metaphorical riches of cultural accomplishment to Piers's imagining of the literal riches that allow culture, and love, to exist. ' "I think there is no harm in telling you that I hope to make money. If I do so, it will be done, I think, honourably, as the result of hard work." '[112]

Throughout the novel, Piers insists that he is not interested in making money for its own sake, but as a means to an end. All of his business is transacted within strict moral limits: he declines a deserved share of his father's estate, does not reclaim loans to his brothers and refuses interest on them, curtly informing Alexander ' "I'm not a money-lender." '[113] Piers delivers an impassioned attack on the immoral commercial spectacle of corporate topography, but tries to emphasize how the individual businessman can be separated from the process of money-making.

> The weather was hot; one should have been far away from these huge rampart-streets, these stifling burrows of commerce. But here toil and stress went on as usual, and Piers Otway saw it all in a lurid light. These towering edifices with inscriptions numberless, announcing every imaginable form of trade with every corner of the world; here a vast building, consecrate in all its commercial magnificence, great windows and haughty doorways, the gleam of gilding and of brass, the lustre of polished woods, to a single company or firm; here is a huge structure which housed on its many floors a crowd of enterprises, names by the score signalled at the foot of the gaping staircase; arrogant suggestions of triumph side by side with desperate beginnings; titles of world-wide significance meeting the eye at every turn, vulgar names with more weight than those of princes, words in small lettering which ruled the fate of millions of men; – no nightmare was ever so crushing to one in Otway's mood. The brute force of money; the negation of the individual – these, the evils of our time, found their supreme expression in the City of London. Here was opulence at home and superb; here must poverty lurk and shrink, feeling itself alive only on sufferance; the din of highway and byway was a voice of blustering conquest, bidding the weaker to stand aside or be crushed. Here no man was a human being, but each merely a portion of an inconceivably complicated mechanism. The shiny-hatted figure who rushed or sauntered, gloomed by himself at corners or made one of a talking group, might elsewhere be found a reasonable and kindly person, with traits, peculiarities; here one could see in him nothing but a money-maker of this or that class, ground to a certain pattern. The smooth working of the huge machine made it only the more sinister; one had but to remember what cold tyranny, what elaborate fraud, were served by its manifold ingenuities, only to think of the cries of anguish stifled by its monotonous roar.[114]

In contrast to Gissing's organic, totalizing vision of a local micro-economy in *The Nether World*, the discourse here temporarily allows the separation of professional from personal life.[115] What is perhaps most surprising about this passage in the context of the rest of Gissing's work is its political quietism. The voice of protest at market conditions is registered, but the possibility of the separation of the individual from the commodified environment in which Piers labours, at last seemingly accepted in Gissing's fiction, allows him to work and continue to be narrated. He can earn money without losing authenticity as long as he maintains sufficient distance from the 'machine'.

Irene, whose name, significantly, means 'peace', is valorized as Piers's just reward for fair-dealing economic success; consequently, unlike *The Whirlpool*, business in this novel can be gendered as a masculine activity. While making money, Piers also makes 'a cult of physical soundness' so that he can attract Irene, 'the prize of wealth, distinction, and high manliness.'[116] Imperialism, however, is characterized as the grotesque over-performance of aggressive masculinity, as embodied in the near-homicidal weapons designer Hannaford. (Dr Derwent's honest patriotism suggests that over-attachment to imperial aggression, not love of country, is for Gissing the real social evil.)[117] *The Whirlpool* dramatizes Gissing's belief that Empire is capitalism writ large, imperialism the self-justifying ideology of 'the buccaneering shopkeeper, the whisky-distiller with a rifle', a petty despot like Robert Louis Stevenson's Attwater.[118] Gissing presciently wrote to Bertz in 1896:

> The late troubles in S. Africa are of course due entirely to capitalist greed. I cannot see any hope for peace, so long as these men of the money-market are permitted to control public life – as they now practically do. But, alas, we must remember that humanity is most imperfectly civilized.[119]

Jerome Otway's interpolated fairy tale, for instance, dramatizes the belief that war is market-driven, especially by the arms and newspaper industries:

> "They say," ventured Irene, with a smile, "that, but for such men, we may really become a mere nation of shopkeepers."
> "Do they? But may we not fear that their ideal is simply a shopkeeper ready to shoot anyone who rivals him in trade?"[120]

Gissing was appalled by the resurgence in nationalistic imperialism in the late 1890s, and by the possibility of a European war.[121] *The Crown of Life* suggests that if money has to be made, it is much better to do so by peaceful means, such as trading with other nations, than violent ones, such as fighting them.

The spokesman for imperialism in *The Crown of Life* is the nationalist politician Arnold Jacks, the next in Gissing's succession of triumphant charlatans; his ancestors are the clergymen Whiffle and Chilvers.[122] Like Chilvers, Jacks's behaviour is governed entirely by how his actions will appear to others; he even values Irene largely for the impression she will make. As her sometime fiancé, Arnold Jacks threatens the possibility of Piers's possible success: in spite of a successful negotiation in which he maintains his authenticity, the hero still might fail to gain that which he desires the most. However, Irene establishes her true value by refusing Jacks when she feels he is more concerned with appearances than reality in the matter of her aunt's supposed affair with Daniel Otway. The novel's other marriages seem governed by desire for social success: Mrs Jacks marries her first husband for money in a transaction in which she is 'nothing but a socially sanctioned purchase'; after she is widowed, Eustace Derwent then marries her for the sake of his own social advancement.[123]

When he first falls in love with Irene, Otway imagines her to be the antithesis of commercial values of sale and profit: 'This girl could not but bestow something of herself on all with whom she came together'.[124] Otway's value is finally established in turn for Irene by his charitable purchase of her aunt's compromising letters; the happy ending is finally possible once she no longer believes Piers to be in debt to his brother. Irene's breaking of her first engagement is described by Gissing as a resistance to British imperialism: 'it was as though a British admiral on his ironclad found himself mocked by some elusive little gunboat, newly invented by the condemned foreigner.'[125] Their union is an act of private resistance to society's predominant values: Gissing was aware that his anti-imperialist stance was, typically, an unpopular one.[126] Both Piers and Irene recognize the nature of the public world: its sham exteriors, aggressive martial capitalism and violations of culture and feeling; the rural setting of the final chapters suggest that in marrying they renounce it.

High-cultural art forms again have no place in this happy ending, Jerome's harmless Dante obsession notwithstanding. Alexander quotes freely from Homer and Tennyson, but by the end of the novel makes his living from the degraded artistic form of the music hall. The novel's most conspicuous model of worldly success, Arnold Jacks, deprecates *In Memoriam* as 'a shocking instance of wasted energy' and suggests compression of the poem by rewriting it as prose.[127] Irene mocks as 'imbecile' a novel whose hero's ' "prospects in life are supposed to be utterly blighted [...] because his father and mother forgot the marriage ceremony" ', only pages after the prospects of *The Crown of Life*'s hero do seem blighted because of his illegitimacy.[128] She dismisses Piers's poetry and suit as 'pure romance': work, not poetry, operates as the means of sexual selection.[129] Even more emphatically than *New Grub Street*, *The Crown of Life* refuses the possibility of art's autonomy from the market. Olga Hannaford has artistic talent, but supports herself by providing illustrations to women's magazines: ' "It isn't high art, you know, but they pay me." '[130] As *In the Year of Jubilee* makes clear, Gissing regarded these periodicals as a debased form of publication, yet here the narrator's voice is uncritical of the way she has chosen to support herself.[131] However, even a commercialized, pseudo-Bohemian artistic life proves too uncomfortable, and when her mother inherits a fortune, Olga returns to 'a respectable, plodding, money-saving married life' after all.[132] Well-dressed, she becomes a 'wonderful illustration of the effect of apparel'; after the fortune is lost, Olga marries not the artist Kite, but the vulgar Florio, 'who, in his elegant attire, rather reminded one of a fashion plate'.[133] As for Eve Madeley in *Eve's Ransom*, Gissing's narrator has some sympathy with her morally compromised choice from among a very limited number of options (although he notes the decline in Olga's looks after she goes into society).[134] In Florio, ironically named after the translator of Montaigne, pure aestheticism meets pure commercialism: a man who is all surface, he wants to cover every empty space he sees with advertisements, from public railings to the backs of bus drivers. As Miss Bonnicastle cheerfully admits, even Gissing's cherished classical culture is not safe from debasement:

> "Yes, it's Ariadne – but I doubt if I shall have the brutality to finish out my idea. She is to have lying on the sand by her a case of Higginson's Hair-wash, stranded from a wreck, and a bottle of it in her hand."[135]

Not long after *The Crown of Life* was published, Royal Academy artist and socialist Walter Crane could use classical images to promote Pears Soap (see Figure 2).[136]

In spite of this novel's uncharacteristically happy ending, *The Crown of Life* retains some continuity with Gissing's earlier realist pessimism. While virtue, identified here as liberal politics, is its own reward, it is able to survive only when it brings material reward as well. Although Irene and Piers do not become casualties of the competitive economy, the visible results of its processes on the other characters, even those who are initially decent, like Alexander and Olga, are dispiriting. Piers succeeds in a world of charlatans and fake surfaces, but, having achieved his object, withdraws from this world when, finally, an inheritance works to a character's advantage: John Jacks's death allows Piers's independence from the business if he wishes. (Even this business will be threatened should Britain and Russia go to war over the North West frontier, as Mr March suggests.) Gissing's protest against the

Figure 2. Even Gissing's cherished classical culture was not safe from debasement by advertising; here, the Royal Academy artist Walter Crane uses classical images to promote Pears' Soap.

market is at its most muted in this novel. The logic of Jasper Milvain has become so strong that it is embodied in the shiny façades of the City of London's architecture: unexplaining, irresistible, immanent and untouchable by the free play of criticism.

Death by Utopia: *The Private Papers of Henry Ryecroft*

Despite the greater financial freedom of the later heroes, few options are still available to them: to become an absolute fraud like *Our Friend the Charlatan*'s Dyce Lashmar, or a shopkeeper like Will Warburton. *Veranilda*, published posthumously and incomplete in 1904, although Gissing had been planning it for years, is as far removed as possible from the realist economic processes the middle-aged author has come to accept as irresistible (although it does contain an intrigue about a will, and a great deal of alienable property changes hands). *The Private Papers of Henry Ryecroft* (1903), one of Gissing's most popular books, is a kind of fantasy, a resignation from the battle of life. Even this book's assertions, however, may be as ironic as those of Gissing's earlier creations.[137] Ryecroft may be read as a typical Gissing hero with all of his desires fulfilled, the impossible dream of a benevolent legacy realized at last: the book is 'more an aspiration than a memory', Gissing admitted to Frederic

Harrison.[138] Fredric Jameson identifies Ryecroft's mode of life as a desired absence in the early novels:

> The exclusive preoccupation in Gissing with the anxieties of money, the misery of hand-to-mouth survival, the absence of independent means or a fixed income, is a way of short-circuiting this intolerable alternative, for it positions the realization of genuine desire in the future, in that Utopian fantasy of a life situation in which one would finally have the leisure necessary to write.[139]

Gissing's fiction is always highly self-conscious: in this book Gissing seems to be toying with the conventions of his own corpus of work. Inheritance releases Ryecroft from the necessity of labour, and immediately he leaves both writing and London. Although Ryecroft repeatedly expresses his contentment with his life, much of the material of the book is comprised of the backward-looking relation of sentiments very similar to those of Gissing's earlier, unhappier heroes. The self and the world are in hostile relation. Happiness is commodified as the purchase of food and books; each commodity can be traded off against the other. Ryecroft had in his youth valued the career of writing, but realizes in time literature's dependence on the laws of the marketplace. Literary labour is unremunerative, injurious to the health, as commercial as any other form of labour, but even more competitive. Ryecroft admits the malleability of his own character in harsh or uncomfortable economic circumstances, and that those of different temperament might thrive better under the same conditions. His duty is to be true to his temperament, where conditions permit him.[140]

Although 'There is no moral good which has not to be paid for in coin of the realm', the pursuit of money for its own sake is odious. Ryecroft is as aware as the narrator of any Gissing book of the pedigree of his wealth. This being late Gissing, however, he discriminates between morally acceptable and repugnant forms of labour, honest agricultural work being the best example of the former, and war the worst of the latter.[141] Ryecroft iterates once more a familiar nineteenth-century paradox:

> One symbol, indeed, has obscured all others – the minted round of metal. And one may safely say that, of all the ages since a coin first became the symbol of power, ours is that in which it yields to the majority of its possessors the poorest return in heart's contentment.[142]

Value can be found in experiences which labour might fund, such as the private contemplation of books and nature, a knowledge of the former increasing one's enjoyment of the latter. Classical culture is valued, but as something with no referent or relevance outside itself. Essential even before these values is 'comfort', a particularly English virtue. Sacrifices are thus worth making for this virtue, including the sacrifice of youthful socialist principles. Like his author, Ryecroft feels easier dealing with exceptional individuals of a class than the class itself. 'Education is a thing of which only the few are capable' he rules; one should be raised, like *The Whirlpool*'s Minnie Wager, to one's calling. Ryecroft's mutely acquiescent working-class housekeeper is 'fulfilling the offices for which she was born'. Even this transaction is outside the market, her primary motivation duty more than wages. Ryecroft's fear of the mob is rooted in his Spencerian belief in the harsh competitiveness of social life and his disgust at the vulgarity of majority taste. This sits uneasily, as he confesses, with his love of occasional conviviality and sympathy with the Kipps-like holidaying artisan in the inn.[143]

Ryecroft admits that what he possesses bears no relation to what he deserves:

> I ask myself whether I shall not have to pay, by some disaster, for this period of sacred calm. For a week or so I have been one of a small number, chosen out of the whole human race by fate's supreme benediction. [...] That my own lot seems so much better than that of ordinary men, sometimes makes me fearful.[144]

Ryecroft's money thus makes him the ending of a novel without plot: 'My life is over.'[145] This book can assert values so freely because it is all discourse, with little narrative, hence the circular, seasonal structure: indeed Gissing admitted to Pinker, his agent, that the book was 'not a novel'.[146] Once Gissing has provided his protagonist with a happy ending, there is nothing more to tell, only short essays on national characteristics, weak pastoral lyricism and short narratives of Ryecroft's time in London of poverty, labour and disease. For the first time, Gissing's ideological position is a nostalgia neither narratable nor, indeed, especially engaging. The decline into vulgar showiness of Chaffey's in *The Town Traveller* is far more convincing than Ryecroft's notorious musings on the poor quality of English butter.

Yet for a utopian existence, Ryecroft's life does not seem particularly attractive, at least for those who do not share Ryecroft's peculiar temperament. Eileen Sypher writes of *Demos*, 'like all nostalgic texts, it simultaneously inscribes its subtle knowledge of its vision's outdatedness, impossibility, and even undesirability'; the same might be said of *The Private Papers of Henry Ryecroft*.[147] Ryecroft's renunciation of life, his non-narratability, his near-withdrawal from utterance make this book almost as self-negating as most of Gissing's other work. 'I have always regarded as a fact of infinite pathos the ability men have to subdue themselves to the conditions of life. Contentment so often means resignation, abandonment of the hope seen to be forbidden.'[148] There is as much pathos in *Ryecroft* as genuine contentment. Freed from economic necessity, the protagonist has supposedly given up writing, but the proof that he has been unable to free himself from this 'mechanic' labour is before the reader's eyes. Ryecroft has not escaped as far as he believes; his papers are collected, 'edited' by George Gissing and sold. Mark Storey notices the irony of the Preface's opening sentence: 'The name of Henry Ryecroft never became familiar to what is called the reading public.'[149] Ryecroft has become a commodity after all, caught in Gissing's favourite irony, that of the impossibility of escape from the marketplace.

Gissing's art springs from multiple impulses: Alfred Gissing suggests that his father's work was generated by separate 'imaginative' and 'intellectual' faculties.[150] His work is continually in a state of negotiation between opposing polarities: the duty of the artist to represent the world both truthfully and morally, even if the world appears deceptive and immoral, and to write from personal conviction while maintaining rational objectivity. He dramatizes how environment can determine character, but refuses to admit that such determination wholly relieves the self from moral responsibility. Gissing's achievement is to write eloquently of failure, a theme that, in various guises, runs throughout his work, while allowing a realm of value to be precariously established beyond the money-ordered reality that he portrays with such fidelity.[151] 'The Hope of Pessimism' exhorts Man to 'cultivate our perception of man's weakness, learn thoroughly the pathos inherent in a struggle between the finite and the infinite.'[152] As Gisela Argyle notes, Gissing's pessimism was un-Schopenhauerian in being dialectical: his fictions are in a constant state of negotiation, of struggle.[153] He deploys the inherited narrative conventions of Victorian fiction ironically, in order to resist the authoritarian judgements of the classic Victorian ending. While deeply morally engaged, even at times opinionated, Gissing's work is so structured that its meanings should not be read as closed. If resistance to the monologic determinations of received wisdom is a characteristic of great literary writing, then Gissing deserves perhaps a more prominent place in the canon of Victorian fiction than he has occupied up to now.

NOTES

INTRODUCTION

1 In Anne Digby and Peter Searby, *Children, School and Society in Nineteenth Century England* (London: Macmillan, 1981), p. 113.

2 *The Collected Letters of George Gissing*, ed. by Pierre Coustillas, Paul F Mattheisen and Arthur C Young, 9 vols (Athens: Ohio University Press, 1990–7), VII, p. 172.

3 *Letters*, VI, p. 60.

4 *London and the Life of Literature in Late Victorian England: The Diary of George Gissing, Novelist*, ed. by Pierre Coustillas (Hassocks: Harvester Press, 1978), pp. 130–1.

5 *A Life's Morning*, ed. by Pierre Coustillas (London: Smith, Elder, 1888; repr. Brighton: Harvester Press, 1984), p. 84.

6 John Vernon, *Money and Fiction: Literary Realism in the Nineteenth and Early Twentieth Centuries* (Ithaca: Cornell University Press, 1984), p. 7.

7 See Jacob Korg, 'George Orwell and his Favorite Novelist', *Gissing Newsletter*, 21.4 (1985), 1–10.

8 *The Complete Works of George Orwell*, ed. by Peter Davison, Ian Angus and Sheila Davison, 20 vols (London: Secker and Warburg, 1986–98), IV: *Keep the Aspidistra Flying*, [n.p.]. In his essay, 'Not Enough Money: A Sketch of George Gissing', Orwell calls Gissing 'perhaps the best novelist England has produced', *Tribune* 2 April 1943, *Works* XV: *Two Wasted Years*, pp. 45–7 (p. 45).

9 Patrick Brantlinger, *The Reading Lesson: The Threat of Mass Literacy in Nineteenth-Century British Fiction* (Bloomington: Indiana University Press, 1998), p. 123.

10 Vladimir Propp, *Morphology of the Folktale*, 2nd edn, trans. by Laurence Scott, ed. by Svatava Pirkova-Jakobson, Louis Wagner and Alan Dundes (Austin: University of Texas Press, 1968), pp. 21, 64.

11 *Shirley*, ed. by Herbert Rosengarten and Margaret Smith (Oxford: Clarendon Press, 1979), p. 274.

12 On the universal equivalence of money, see Marc Shell, *Money, Language and Thought: Literary and Philosophical Economies from the Medieval to the Modern Era* (Berkeley: University of California Press, 1982), pp. 105–11.

13 Grahame Smith, *Dickens, Money and Society* (Berkeley: University of California Press, 1968), pp. 64–5.

14 Thomas Carlyle, *Past and Present*, ed. by Richard D Altick (New York: New York University Press, 1965), p. 148.

15 For a reading that attempts to relate some of these arguments to *Our Mutual Friend* in this context, see Mary Poovey, 'Speculation and Virtue in *Our Mutual Friend*', in *Making*

a Social Body: British Cultural Formation 1830–1864 (Chicago: Chicago University Press, 1995), pp. 155–81. See also Kurt Heinzelman, *The Economics of the Imagination* (Amherst: University of Massachusetts Press, 1980), pp. 70–109. For Gissing's reading of Mill, see *George Gissing at Work: a Study of his Notebook Extracts From my Reading*, ed. by Pierre Coustillas and Patrick Bridgwater (Greensboro: ELT, 1988), pp. 66–7.

16 Barbara Weiss, *The Hell of the English: Bankruptcy and the Victorian Novel* (London: Associated University Presses, 1986), pp. 29–30.

17 *David Copperfield*, ed. by Nina Burgis (Oxford: Clarendon Press, 1981), p. 650. Cf. William Morris, 'Useful Work versus Useless Toil', *Works*, ed. by May Morris, 24 vols (London: Longmans Green, 1915), XXIII: *Signs of Change; Lectures on Socialism*, pp. 98–120.

18 Robin Gilmour, *The Idea of the Gentleman in the Victorian Novel* (London Allen and Unwin, 1981), pp. 97–8.

19 Malthus, *An Essay on the Principle of Population; and a Summary View of the Principle of Population*, ed. by Anthony Flew (Harmondsworth: Penguin, 1982), p. 183.

20 Daniel Born, *The Birth of Liberal Guilt in the English Novel: Charles Dickens to H G Wells* (Chapel Hill: University of North Carolina Press, 1995), pp. 27–8.

21 Heinzelman, p. 74; Josephine Guy, 'Aesthetics, Economics and Commodity Culture: Theorizing Value in Late Nineteenth-Century Britain', *English Literature in Transition*, 42.2 (1999), 143–71.

22 'The Storyteller', in *Illuminations*, ed. by Hannah Arendt, trans. by Harry Zohn (London: Cape, 1970), pp. 83–109 (pp. 86–7).

23 A comprehensive defence of this statement above would, admittedly, require another volume considerably longer than this one. For a very readable discussion of this subject, albeit one with which I am not wholly in agreement, see Wayne C Booth, *The Company We Keep: An Ethics of Fiction* (Berkeley: University of California Press, 1988). In an influential essay on the writing of history, Hayden White has argued that inherently 'narrativizing discourse serves the purpose of moralizing judgements'. 'The Value of Narrativity in the Representation of Reality', in *On Narrative*, ed. by WJT Mitchell (Chicago: Chicago University Press, 1981), pp. 1–23 (p. 23). See also Peter Brooks, *Reading for the Plot: Design and Intention in Narrative* (Cambridge MA: Harvard University Press, 1992), pp. 92–7.

24 Brooks, p. 103.

25 'Utilitarianism', in *The Collected Works of John Stuart Mill*, ed. by JM Robson and others, 33 vols (Toronto; London: University of Toronto Press; Routledge and Kegan Paul, 1963–81), X: *Essays on Ethics, Religion and Society*, pp. 205–59 (p. 236).

26 Samuel Smiles, *Self-Help*, ed. by Peter W Sinnema (Oxford: Oxford University Press, 2002), p. 242.

27 See in this respect Frank Kermode, *The Sense of an Ending: Studies in the Theory of Fiction* (Oxford: Oxford University Press, 1967). JRR Tolkien, in 'On Fairy-Stories', makes a case for 'the joy of the happy ending' as an image, or even a glimpse, of grace. *The Monsters and the Critics and Other Essays*, ed. by Christopher Tolkien (London: Allen and Unwin, 1983), pp. 109–61 (p. 153).

28 John R Reed, *Dickens and Thackeray: Punishment and Forgiveness* (Athens: Ohio University Press, 1995), p. 30.

29 *Shirley*, p. 722.

30 John R Reed, *Dickens and Thackeray*, p. 285.

31 Roland Barthes, *S/Z*, trans. by Richard Miller with an introduction by Richard Howard (Oxford: Blackwell, 1990), pp. 88–9.

32 *Our Mutual Friend*, ed. by Adrian Poole (Harmondsworth: Penguin, 1997), p. 782.

33 Henry James, 'The Art of Fiction', *Literary Criticism: Essays on Literature, American Writers, English Writers*, ed. by Leon Edel and Mark Wilson (New York: Library of America, 1984), pp. 44–65 (p. 48).

34 Patrick Brantlinger, *Fictions of State: Culture and Credit in Britain, 1694–1994* (Ithaca: Cornell University Press, 1996), p. 144.

35 Vernon, p. 23.

36 For recent work in this area, see, for instance, Daniel J Schneider, *The Crystal Cage: Adventures of the Imagination in the Fiction of Henry James* (Lawrence: The Regents Press of Kansas, 1978); Jean-Christophe Agnew, 'The Consuming Vision of Henry James', in *The Culture of Consumption: Critical Essays in American History*, ed. by Richard Fox and TJ Jackson Lears (New York: Pantheon Books, 1983), pp. 65–100; Mark Seltzer, *Henry James and Power* (Ithaca: Cornell University Press, 1984); Peggy McCormack, *The Rule of Money: Gender, Class and Exchange Economics in the Fiction of Henry James* (Ann Arbor: UMI Research Press, 1990); Ian FA Bell, *Henry James and the Past: Readings in Time* (Basing-stoke: Macmillan, 1991).

37 See Andrew H Miller's reading of *Cranford* in this respect: *Novels Behind Glass: Commodity Culture and Victorian Narrative* (Cambridge: Cambridge University Press, 1995), pp. 115–18.

38 For different versions of this approach, see James M Brown, *Dickens: The Novelist in the Marketplace* (London: Macmillan, 1982); Michael Anesko, *"Friction with the Market": Henry James and the Profession of Authorship* (Oxford: New York University Press, 1986); NN Feltes, *Modes of Production of Victorian Novels* (Chicago: University of Chicago Press, 1986); Gillian Beer, 'Circulatory Systems: Money, Gossip and Blood in Middlemarch', in *Arguing with the Past: Essays in Narrative from Woolf to Sidney* (London: Routledge, 1989), pp. 99–117; Jeff Nunokawa, *The Afterlife of Property: Domestic Security and the Victorian Novel* (Princeton: Princeton University Press, 1994); John A Jordan and Robert L Patten, eds., *Literature in the Marketplace* (Cambridge: Cambridge University Press, 1995).

39 *The Way we Live Now*, ed. by John Sutherland (Oxford: Oxford University Press, 1982), p. 423. Cf. Jacques Derrida, *Given Time: I. Counterfeit Money*, trans. by Peggy Kamuf (Chicago: University of Chicago Press, 1992), p. 61.

40 David E Musselwhite, *Partings Welded Together: Politics and Desire in the Nineteenth-Century Novel* (London: Methuen, 1987), pp. 136–7.

41 *The Reading Lesson*, pp. 132–3.

42 See also Brantlinger, *Fictions of State*, pp. 45, 78, 150.

43 *Capital: A Critique of Political Economy*, ed. by Frederick Engels, 4th edn (New York: Modern Library, 1906), p. 123. Cf. Sigmund Freud, 'Character and Anal Erotism', in *The Standard Edition of the Complete Psychological Works of Sigmund Freud*, trans. by James Strachey et al., 24 vols (London: Hogarth Press, 1959 [1995]), IX: *Jensen's Gradiva and Other Works*, pp. 167–75.

44 Harriet Martineau, 'An Account of Some Treatment of Gold and Gems', *Household Words*, 4 (1851), 449–55; WH Wills, 'Review of a Popular Publication in the Searching Style', *Household Words*, 1 (1850), 423–6; Charles Dickens, 'The Old Lady in Thread-needle Street', Charles Dickens and Mark Lemon, 'A Paper Mill', *Uncollected Writings from Household Words*, ed. by Harry Stone, 2 vols (Bloomington: Indiana University Press, 1968), I, pp. 123–35, pp. 137–42.

45 Vernon, p. 7.

46 Shell, *Money, Language and Thought*, p. 7, pp. 18–19.

47 Shell, *Money, Language and Thought*, p. 156.

48 On gold's status as both money and the representation of money, see Walter Benn Michaels, *The Gold Standard and the Logic of Naturalism: American Fiction at the Turn of the Century* (Berkeley: University of California Press), pp. 139–80.

49 John Stuart Mill, *Works*, II: *Principles of Political Economy with Some of their Applications to Social Philosophy* (London: Routledge and Kegan Paul, 1965), p. 6. Cf. *Capital*, p. 641.

50 Heinzelman, p. 40.

51 Carlyle, *Past and Present*, p. 194.

52 Millicent Garrett Fawcett, *Political Economy for Beginners* (London: Macmillan, 1870), p. 2.

53 *Silas Marner*, ed. by Terence Cave (Oxford: Oxford University Press, 1996), p. 16. Cf. Georg Simmel, *The Philosophy of Money*, trans. by Tom Bottomore and David Frisby (London: Routledge and Kegan Paul, 1978), p. 245.

54 Published as 'A Joy for Ever', *Works*, ed. by ET Cook and Alexander Wedderburn, 39 vols (London: Allen, 1905), XVI: *A Joy for Ever; and the Two Paths*, pp. 9–169 (p. 99).

55 'Seminar on "The Purloined Letter"', *Yale French Studies*, 48 ([1972]), 38–72 (68).

56 Mark Shell, *The Economy of Literature* (Baltimore: Johns Hopkins University Press, 1978), p. 92.

57 Charles Dickens, *Dombey and Son*, ed. by Alan Horsman (Oxford: Clarendon Press, 1974), p. 93.

58 Adam Smith, *The Wealth of Nations*, ed. by RH Campbell, AS Skinner and WB Todd, 2 vols (Oxford: Clarendon Press, 1976), I, pp. 37–46, p. 48.

59 *The Wealth of Nations*, p. 54.

60 'We therefore find that economists, who are thoroughly agreed as to the labour time being the measure of the magnitude of value, have the most strange and contradictory ideas of money, the perfected form of the general equivalent.' *Capital*, p. 93n.; see also p. 106. For Marx's response to Smith, see the notes for the fourth volume of *Capital*, published as *Theories of Surplus Value*, ed. by Karl Kautsky, trans. by GA Bonner and Emile Burns (London: Lawrence and Wishart, 1951), pp. 107–97.

61 Jean Baudrillard, *The Mirror of Production*, trans. by Mark Poster (St Louis: Telos Press, 1975).

62 *New Grub Street*, ed. by Bernard Bergonzi (Harmondsworth: Penguin, 1985), p. 434. See, for instance, Henry Sidgwick, 'What is Money?', *Fortnightly Review*, 31 (1879), 563–75.

63 Brantlinger, *Fictions of State*, p. 7.

64 'Gold Standards', David Trotter, *The English Novel in History 1895–1920* (London: Routledge, 1992), pp. 49–61 (p. 58, p. 61).

65 DA Miller, *Narrative and its Discontents: Problems of Closure in the Traditional Novel* (Princeton: Princeton University Press, 1981), p. ix.

66 *Nicholas Nickleby*, ed. by Paul Schlicke (Oxford: Oxford University Press, 1990), p. 830.

67 Anny Sadrin, *Parentage and Inheritance in the Novels of Charles Dickens* (Cambridge: Cambridge University Press, 1994), pp. 5–9; Franco Moretti, *The Way of the World: The Bildungsroman in European Culture* (London: Verso, 1987), p. 205.

68 Cedric Watts, *Literature and Money: Financial Myth and Literary Truth* (Hemel Hempstead: Harvester Wheatsheaf, 1990), pp. 144–6.

69 John R Reed, *Victorian Conventions* (Ohio: Ohio University Press, 1975), p. 268.

70 For this transition's economic and social implications, see Eric Hobsbawm and Chris Wrigley, *Industry and Empire*, new edn (Harmondsworth: Penguin, 1999), pp. 173–81; David Cannadine, *The Decline and Fall of the British Aristocracy* (New Haven and London:

Yale University Press, 1990); Martin J Wiener, *English Culture and the Decline of the Industrial Spirit 1850–1980* (Harmondsworth: Penguin, 1985). On the shift from land to money, see James Thompson, *Models of Value: Eighteenth-Century Political Economy and the Novel* (Durham, NC: Duke University Press), p. 71.

71 *The Mill on The Floss*, ed. by Gordon S Haight (Oxford: Clarendon Press, 1980), p. 198.

72 Thomas Hardy, *Under the Greenwood Tree or The Mellstock Quire: A Rural Painting of the Old School*, ed. by Geoffrey Grigson (London: Macmillan, 1975), p. 191.

73 Richard D Altick, 'Speculation and Bankruptcy', in *The Presence of the Present: Topics of the Day in the Victorian Novel* (Columbus: Ohio State University Press, 1991), pp. 638–67 (pp. 654–5).

74 Ranald C Michie, *The City of London: Continuity and Change, 1850–1900* (London: Macmillan, 1992), pp. 1–2. See also Paul Russell, *The Novelist and Mammon: Literary Responses to the World of Commerce in the Nineteenth Century* (Oxford: Clarendon Press, 1986).

75 Reed, *Victorian Conventions*, pp. 172–92.

76 *In the Year of Jubilee*, ed. by Gillian Tindall with notes by PF Kropholler (London: Lawrence and Bullen, 1895; repr. Hassocks: Harvester Press, 1976), p. 106.

77 Reed, *Victorian Conventions*, p. 477.

78 Alexander Welsh, *The City of Dickens* (Oxford: Clarendon Press, 1971), p. 78.

79 'Useful Work *versus* Useless Toil', in *Works*, XXIII: *Signs of Change; Lectures on Socialism*, pp. 98–120. Cf. 'Constant labour of one uniform kind disturbs the intensity and flow of man's animal spirits, which find recreation and delight in mere change of activity' (Marx, *Capital*, p. 374).

80 *Mary Barton: A Tale of Manchester Life*, ed. by Macdonald Daly (Harmondsworth: Penguin, 1996), p. 3.

81 Deirdre David, *Fictions of Resolution in Three Victorian Novels: North and South, Our Mutual Friend, Daniel Deronda* (London: Macmillan, 1981), p. 46.

82 *Dickens's Working Notes for His Novels*, ed. by Harry Stone (Chicago: University of Chicago Press, 1987), pp. 370–1.

83 George Orwell, 'Charles Dickens', *Works*, XII: *A Patriot After All 1940–1941*, pp. 20–57 (pp. 45–7). Cf. Derrida, p. 159.

84 Tom Winnifrith, *Fallen Women in the Nineteenth-Century Novel* (Basingstoke: Macmillan, 1994), p. 1.

85 For Defoe's novels, for instance, charting individual 'psychologies of money', see Thompson, *Models of Value*, pp. 87–131.

86 *Middlemarch*, ed. by David Carroll (Oxford: Clarendon Press, 1986), p. 801.

87 'Our Mr Jupp', *Human Odds and Ends* (London: Sidgwick and Jackson, 1911), pp. 155–76 (pp. 175–6).

88 Ruskin, 'The Veins of Wealth', in *Unto this Last*, *Works*, XVII: *Unto this Last; Minera Pulveris; Time and Tide, with Other Writings on Political Economy 1860–1873*, pp. 47–56 (p. 52).

89 *OED*, 1–16.

90 *Martin Chuzzlewit*, ed. by Margaret Cardwell (Oxford: Clarendon Press, 1982), p. 833.

91 'A Christmas Carol', in *Christmas Books*, ed. by Ruth Glancy (Oxford: Oxford University Press, 1988), pp. 3–90 (pp. 17–18).

92 *Oliver Twist*, ed. by Kathleen Tillotson (Oxford: Clarendon Press, 1966), p. 101.

93 *Oliver Twist*, p. 316. Martha similarly refuses money in *David Copperfield* (p. 585).

94 Kate Flint, *Dickens* (Brighton: Harvester Press, 1986), p. 40; FS Schwarzbach, *Dickens and the City* (London: Athlone Press, 1979), p. 72.

95 David Trotter, *Circulation: Defoe, Dickens and the Economics of the Novel* (London: Macmillan, 1988), p. 81.

96 WJ Holdsworth, *Dickens as a Legal Historian* (New Haven: Yale University Press, 1929).

97 *Oliver Twist*, p. 351.

98 *Oliver Twist*, p. lxii.

99 Georg Lukàcs, *The Theory of the Novel: A Historico-Philosophical Essay on the Forms of Great Epic Literature*, trans. by Anna Bostock (London, Merlin, 1971), p. 61.

100 *Nicholas Nickleby*, pp. 730–1.

101 Here I disagree with John Kucich, who claims that Nicholas is 'hardly tormented by self-denial': *Repression in Victorian Fiction* (Berkeley: University of California Press, 1987), p. 214.

102 Moretti, p. 8.

103 Sadrin, p. 119.

104 *Bleak House*, ed. by Nicola Bradbury (Harmondsworth: Penguin, 1996), p. 93.

105 *Little Dorrit*, ed. by Harvey Peter Sucksmith (Oxford: Clarendon Press, 1979), p. 412.

106 *The Old Curiosity Shop*, ed. by Elizabeth M Brennan (Oxford: Clarendon Press, 1997), p. 22.

107 *The Old Curiosity Shop*, p. 520.

108 *The Old Curiosity Shop*, p. 571.

109 *Great Expectations*, ed. by Margaret Cardwell (Oxford: Clarendon Press: 1993), p. 379. See Charles Dickens and WH Wills, 'My Uncle', in *Uncollected Writings for Household Words*, II, pp. 367–78.

110 *Great Expectations*, p. 179.

111 *Great Expectations*, p. 195.

112 *Great Expectations*, p. 336.

113 *Great Expectations*, p. 176.

114 *Our Mutual Friend*, p. 147.

115 *Our Mutual Friend*, p. 23, p. 92, p. 163, p. 300, p. 335, p. 41.

116 *Our Mutual Friend*, p. 605.

117 See 'The Pill', in Bernard Darwin, *The Dickens Advertiser: A Collection of the Advertisements in the Original Parts of Novel by Charles Dickens* (London: Mathews and Marrot, 1930), pp. 179–96.

118 *Our Mutual Friend*, p. 497.

119 *Our Mutual Friend*, p. 118.

120 Adrian Poole, *Gissing in Context* (London: Macmillan, 1975), p. 10.

121 *Our Mutual Friend*, p. 45, p. 371.

122 For the persistence of this theme in Dickens, see Ross H Dabney, *Love and Property in the Novels of Dickens* (London: Chatto and Windus, 1967).

123 *Our Mutual Friend*, p. 50.

124 Peter K Garrett, *The Victorian Multiplot Novel: Studies in Dialogical Form* (New Haven: Yale University Press, 1980), p. 222; Catherine Waters, *Dickens and the Politics of the Family* (Cambridge: Cambridge University Press, 1997); Monica F Cohen, *Professional Domesticity in the Victorian Novel* (Cambridge: Cambridge University Press, 1998).

125 Marc Shell, *The Economy of Literature*, p. 92; Nancy Armstrong, *Desire and Domestic Fiction: A Political History of the Novel* (New York: Oxford University Press, 1987); DA Miller, *The Novel and the Police*, (Berkeley: University of California Press, 1988), p. 82; Catherine Gallagher, 'The Bio-Economics of *Our Mutual Friend*', in *Subject to History: Ideology, Class, Gender*, ed. by David Simpson (Ithaca: Cornell University Press, 1991),

pp. 47–64.

126 Maurice Bloch and Jonathan Parry, 'Money and the Morality of Exchange', in *Money and the Morality of Exchange*, ed. by Maurice Bloch and Jonathan Parry (Cambridge: Cambridge University Press, 1989), pp. 1–32 (p. 2).

127 *Bleak House*, p. 941.

128 *Our Mutual Friend*, p. 667, p. 734, p. 735.

129 *Little Dorrit*, p. 20.

130 *Great Expectations*, p. 457; HM Daleski, *Dickens and the Art of Analogy* (London: Faber, 1970), p. 121.

131 Thomas Hardy, *Tess of the d'Urbervilles*, ed. by Juliet Grindle and Simon Gatrell (Oxford: Clarendon Press, 1983), p. 51.

132 Donald L McLoskey, 'Storytelling in Economics', in *Narrative in Culture: The Uses of Storytelling in the Sciences, Philosophy, and Literature*, ed. by Christopher Nash (London: Routledge, 1990), pp. 5–22 (p. 9).

133 Georg Simmel, 'The Metropolis and Mental Life', in *The Sociology of Georg Simmel*, ed. and trans. by Kurt H Wolff (New York: Free Press, 1950*)*, pp. 409–24 (p. 414). Cf. *Capital*, p. 148.

134 Harry Levin, *The Gates of Horn: A Study of Four French Realists* (New York: Oxford University Press, 1966), p. 193. For James's mingled admiration and objection, see *Literary Criticism: French Writers; Other European Writers; The Prefaces to the New York Edition*, ed. by Leon Edel and Mark Wilson (New York: Library of America, 1984), pp. 31–152.

135 'The Veins of Wealth', p. 45.

136 Grahame Smith, p. 68.

137 Rachel Bowlby, *Just Looking: Consumer Culture in Dreiser, Gissing and Zola* (London: Methuen, 1985), p. 26.

138 See also Roland Barthes, 'Introduction to the Structural Analysis of Narrative', *Image-Music-Text*, ed. and trans. by Stephen Heath (London: Fontana, 1977), pp. 179–124 (pp. 92–7).

139 'Authentic *Ressentiment*: Generic Discontinuities and Ideologemes in the "Experimental" Novels of George Gissing', *The Political Unconscious: Narrative as a Socially Symbolic Act* (London: Methuen, 1981), pp. 185–205 (p. 204).

140 'The Ideology of Modernism', in *The Meaning of Contemporary Realism*, trans. by John and Necke Mander (London: Merlin, 1963), pp. 17–46 (pp. 23–4).

141 *Life and Labour*, ed. by Charles Booth, 2 vols (London: Williams and Norgate, 1889), I: *East London*, p. 157. *Letters*, IV, p. 249.

142 *Selections Autobiographical and Imaginative from the Works of George Gissing*, with an Introduction by Virginia Woolf, ed. by Alfred Gissing (London: Cape, 1929), p. 149.

143 *Letters*, VIII, p. 202; see also p. 208.

144 *Diary*, pp. 22–3.

145 John Goode, 'George Gissing's *The Nether World*' in *Tradition and Tolerance in Nineteenth-Century Fiction: Critical Essays on Some English and American Novels*, ed. by David Howard, John Lucas and John Goode (London: Routledge, 1966), pp. 207–41 (p. 210).

146 *Charles Dickens: A Critical Study* (London: Gresham, 1903), p. 206.

147 Raymond Williams, *The Country and the City* (London: Hogarth, 1993), p. 156.

148 John Goode, *George Gissing: Ideology and Fiction* (London: Vision Press, 1978), p. 29.

149 Michael Irwin, *Picturing: Description and Illusion in the Nineteenth-Century Novel* (London: Allen and Unwin, 1979), pp. 93–4.

150 For a short story on the theme of the transitions between clothing and money, see 'A Poor Gentleman', in *The Day of Silence and Other Stories*, ed. by Pierre Coustillas (London: Dent, 1993), pp. 126–38 (p. 135).

151 *Letters*, V, p. 296.

152 *New Grub Street*, p. 289.

153 P Villars, *London and Its Environs: A Picturesque Survey of the Metropolis and its Suburbs*, trans. by Henry Frith (London: Routledge, 1888), p. 59.

154 In *Pawnbroking: An Aspect of British Social History* (London: Bodley Head, 1982), Kenneth Hudson draws attention to the historical silence around the subject of pawning, suggesting that even among the poor the subject is taboo (pp. 16–18, p. 71).

155 Marx, pp. 48–69, Mill, *Principles*, III, p. 502.

156 See Thorstein Veblen, 'Dress as an Expression of the Pecuniary Culture', *The Theory of the Leisure Class* (New York: Dover, 1994), pp. 103–15.

157 *New Grub Street*, p. 161, p. 172, p. 248, p. 35, p. 100, p.181, p. 283, p. 494, p. 285, p. 93, p. 489, p. 304, p. 435, p. 174.

158 *New Grub Street*, pp. 381–3.

159 For an investigation of these codes in a different medium, see Mary Cowling, *The Artist as Anthropologist: The Representation of Type and Character in Victorian Art* (Cambridge: Cambridge University Press, 1989). See also Arthur Schopenhauer, *Essays and Aphorisms*, ed. and trans. by RJ Hollingdale (Harmondsworth: Penguin, 1970), p. 232.

160 *Isabel Clarendon*, ed. by Pierre Coustillas, 2 vols (London: Chapman and Hall, 1886; repr. Brighton: Harvester Press, 1969), I, p. 213.

161 *New Grub Street*, p. 182; cf. p. 267.

162 *The Nether World*, ed. by John Goode (London: Smith, Elder, 1890; Brighton, Harvester Press, 1974), p. 377.

163 *Shelley's Poetry and Prose: Authoritative Texts, Criticism*, 2nd edn, ed. by Donald H Reiman and Neil Fraistat (New York: Norton, 2002), pp. 509–35 (p. 531).

164 'Realism and the Contemporary Novel', in *The Long Revolution* (London: Hogarth, 1961), pp. 274–89 (p. 288).

165 *Letters*, I, pp. 282–3.

1: DICKENS IN MEMORY

1 *Letters*, p. IV, p. 75. 'To realise the inferiority of Dickens to Thackeray', *George Gissing's Commonplace Book: A Manuscript in the Berg Collection of the New York Public Library*, ed. by Jacob Korg (New York: New York Public Library, 1962), p. 34; 'In no modern writer have I such intense *personal* interest as in Charlotte Brontë', *ibid.*, p. 29. See also *Letters*, III, p. 101, IV, pp. 169–70.

2 Richard J Dunn, 'Gissing's Introduction to the Rochester *David Copperfield*', *The Dickensian* 77:1 (1981), 3–11 (5).

3 George Gissing, *The Immortal Dickens* (London: Palmer, 1925), p. 10. See also p. 80 and Gissing's essay 'Dickens', in *Homes and Haunts of Famous Writers* (London: Wells Gardner, Darton and Co. [1906]), pp. 107–20; and Goode, *Ideology and Fiction*, pp. 33–4.

4 Cf. 'the world saw with [Dickens] – much better than with its own poor, purblind eyes.' *Critical Study*, p. 226.

5 *Letters*, VI, p. 358. In 1901, Gissing was still uneasy averring to his agent James B Pinker, 'I am not at all a Dickens specialist – though people seem to be regarding me in that light.' *Letters*, VIII, p. 261.

6 *Letters*, VI, p. 327, p. 249.

7 *Critical Study*, p. 12, pp. 98–9.

8 *Letters*, VI, p. 254.

9 *George Gissing at Work*, p. 8.

10 Pierre Coustillas, 'Gissing's Reminiscences of His Father: An Unpublished Manuscript', *English Literature in Transition*, 32:4 (1989), 419–39.

11 Goode, *Ideology and Fiction*, p. 20. In 'Dickens in Memory', Gissing seems to associate *Our Mutual Friend* in particular with his father and with his first contact with Dickens. The novel attracts some of Gissing's strongest praise and blame in the critical writing: see for instance *Critical Study*, pp. 64–5, p. 149.

12 *Forster's Life of Dickens*, ed. and abridged by George Gissing (London: Chapman and Hall, 1903), p. vi.

13 Goode, *Ideology and Fiction*, p. 34.

14 Goode, *Ideology and Fiction*, p. 15.

15 *Critical Study*, p. 27, p. 25. See also 'Gissing's Introduction to the Autograph Edition of *David Copperfield*', *Gissing Journal*, 33.1 (1997), 10–19 (19).

16 See, of course, Dickens's 'Autobiographical Fragment' in John Forster, *The Life of Charles Dickens*, with an Introduction by GK Chesterton, 2 vols (London; New York: Dent; Dutton, 1927), I, pp. 20–33. Gissing, strikingly for a supposedly highly-autobiographical novelist, left no extant autobiographical record of his prison experiences.

17 Peter Keating, *The Working Classes in Victorian Fiction* (London: Routledge, 1971), p. 73.

18 *The Nether World*, ed. by Stephen Gill (Oxford: Oxford University Press, 1992), pp. xxi–xxii (xxi). But for its ending, Gissing thought *Great Expectations* 'nearly perfect in its mechanism', *Critical Study*, p. 66.

19 Moretti, pp. 207–11. See John R Reed, *Dickens and Thackeray*, for the ending of *The Old Curiosity Shop*, pp. 109–10. Cf. *Critical Study*, p. 211.

20 *Critical Study*, p. 93.

21 The phrase is from Raymond Williams, *Culture and Society* (London: Hogarth, 1983), pp. 175–6.

22 Moretti, p. 55.

23 'Jacob Korg, 'The Paradox of Success and Failure in the Novels of George Gissing', *Gissing Newsletter*, 19.3 (1983), 16–23 (17).

24 Letter to Morley Roberts, *Letters*, V, p. 296.

25 *New Grub Street*, p. 403.

26 *Letters*, IV, p. 288.

27 John Middleton Murry, 'George Gissing', in *Katherine Mansfield and Other Literary Studies* (London: Constable, 1959), pp. 1–68 (p. 17, pp. 9–10).

28 *New Grub Street*, p. 239.

29 *New Grub Street*, p. 179.

30 Constance Harsh, 'George Gissing's *Thyrza*: Romantic Love and Ideological Co-Conspiracy', *Gissing Journal*, 30.1 (1994), 1–12 (1).

31 Patricia Alden, *Social Mobility in the English Bildungsroman: Gissing, Hardy, Bennett and Lawrence* (Ann Arbor: UMI Research Press, 1986), p. 11.

32 Barbara Hardy, *The Moral Art of Dickens: Essays* (London: Athlone Press, 1970), p. 13; Marianna Torgovnick, *Closure in the Novel* (Princeton: Princeton University Press, 1981), pp. 37–60; Robert L Caserio, *Plot, Story, and the Novel: from Dickens and Poe to the Modern Period* (Princeton: Princeton University Press, 1979), p. 169.

33 Gissing praised Hogarth's realism over Dickens's, for representing the real world faith-

fully without overpowering with moral judgement. See *Critical Study*, p. 31, p. 103, *Immortal Dickens*, pp. 82–3, *The Unclassed*, 3 vols (London: Chapman and Hall, 1884), III, p. 11.

34 In making this distinction throughout, I use 'plot' to indicate that which is narrated, the represented, and 'discourse' the language which does the work of representing. For discussions of this terminology, see Caserio, pp. 2–3, Brooks, pp. 12–14, Moretti, p. 250, Tsvetan Todorov, 'Language and Literature', in *The Poetics of Prose*, ed. by Jonathan Culler, trans. by Richard Howard (Oxford: Blackwell, 1977), pp. 19–28 (pp. 25–8), Seymour Chatman, *Story and Discourse: Narrative Structure in Fiction and Film* (Ithaca: Cornell University Press, 1978), pp. 19–26.

35 *Letters*, VII, p. 310.

36 *Letters*, IX, 272.

37 *The Woman Who Did*, ed. by Sarah Wintle (Oxford: Oxford University Press, 1995), p. 96. Gissing's approval of the novel is recorded in *Letters*, V, p. 343.

38 *Letters*, VI, p. 320.

39 *George Gissing: The Cultural Challenge* (Basingstoke: Macmillan, 1989), p. 150; see also Goode, *Ideology and Fiction*, pp. 200–1. The most useful sustained analysis of Gissing in this multiple-perspectived way is David Grylls, *The Paradox of Gissing* (London: Allen and Unwin, 1986).

40 For differing views of one novel, see, for instance, John Goode and Alan Lelchuk, 'Gissing's *Demos*: A Controversy', *Victorian Studies*, 12.4 (1969), 432–40; or for a reading of this novel that is contrary to my own, CJ Francis, '*Demos*', *Gissing Newsletter*, 10.2 (1974), 1–13. For two excellent critiques of the pitfalls of reading Gissing's work as autobiographical, see Christina Sjöholm, *The Vice of Wedlock: The Theme of Marriage in George Gissing's Novels* (Uppsala: Uppsala University Press, 1994), pp. 11–18; and David Grylls, 'The Teller not the Tale: George Gissing and Biographical Criticism', *English Literature in Transition*, 32.4 (1989), 454–73.

41 *Letters*, VII, p. 318.

42 *Letters*, VI, p. 320.

43 *Letters*, V, p. 36. Gissing also wrote to Algernon in 1880 of *Workers in the Dawn*, 'It is not *I* who propagate a doctrine, but the characters whose lives I tell.' *Letters*, I, p. 236. See also pp. 290–1, and VI, p. 219.

44 *Letters*, V, p. 176.

45 Eileen Sypher suggests that, '*Demos* is produced by an implied author who feels trapped in this environment and so feels resentful.' *Wisps of Violence: Producing Public and Private Politics in the Turn-of-the-Century British Novel* (London: Verso, 1993), p. 50; see also p. 200.

46 Sjöholm, pp. 13–14.

47 Jameson, p. 202.

48 Ruth Capers McKay, 'George Gissing as a Portrayer of Society', in *Collected Articles on George Gissing*, ed. by Pierre Coustillas (London: Cass, 1968), pp. 27–42 (p. 40).

49 *New Grub Street*, p. 154.

50 *Letters*, III, p. 160. See also IV, p. 140; also John Sloan, 'The Literary Affinity of Gissing and Dostoevsky: Revising Dickens', *English Literature in Transition*, 32.4 (1989), 441–553.

51 In the *Critical Study*, p. 261, pp. 267–70, Gissing praises Dostoevsky as a better writer than Dickens.

52 Mikhail Bakhtin, *Problems of Dostoevsky's Poetics*, ed. and trans. by Caryl Emerson, with an Introduction by Wayne C Booth (Minneapolis: University of Minnesota Press, 1984), p. 226.

53 *Letters*, IV, p. 209.

54 *Problems of Dostoevsky's Poetics*, p. 7, p. 30, p. 62, p. 20, p. 7, p. 15.

55 *The Nether World*, p. 297.

56 *Problems of Dostoevsky's Poetics*, p. 115.

57 'A combination of carnivalization with a sentimental perception of life was found by Dostoevsky in Sterne and Dickens.' *Problems of Dostoevsky's Poetics*, p. 159.

58 'Forms of Time and Chronotope in the Novel', *The Dialogic Imagination: Four Essays*, ed. by Michael Holquist, trans. by Caryl Emerson and Michael Holquist (Austin: University of Texas Press, 1981), pp. 84–258 (pp. 234–5).

59 Mabel Collins Donnelly, *George Gissing: Grave Comedian* (Cambridge, MA: Harvard University Press, 1954), p. 106; Poole, p. 93.

60 Jameson, p. 186. Cf. Gissing's commercially successful and despised contemporary Hall Caine, who wrote in 'The New Watchwords of Fiction', 'justice is the only end for a work of imaginative art, whatever may be the frequent end of life.' *Contemporary Review* 57 (April 1890), 479–88, reprinted in *A Victorian Art of Fiction: Essays on the Novel in British Periodicals 1870–1900*, ed. by John Charles Olmsted, 3 vols (New York: Garland, 1979), III: *1870–1900*, pp. 469–80 (p. 478).

61 *Letters*, III, p. xvii.

62 *The Private Papers of Henry Ryecroft*, ed. by John Stewart Collis and Pierre Coustillas (London: Constable, 1903; repr. Brighton: Harvester Press, 1982), p. 187. Florence Emily Hardy, *The Early Life of Thomas Hardy 1840–1891* (London: Macmillan, 1928), p. 163.

63 On the late nineteenth-century debate over whether the novel should strive first to be realistic or pleasing, see Kenneth Graham, *English Criticism of the Novel, 1865–1900* (Oxford: Clarendon Press, 1965), pp. 30–4.

64 *Letters*, VI, p. 91. *Gissing: The Critical Heritage* ed. by Pierre Coustillas and Colin Partridge (London: Routledge and Kegan Paul, 1972, p. 144. Gissing thought the review was 'written coldly and poorly' (*Diary*, p. 166).

65 *George Gissing on Fiction*, ed. by Jacob and Cynthia Korg (London: Enitharmon, 1978), p. 84.

66 *Letters*, VI, p. 94.

67 *Gissing on Fiction*, pp. 85–6.

68 According to Gabrielle Fleury (*Commonplace Book*, p. 67). See also *Ryecroft*, pp. 212–13.

69 *The Immortal Dickens*, p. 125.

70 Jameson, p. 185.

71 *The Unclassed*, ed. by Jacob Korg, (London: Lawrence and Bullen, 1895; repr. Brighton: Harvester Press, 1976), p. xv.

72 *Letters*, II, p. 328. See also II, pp. 178–9.

73 *The Unclassed*, I, 229–30. Cf. II, pp 150–1: 'Life is an incomplete novel, consisting, for the most part, of blurred and fragmentary chapters. It interests us, doubtless, as each new situation shadows itself forth; but, as we see these successively come to nothing, we smile, if we are wise, and wonder sadly what the author was about.'

74 *Critical Heritage*, p. 97.

75 *The Colvins and Their Friends*, ed. by EV Lucas (London: Methuen, 1928), pp. 279–80. See also *Henry James: Interviews and Recollections*, ed. by Norman Page (London: Macmillan, 1984), p. 51.

76 *Letters*, II, p. 320.

77 Grylls, *The Paradox of Gissing*, p. xii.

78 *Isabel Clarendon*, I, p. 185; I, p. 274; II, p. 164; I, p. 210.

79 'The English Novel of the Eighteenth Century', *Gissing on Fiction*, p. 108.

80 *George Gissing's American Notebook: Notes – G.R.G. – 1877*, ed. by Bouwe Postmus (Lewiston: Mellen, 1993), p. 21.

81 Michel Ballard, '*Born in Exile* as an Organic Study in Behaviour and Motivation', *English Studies*, 58.4 (1977), 324–33 (333).

82 Théodule-Armand Ribot, *Heredity: a Psychological Study of its Phenomena, Laws, Causes and Consequences* (London: King, 1875), p. 216. *Diary*, p. 170; Robert L Selig, 'Gissing's *Born in Exile* and Théodule-Armand Ribot's *L'hérédité psychologique*', *Gissing Journal*, 32.4 (1996), 1–10.

83 *Thyrza: A Tale*, ed. by Jacob Korg (London: Smith, Elder, 1892; repr. Brighton: Harvester Press, 1974), p. 413.

84 *Critical Heritage*, p. 204.

85 *Critical Heritage*, p. 28; *Charles Dickens: The Critical Heritage*, ed. by Philip Collins (London: Routledge, 1971), pp. 344–9, pp. 366–74, pp. 469–73. For posthumous attacks on Dickens's reputation, see also GH Lewes, 'Dickens in Relation to Criticism', *Fortnightly Review*, 17 (1872), 141–54; and Mowbray Morris, 'Charles Dickens', *Fortnightly Review*, 38 (1882), 762–79, both reprinted in *A Victorian Art of Fiction*, III, pp. 19–32, pp. 203–20.

86 George Ford, *Dickens and his Readers* (Princeton: Princeton University Press, 1955), p. 172. Writing to Algernon in 1890, Gissing notes the large number of cheap reprints of Dickens available (*Letters*, IV, 202–3).

87 *Letters*, II, p. 72; TT Sykes, 'The Early School Life of George Gissing', reprinted in Pierre Coustillas, *George Gissing at Alderley Edge* (London: Enitharmon: 1969), p. 23.

88 *Letters*, I, p. 86, p. 105; II, p. 93; *Diary*, p. 18, p. 36, p. 152.

89 See Gissing's abridgement of Forster's *Life*, p. 267; Charles Dickens, 'His General Line of Business/The Shipment', in *The Uncommercial Traveller and Other Papers 1859–70*, ed. by Michael Slater and John Drew (London: Dent, 2000), pp. 26–40 (p. 28).

90 Poole, pp. 112–13.

91 Garrett, p. 96.

92 *Commonplace Book*, p. 69. Gissing, however, felt that Thackeray betrayed the trust of the artist when confessing in the Preface to *Pendennis* that he had to soften the fidelity of his representations for fear of offending his public (*Letters*, II, p. 276). See George Moore, '*Literature at Nurse', or, Circulating Morals: A Polemic on Victorian Censorship*, ed. by Pierre Coustillas (Brighton: Harvester Press, 1976).

93 When Gissing does compare Dickens to Thackeray, it tends to be to Dickens's disadvantage, but is usually followed by the admission that such a comparison is a pointless exercise (*Critical Study*, p. 148; *Immortal Dickens*, pp. 73–75, p. 114, p. 145).

94 *Critical Study*, p. 11.

95 'Dickens in Memory', *Immortal Dickens*, p. 13; see also *Immortal Dickens*, p. 11; *Diary*, p. 20; *Letters*, III, 226–27.

96 Poole, p. 109.

97 For an excellent study of the literary consequences of the 1870 Act, see Peter Keating, *The Haunted Study: A Social History of the English Novel 1875–1914* (London: Secker and Warburg, 1989).

98 *Letters*, VI, p. 336.

99 Cf. Albert SG Canning, *The Philosophy of Charles Dickens* (London: Smith, Elder, 1880);

Frank T Marzials, *Life of Charles Dickens* (London: Scott, 1887); Thomas Archer, *Charles Dickens: A Gossip about his Life, Works and Characters*, 6 vols (London: Cassell, [1894]); or even the lecture by Gissing's friend Frederic Harrison, *Dickens's Place in Literature* (London: Arnold, 1895). Hippolyte Taine's evaluation of Dickens in his *History of English Literature*, trans. by H Van Laun, 4 vols (Edinburgh: [n.p.], 1874), IV, pp. 113–64, which Gissing read in 1889, is closer in spirit to Gissing's more mixed appreciation.

100 *Critical Study*, p. 146; also pp. 51–2. Cf. *Ryecroft*, p. 68.

101 *Critical Study*, p. 1.

102 *Critical Study*, pp. 70–1.

103 See also *Forster's Life of Dickens*, ed. by Gissing, p. 49; Brantlinger, *The Reading Lesson*, p. 13.

104 *Critical Study*, p. 2.

105 *Critical Study*, pp. 74–5; see also pp. 83–4 for Gissing's disapproval of Dickens's apparent acceptance of censorship in the Preface to *Oliver Twist*.

106 *The Immortal Dickens*, p. 161.

107 *Critical Study*, p. 81; *Immortal Dickens*, p. 115.

108 *Critical Study*, p. 81. For a useful distinction between Gissing's uses of the terms 'theatrical' and 'dramatic', see Michael Cronin, 'Gissing's Criticism of Dickens', in *A Garland for Gissing*, ed. by Bouwe Postmus (Amsterdam: Rodopi, 2001), pp. 23–31 (p. 29).

109 *Critical Study*, p. 73.

110 *Critical Study*, p. 262.

111 *Critical Study*, p. 129.

112 Robert Buchanan, 'The Good "Genie" of Fiction: Thoughts while Reading Forster's "Life of Charles Dickens"', *Saint Paul's*, 10 (1872), 130–48.

113 *Critical Study*, p. 37; see also, e.g., p. 12, p. 195, pp. 225–6, p. 231.

114 *The Immortal Dickens*, p. 158.

115 *Critical Study*, pp. 82–5.

116 Robert Langton, *The Childhood and Youth of Charles Dickens with Retrospective Notes and Elucidations from his Books and Letters* (London: Hutchinson, 1912), p. 173; cf. *The Immortal Dickens*, pp. 150–1.

117 *Critical Study*, p. 238.

118 *The Immortal Dickens*, p. 212.

119 *Critical Study*, p. 52, *Immortal Dickens*, p. 78.

120 *Critical Study*, p. 54.

121 Unsigned review of FG Kitton's *Charles Dickens: his Life, Writings and Personality*, *Times Literary Supplement* 15 August 1902, in Pierre Coustillas, *Gissing's Writings on Dickens: A Bio-bibliographical Study* (London: Enitharmon, 1969), pp. 21–5 (p. 21).

122 *Critical Study*, p. 125, p. 84. Cf. Gissing's language in a letter to JWT Ley supporting the establishment of a Dickens Society, *Letters*, VIII, p. 367.

123 *Critical Study*, p. 200, p. 197. Gissing reads Dickens closely if not always carefully: David's meal in fact consisted of chops. For Gissing's errors in the *Critical Study*, see *Letters* VII, p. 118, John Spiers and Pierre Coustillas, *The Rediscovery of George Gissing: A Reader's Guide* (London: National Book League, 1971), p. 120; Lionel Johnson, 'About Dickens: Mr. Gissing', *The Academy*, 22 April 1899, 461; *Gissing's Writings on Dickens*, p. 4, p. 14.

124 *Immortal Dickens*, p. 175, p. 238.

125 *Critical Study*, p. 229. The younger Gissing had thought this novel 'Dickens's poorest work', *Letters*, II, p. 93.
126 *Critical Study*, p. 261. Cf. 'The details which would to me be most precious, [Dickens] left aside as unsuitable, because unattractive to the multitude of novel-readers.' *Commonplace Book*, p. 33.
127 *Critical Study*, p. 201.
128 *Critical Study*, p. 209.
129 *Critical Study*, p. 48, p. 54.
130 Rochester *David Copperfield* Preface, p. 7.
131 *Critical Study*, p. 90.
132 *Immortal Dickens*, p. 223.
133 See, for instance, J Hillis Miller, *Charles Dickens: The World of his Novels*, pp. 160–224, and throughout the material collected in Jeremy Tambling, ed., *Bleak House: A New Casebook* (Basingstoke: Macmillan, 1998).
134 *Critical Study*, p. 62. Even when condemning Dickens, as in the passage above, a reverential tone can still be detected in the *Critical Study* in the large number of allusions to Shakespeare, unequivocally Gissing's favourite English author. See PF Kropholler, 'Notes to *Charles Dickens: A Critical Study*', *Gissing Newsletter*, 24.1 (1988), 26–36.
135 See, for instance, Harry Stone, *Dickens and the Invisible World: Fairy Tales, Fantasy and Novel-Making* (London: Macmillan, 1980).
136 *Bleak House*, p. 7.
137 *Critical Study*, pp. 29–30; see also p. 230; *Immortal Dickens*, p. 158.
138 GK Chesterton, *Charles Dickens* (London: Methuen, 1906), p. 5.
139 *Critical Study*, p. 92.
140 *Critical Study*, p. 47.
141 *Critical Study*, p. 214.
142 *Immortal Dickens*, p. 50; *Critical Study*, p. 253, p. 58; *Immortal Dickens*, p. 142, p. 126; *Critical Study*, p. 125, p. 187, p. 94; Rochester, *David Copperfield* Preface, p. 7; *Critical Study*, p. 87, p. 89, p. 69, p. 194. In his *Commonplace Book*, Gissing mistakenly suggests that 'Dickens at first intended the change to miserliness in Mr. Boffin for a perfectly real one. I should not wonder if the murmurings of the imbecile public induced him to alter his plan, or perhaps he himself shrank from the worthier course. In either case, the instance illustrates Dickens's grave defect' (p. 31).
143 *Critical Study*, p. 19. Morley Roberts, *The Private Life of Henry Maitland: A Record Dictated by J.H.* (London: Nash, 1912), suggests that Gissing identified himself with Dickens 'in full manhood measuring the abyss which sundered him from all he had hoped' (p. 209).
144 *Immortal Dickens*, p. 118, *Critical Study*, p. 245.
145 *Gissing's Writings on Dickens*, p. 5; *Letters* VII, p. 172.
146 *Critical Study*, p. 275.
147 Forster, *Life*, II, p. 423. See also *Homes and Haunts*, p. 117; see also, however, *Letters*, I, p. 27 for the younger Gissing's apparent admiration of Dickens's energy and *With Gissing in Italy: The Memoirs of Brian Ború Dunne*, ed. by Paul F Mattheisen, Arthur C Young and Pierre Coustillas (Athens: Ohio University Press, 1999), p. 50.

2: POVERTY AND IMAGINATION

1 *Letters*, I, p. 307. Gissing wrote to his brother Will: 'I know very well that [*Workers in the Dawn*] cannot be popular, like Dickens, or Miss Braddon, or Mrs Henry Wood' (I, p. 242).

2 See, for instance, Gissing's response to Tolstoy's *What is Art?* in *Letters*, VII, pp. 162–6.

3 *Workers in the Dawn*, ed. by Pierre Coustillas (New York: Doubleday, 1935; repr. Brighton: Harvester Press, 1985), II, pp. 69–78; *The Unclassed*, I, pp. 70–94. In a passage deleted from *Workers in the Dawn*, the narrator asks, 'What if someone were to steal into these splendid halls and whisper into these children's ears that the gold which procures them all this delight is *stolen* gold, inasmuch as it furnishes forth unspeakable extravagance when Whitecross Street and the like are made Hells from the want of an infinitesimal portion of it?" (p. lxxiv).

4 Gissing wrote an ending for Challenger, but excised it from the final version of the novel (p. lxxx). Gissing's narrator also laments that Lizzie's destiny is to become a prostitute (pp. lxxv–xxvi).

5 *Workers in the Dawn*, I, p. 84.

6 *Workers in the Dawn*, I, p. 40.

7 See Susan Shatto, *The Companion to Bleak House* (London: Allen and Unwin, 1988), p. 28, for the law/wrestling pun.

8 Cf. *Oliver Twist*, pp. 35–8; *Workers in the Dawn*, I, pp. 79–80.

9 In 'Transplanted' and 'A Son of the Soil' in *Human Odds and Ends*, Gissing also shows the unfortunate consequences of transplanting a member of the urban working-class to the country and an agricultural worker to the city.

10 In a cancelled MS passage, Tollady reveals his love of botany, an interest shared with Gissing's own father; Tollady dies in 1870, the same year as Dickens and Thomas Gissing (p. lxxvii).

11 See Adeline Tintner, 'The Gissing Phase in Henry James: The Underclass and the "Essentially Unheroic" ', *The Twentieth-Century World of Henry James: Changes in his Work after 1900* (Baton Rouge: Louisiana State University Press, 2000), pp. 201–14. Tintner's factual errors are corrected by Pierre Coustillas in *The Gissing Journal*, 36.4, (2000), 36.

12 *Critical Heritage*, p. 531, Orwell, 'Not Enough Money', p. 46; Grylls, *The Paradox of Gissing*, p. xi.

13 *Letters*, IX, p. 291.

14 *Immortal Dickens*, p. 235.

15 *George Gissing: Essays and Fiction*, ed. by Pierre Coustillas (Baltimore: Johns Hopkins Press, 1970), pp. 76–97; cf. *Letters*, II, p. 47. See Patrick Bridgwater, *Gissing and Germany* (London: Enitharmon, 1981), pp. 39–57. See William J Scheick, *Fictional Structure and Ethics: The Turn-of-the-Century English Novel* (Athens: University of Georgia Press, 1990), pp. 47–66.

16 Gissing wrote of the hero of this novel, 'the point is this. Egremont has suffered all along from an excess of Idealism.' *Letters*, V, p. 131. Egremont's project of regenerative culture is explicitly identified by his vocabulary as Arnoldian: *Thyrza: A Tale*, ed. by Jacob Korg (London: Smith, Elder, 1892; repr. Brighton: Harvester Press, 1974), for example, p. 16, p. 92.

17 Cf. *Thyrza*, p. 127.

18 *Letters*, I, p. 314.

19 *Critical Study*, p. 249.

20 *Bleak House*, p. 710.

21 *The Unclassed*, III, p. 214.

22 *The Unclassed*, II, p. 16; for Gissing's dent to Brontë see above.

23 *Letters*, VI, p. 155.

24 *The Unclassed*, I, pp. 139–41.

25 *The Unclassed*, III, pp. 9–10.

26 Peter Ackroyd, *Dickens* (London: Sinclair-Stevenson, 1990), pp. 536–7. See Judith Walkowitz, *Prostitution and Victorian Society: Women, Class and the State* (Cambridge: Cambridge University Press, 1980), pp. 13–31 on prostitution 'as the best of a series of unattractive alternatives' for working-class women such as Ida (p. 31).

27 *The Unclassed*, II, pp. 98–9.

28 'A man's wife', generalizes Earwaker in *Born in Exile*, 'may be his superior in whatever you like, *except* social position. That is precisely the distinction that no woman can forget or forgive.' *Born in Exile*, ed. by Pierre Coustillas (London: A and C Black, 1892; repr. Hassocks: Harvester Press, 1978), p. 139.

29 *The Unclassed*, III, p. 257.

30 *The Unclassed*, III, pp. 230–1.

31 *The Unclassed*, II, p. 304; I, p. 30, p. 80. Mrs Enderby, like *The Whirlpool*'s Alma, takes chloral to help her sleep (III, p. 150).

32 *The Unclassed*, I, p. 193.

33 *The Unclassed*, II, pp. 33–4.

34 For example, *Letters*, I, p. 234, II, p. 116, p. 135, p. 146, IV, pp. 292–3; Grylls, *The Paradox of Gissing*, p. 35. Cf. also Schopenhauer, p. 156.

35 *Letters*, II, p. 228.

36 *The Unclassed*, II, p. 287; Grylls, *The Paradox of Gissing*, p. 37. For a recent assessment of Gissing's turning-away from aestheticism, see Diana Maltz, 'Gissing as Thwarted Aesthete', in *A Garland for Gissing*, pp. 203–13.

37 *The Unclassed*, III, p. 2.

38 *The Unclassed*, III, p. 74.

39 *Critical Study*, p. 151.

40 *The Unclassed*, 1895 text, p. xv.

41 *The Unclassed*, I, p. 76.

42 *The Unclassed*, III, p. 132. Maud's encounter with a prostitute in Waterloo Place (III, pp. 35–8) does not appear in the 1895 text. See Jacob Korg, 'Cancelled Passages in Gissing's *The Unclassed*', *Bulletin of the New York Public Library*, 80 (1977), 553–8.

43 Karl Marx, *Economic and Philosophical Manuscripts of 1844*, 4th edn, ed. by Dirk Struik, trans. by Martin Milligan (Moscow: Progress, 1974), pp. 118–22 (p. 122).

44 *The Nether World*, pp. 135–6. For a discussion of Oliver Twist's surprising ability to read, see Brantlinger, *The Reading Lesson*, pp. 69–70.

45 *Letters*, II, p. 360.

46 *Demos: A Story of English Socialism*, ed. by Pierre Coustillas (London: Lawrence and Bullen, 1897; repr. Brighton: Harvester Press, 1972), p. 136.

47 *Demos*, p. 96, p. 100.

48 See *Thyrza*, p. 123.

49 *Demos*, p. 387.

50 *Commonplace Book*, p. 26.

51 WW Jacobs, *The Monkey's Paw* (London: Harper, 1902; repr. Woodbridge: Boydell Press, 1983), pp. 1–25.

52 *Demos*, p. 75.

53 *Demos*, p. 67.

54 *Demos*, p. 419.

55 *Demos*, p. 110. Note the feminizing of happy endings in the 'gentle milky stream of English romance'. In *The Whirlpool*, ed. by Patrick Parrinder (London: Lawrence and Bullen, 1897; repr. Hassocks: Harvester Press, 1977), Carnaby complains of a 'draggle-tailed, novelette-reading feminine democracy' (p. 15); in Gissing's *American Notebook*, there is a note for a story about a 'woman who has weakened her mind by reading romances, and acts in daily life accordingly' (p. 52). In 'Raw Material' in *Human Odds and Ends*, the slatternly servant Minnie is found asleep over a 'penny novelette' (p. 187). The literary man Sykes claims in *New Grub Street* that ' "nothing can induce working men or women to read stories that treat of their own world. They are the most consumed idealists in creation, especially the women." ' (*New Grub Street*, p. 416).

56 *Demos*, p. 38.

57 *Demos*, p. 54.

58 *Demos*, p. 394.

59 *Demos*, pp. 42–3, p. 301.

60 *Demos*, p. 21.

61 *Demos*, p. 246.

62 *Demos*, p. 46, p. 209.

63 Sadrin, p. 119.

64 *Demos*, pp. 134–38; see also p. 272.

65 *Demos*, p. 49.

66 *Demos*, p. 103.

67 *Demos*, p. 118, p. 406.

68 *Demos*, p. 350.

69 *Demos*, p. 313.

70 *Demos*, p. 311.

71 *Demos*, p. 439.

72 *Demos*, p. 105, p. 137, p. 278.

73 *Demos*, p. 460.

74 Cf. John Carey, 'George Gissing and the Ineducable Masses', in *The Intellectuals and the Masses: Pride and Prejudice among the Literary Intelligentsia 1880–1939* (London: Faber, 1992), pp. 93–107 (pp. 110–12).

75 *Demos*, p. 338.

76 Reed, *Victorian Conventions*, p. 286.

77 *Letters*, III, p. 8.

78 *Letters*, III, p. 220; see also *Diary*, p. 28.

79 *Demos*, p. 207.

80 Goode, *Ideology and Fiction*, pp. 72–4; Jameson, p. 190. Cf. J Hillis Miller, p. xv.

81 John Sloan, *George Gissing: The Cultural Challenge* (New York: St Martin's Press, 1989), p. 58.

82 *Thyrza*, p. 352.

83 *The Nether World*, p. 11.

84 *Critical Heritage*, p. 59, p. 79, p. 81. Gissing recommended *Alton Locke* to his sister Ellen (*Letters*, I, 257), and reread it himself in 1889 (*Diary*, p. 158).

85 'See 'Pessimism and Will Power', Grylls, *The Paradox of Gissing*, pp. 1–18.

86 *Letters*, II, p. 88.

87　*The Nether World*, p. 343. 'Heavens! the labour that book cost me! […] I exhaust myself in toil,' Gissing wrote to Bertz of *The Nether World*, *Letters*, IV, p. 67.

88　*New Grub Street*, p. 9.

89　*George Gissing and H G Wells: A Record of their Friendship and Correspondence*, ed. by Royal A Gettmann (London: Hart-Davis, 1961), p. 237, *Letters*, VI, p. 265, 'George Gissing: Poet of Fatigue', in Coustillas, ed., *Collected Articles*, pp. 119–25 (p. 121).

90　*Letters*, V, p. 262.

91　*Thyrza*, p. 374.

92　*The Nether World*, p. 84.

93　*Notes on Social Democracy*, ed. by Jacob Korg (London: Enitharmon, 1968); Martha S Vogeler, 'Gissing and the Positivists: The *Vestnik Evropy* Articles', *Gissing Newsletter*, 21.1 (1985), 1–13; *Letters*, I, p. 142.

94　*The Nether World*, p. 5. See also p. 210, p. 281, p. 377.

95　*The Nether World*, p. 364.

96　*The Nether World*, pp. 193–4.

97　Cf. *The Unclassed*, I, p. 17. For the theme of 'living *actual* life in the shadow of an *alternative*', see Lucy Crispin, 'Living in Exile: Self-Image, Social Role and the Problem of Identity', in *A Garland for Gissing*, pp. 41–9 (p. 43).

98　*The Nether World*, p. 94.

99　Poole, p. 88, p. 94.

100　*The Nether World*, pp. 368–9.

101　Grylls, *The Paradox of Gissing*, p. 54, also notes the similarity of Gissing's sentiments to Arnold White's *Problems of a Great City* (1886), which Gissing read while preparing *The Nether World*. Gissing does not advocate, however, White's proposed remedy of emigration.

102　For the 'rescue into love', see Barbara Hardy, 'Implication and Incompleteness in *Middlemarch*', in *Particularities: Readings in George Eliot* (London: Owen, 1982), pp. 15–36 (p. 19).

103　*The Nether World*, pp. 391–2.

104　*The Nether World*, p. 369.

105　*The Immortal Dickens*, p. 159.

106　*Thyrza*, p. 422.

107　*The Nether World*, p. 109.

108　*Demos*, pp. 62–4.

109　*Workers in the Dawn*, I, p. 275.

110　*Workers in the Dawn*, II, p. 15

111　*Letters*, I, pp. 281–2.

112　Gissing wrote to Bertz in 1893, 'My own hope is that the world will some day be reconstituted on a basis of *intellectual aristocracy*. I believe that, relatively speaking, there must always be much the same social distinctions as now exist. All classes will be elevated, but between higher & lower the distinction will remain.' *Letters*, V, p. 114. See also V, p. 141.

113　See 'The Coming of the Preacher', in *George Gissing on Fiction*, pp. 94–7; *Letters*, II, p. 349.

3: THE PRICE OF CULTURE

1 Maltz, *A Garland for Gissing*, p. 210.
2 *Critical Heritage*, p. 132, see also p. 431.
3 *American Notebook*, pp. 32–4. See also 'The Coming of the Preacher', *Gissing on Fiction*, p. 96.
4 *George Gissing at Work*, pp. 37–8.
5 Samuel Butler, *Erewhon or Over the Range*, ed. by Hans-Peter Breuer and Daniel F Howard (Newark; London: University of Delaware Press; Associated University Presses, 1981), pp. 169–70.
6 *Selections*, pp. 54–8 (58), *New Grub Street*, pp. 58–9, *Ryecroft*, pp. 128–9.
7 *Gissing and Wells*, p. 258.
8 Lionel Trilling, 'Freud: Within and Beyond Culture', in *Beyond Culture: Essays on Literature and Learning* (Harmondsworth: Penguin, 1967), pp. 87–110 (p. 110).
9 See Raymond Williams, *Keywords: A Vocabulary of Culture and Society* (London: Fontana, 1988), pp. 87–92.
10 *New Grub Street*, p. 397.
11 To Ellen: 'I had rather have a girl well acquainted with Dickens & George Eliot & Shelley & Browning than with all the science in all the text-books.' *Letters*, II, p. 72.
12 Letter of 2 January 1886, *The Letters of Robert Louis Stevenson*, ed. by Bradford A Booth and Ernest Mehew, 8 vols (New Haven: Yale University Press, 1994–7), V, p. 171.
13 *Letters*, IV, p. 99, p. 214; V, pp. 6–7, 26, 93, 225–6; VII, p. 67; VIII, p. 74; *Diary*, p. 22, p. 266, p. 267, p. 278, p. 343.
14 *Diary*, p. 247; *Letters*, VII, p. 29.
15 *Thyrza*, p. 423.
16 Brantlinger, *The Reading Lesson*, p. 129, pp. 192–7.
17 In his *Diary*, p. 148, Gissing records a conversation with Roberts in which he wishes for a patron like Gillman.
18 *The Reading Lesson*, p. 190, *Fictions of State*, p. 200.
19 'Introduction to the Autograph Edition of *David Copperfield*', 15. Cf. *Forster's Life*, ed. by Gissing, p. 205.
20 *Maitland*, p. 38.
21 *Letters*, VI, p. 310.
22 *Ryecroft*, p. 37; *Born in Exile*, pp. 48–9. See Maud Ellmann, *The Hunger Artists: Starving, Writing and Imprisonment* (London: Virago, 1993) for a brilliant imagining of the reciprocities between writing and starvation. 'Have you ever been conscious, when so fearfully hungry, of an unusual lucidity of thought, an extreme enthusiasm for work of every description?' Gissing wrote to Algernon in 1880 (*Letters*, I, p. 246).
23 *New Grub Street*, p. 79, p. 55.
24 *New Grub Street*, p. 547.
25 *New Grub Street*, p. 138, p. 137.
26 *New Grub Street*, p. 206.
27 *New Grub Street*, p. 187, p. 54.
28 Benjamin, 'The Work of Art in the Age of Mechanical Reproduction', *Illuminations*, pp. 219–53 (p. 223).
29 *New Grub Street*, p. 38.
30 Sloan, p. 89. For the accuracy of the novel, see Nigel Cross, 'Gissing's New Grub Street, 1880–1900', in *The Common Writer: Life in Nineteenth-Century Grub Street* (Cambridge: Cambridge University Press, 1985), pp. 204–40.

31 Keating, *Haunted Study*, pp. 23–7; Guinevere Griest, *Mudie's Circulating Library and the Victorian Novel* (Newton Abbot: David and Charles, 1970), pp. 166–212.

32 *New Grub Street*, pp. 425–6; Bergonzi, Introduction to *New Grub Street*, p. 25; Coustillas, Introduction to *Literature at Nurse*, pp. 11–12; *Diary*, p. 247. James Hepburn suggests that with a good agent, Reardon could have made four times as much on his novel: *The Author's Empty Purse and the Rise of the Literary Agent* (London: Oxford University Press, 1968), p. 21.

33 *Letters*, V, p. 155.

34 *Letters*, V, p. 149.

35 *Gissing on Fiction*, p. 86; *Letters*, V, p. 163.

36 *Critical Heritage*, pp. 343–5.

37 Editors' Introduction, *Letters*, V, p. xxii.

38 *Letters*, II, p. 253; IV, p. 61; VI, pp. 322–3.

39 *New Grub Street*, pp. 81–2.

40 *New Grub Street*, p. 83.

41 Eugene M Baer, 'Authorial Intrusion in Gissing's *New Grub Street*', *Gissing Newsletter* 21.1 (1985), 14–25 (16). I am not in full agreement with Baer's conclusions, however.

42 *New Grub Street*, p. 462.

43 *New Grub Street*, p. 230.

44 Grylls, *The Paradox of Gissing*, p. 88.

45 *New Grub Street*, p. 418.

46 *New Grub Street*, p. 118, p. 325.

47 *New Grub Street*, pp. 453–4.

48 *New Grub Street*, p. 362.

49 Jacob Korg, *George Gissing: A Critical Biography* (London: Methuen, 1965), p. 94.

50 *New Grub Street*, pp. 232–3. Cf. *A Life's Morning*, pp. 40–1.

51 *New Grub Street*, p. 279.

52 Trotter, *The English Novel in History*, pp. 17–18; Edward Copeland, *Women Writing about Money: Women's Fiction in England 1790–1820* (Cambridge: Cambridge University Press, 1995), pp. 4–5.

53 *The Town Traveller*, ed. by Pierre Coustillas (London: Methuen, 1898; repr. Brighton: Harvester Press, 1981), p. 291, p. 305.

54 *New Grub Street*, p. 279.

55 'George Orwell, 'George Gissing', in *Works*, XIX: *It is What I think 1947–1948*, pp. 346–52 (p. 349). Robert L Selig, 'Alienation in George Gissing's *New Grub Street*', in *George Gissing: Critical Essays*, ed. by Jean-Pierre Michaux (London; Totowa: Vision; Barnes and Noble, pp. 162–73 (p. 172); Patricia Stubbs, *Women and Fiction: Feminism and the Novel* (Sussex; New York: Harvester Press; Barnes and Noble, 1979), p. 144.

56 *New Grub Street*, p. 275.

57 *New Grub Street*, p. 81.

58 *New Grub Street*, p. 421.

59 *New Grub Street*, p. 422.

60 Thomas Richards, *The Commodity Culture of Victorian England: Advertising and Spectacle 1851–1914* (London: Verso, 1991); ES Turner, *The Shocking History of Advertising*, rev edn (Harmondsworth: Penguin, 1965); W Hamish Fraser, *The Coming of the Mass Market 1850–1914* (London: Macmillan, 1981), pp. 134–46.

61 *New Grub Street*, p. 193.

62 *New Grub Street*, p. 124.

63 *Letters*, VI, p. 335; *Diary*, p. 295.

64 *New Grub Street*, p. 544, p. 539.

65 Goode, *Ideology and Fiction*, p. 116.

66 *New Grub Street*, p. 502.

67 *OED*, 2a, recorded as still in use by 1905.

68 *New Grub Street*, p. 70.

69 *New Grub Street*, p. 545.

70 Gissing wrote to Gabrielle, 'a woman (the high-minded woman) is content with love afar off – with its spiritual gifts; she can live her whole life long on imagination. Alas! it is not so with a man.' *Letters*, VII, p. 156.

71 *Letters*, IV, p. 117.

72 Bowlby observes that Gissing writes 'with the hindsight of a decade', but does not go on to suggest that the historical distance ironizes Jasper (p. 102).

73 Grylls, *The Paradox of Gissing*, p. 105.

74 Poole, pp. 154–5.

75 Grylls, *The Paradox of Gissing*, p. 98.

76 Alden, p. 43, pp. 67–8. John Goode claims that '*Born in Exile* is *Jude* in reverse' (*Ideology and Fiction*, p. 60). Interestingly, given the novels' similarities in the ironizing of their central characters' despair, Gissing thought poorly of *Jude the Obscure*, writing in a letter to Henry Hick: 'Poor Thomas is utterly on the wrong tack, & I fear he will never get back into the right one. At his age a habit of railing against the universe is not overcome.' He adds later that the novel 'suffers from Hardy's determination to arraign life', (*Letters*, VI, p. 62, 76); to Algernon he complained that the novel lacked humour (VI, p. 49).

77 *Born in Exile*, pp. 168–9.

78 *Born in Exile*, p. 449, 304.

79 *Born in Exile*, pp. 170–1.

80 *Seven Types of Ambiguity* (London: Hogarth, 1984), p. vi, p. 226.

81 *Born in Exile*, p. 86.

82 For a famous diagnosis of the plight of the twentieth-century 'scholarship boy', see Richard Hoggart, *The Uses of Literacy: Aspects of Working-class Life with Special Reference to Publications and Entertainments* (Harmondsworth: Penguin, 1958), pp. 291–304.

83 *Born in Exile*, pp. 38–9.

84 VS Pritchett, '*Grub Street*', in *Collected Articles on George Gissing*, pp. 126–30 (p. 127).

85 *Born in Exile*, p. 30.

86 Sigmund Freud, 'Family Romances', *Works*, IX, pp. 237–41 (p. 239).

87 *Born in Exile*, p. 129.

88 Brooks, pp. 25–32 *et seq.*

89 *Born in Exile*, p. 246.

90 Peak's Conradian fantasy parodies the emigration-ending so well that it is worth quoting at length: 'He must resume his purpose of seeking some distant country, where new conditions of life would allow him to try his fortune at least as an honest adventurer. In many parts of colonial England his technical knowledge would have a value, and were there not women to be won beneath other skies – women perhaps of subtler charm than the old hidebound civilisation produced? Reminiscences of scenes and figures in novels he had read nourished the illusion. He pictured some thriving little town at the ends of the earth, where a young Englishman of good manners and unusual culture would easily be admitted to the intimacy of the richest families; he saw

the ideal colonist (a man of good birth, but a sower of wild oats in his youth) with two or three daughters about him – beautiful girls, wondrously self-instructed – living amid romantic dreams of the old world, and of the lover who would some day carry them off (with a substantial share of papa's wealth) to Europe and the scenes of their imagination' (*Born in Exile*, pp. 259–60).

91 *Great Expectations*, p. 106; *Born in Exile*, p. 53.
92 *Born in Exile*, p. 67.
93 *Born in Exile*, p. 127.
94 Poole, p. 172.
95 *Born in Exile*, p. 76.
96 *Born in Exile*, p. 15.
97 *Born in Exile*, p. 22.
98 *Born in Exile*, pp. 8–9.
99 *Born in Exile*, p. 197.
100 *Born in Exile*, p. 302, pp. 156; see also pp. 115, 130, 143–4, 155, 167–8, 252.
101 Lionel Trilling, *Sincerity and Authenticity* (London: Oxford University Press, 1972), pp. 114–15.
102 Trilling, p. 16.
103 Trilling, pp. 10–11. Cf. Schopenhauer, pp. 168–9.
104 Crispin, p. 45. Charles Swann writes very persuasively on this novel from a Nietzschean and existential point of view, but perhaps underrates Gissing's conservatism, and the desirability of the middle-class existence Peak desires. See Charles Swann, 'Sincerity and Authenticity: The Problem of Identity in *Born in Exile*', *Literature and History*, 10 (1984), 165–88 (168).
105 *Born in Exile*, p. 71.
106 *Born in Exile*, p. 252.
107 *Born in Exile*, p. 157.
108 On gaze and discipline, see Michel Foucault, *Discipline and Punish: The Birth of the Prison*, trans. by Alan Sheridan (Harmondsworth: Penguin, 1979).
109 *Born in Exile*, p. 358.
110 Charles Darwin, *The Works of Charles Darwin*, ed. by Paul H Barrett and RB Freeman, 29 vols (London: Pickering and Chatto: 1986–9), XXIII: *The Expression of the Emotions in Man and Animals*, pp. 269–70. The same chapter also has sections on 'Shyness' and 'Shame, from broken moral rules and conventional rules'.
111 Introduction, *Born in Exile*, ed. by David Grylls (London; Rutland: Dent; Tuttle, 1993), pp. vii–xvii (x–xii); *The Paradox of Gissing*, pp. 132–4. See also Stephen Ogden, 'Darwinian Scepticism in George Gissing's *Born in Exile*', in *A Garland for Gissing*, pp. 171–8.
112 *Diary*, p. 170; pp. 234–44 records Gissing's scientific reading for *Born in Exile*.
113 Darwin, *Works*: XV: *On the Origin of Species*.
114 *Born in Exile*, p. 61.
115 *Born in Exile*, pp. 133–4.
116 *Born in Exile*, p. 133.
117 Gillian Beer, *Darwin's Plots: Evolutionary Narrative in Darwin, George Eliot and Nineteenth-Century Fiction* (London: Routledge and Kegan Paul, 1983), p. 117.
118 *Born in Exile*, p. 402.
119 *Born in Exile*, p. 245; see also pp. 436–7.
120 Beer, p. 11.

121 *Born in Exile*, p. 61.

122 *Born in Exile*, pp. 218–19.

123 *Born in Exile*, p. 380.

124 *Born in Exile*, p. 469; Goode, *Ideology and Fiction*, p. 62.

125 *Born in Exile*, p. 479.

126 John Halperin, *Gissing: A Life in Books* (Oxford: Oxford University Press, 1987), pp. 4–5.

127 *Isabel Clarendon*, I, p. 93, II, p. 291.

128 'A Song of Sixpence', *Human Odds and Ends*, pp. 226–7. Cf. *Extracts from my Reading*, pp. 103–4.

129 *Critical Heritage*, p. 525.

130 *Born in Exile*, p. 71.

131 *Born in Exile*, p. 459, p. 118.

132 *Born in Exile*, p. 109, p. 421.

133 *Born in Exile*, p. 443.

134 *Born in Exile*, p. 442; Swann, 183.

135 *Born in Exile*, p. 110.

136 *Born in Exile*, p. 282.

137 *The Emancipated*, ed. by Pierre Coustillas (London: Lawrence and Bullen, 1893; repr. Hassocks: Harvester Press, 1977), p. 199. See *Born in Exile*, p. 231 for Buckland Warricombe's agreement.

138 *Born in Exile*, p. 439.

139 *Born in Exile*, p. 170.

140 *Born in Exile*, p. 480; Jacob Korg, 'The Spiritual Theme of George Gissing's *Born in Exile*', in *From Jane Austen to Joseph Conrad: Essays Collected in Memory of James T Hillhouse* (Minneapolis: University of Minnesota Press, 1958), pp. 246–56 . *Born in Exile* perhaps resembles Turgenev's *Fathers and Sons* in the functional nihilism of its plot: little incident actually occurs in either novel, and neither protagonist comes close to his potential, each dying a fruitless, unheroic death.

141 Korg, 'Spiritual Theme', p. 256.

142 Alden, pp. 35–6.

4: GISSING'S CITY OF WOMEN

1 William Greenslade, *Degeneration, Culture and the Novel 1880–1940* (Cambridge: Cambridge University Press, 1994), pp. 136–7.

2 *Born in Exile*, pp. 287–8.

3 *Critical Study*, pp. 191–2.

4 *Letters*, V, p. 113. Gissing's care for the continuing education of his sisters, especially the more emancipated Ellen, is consistently evident in his letters to them. See also II, p. 72–3, V, p. 79.

5 Sjöholm, pp. 72–3.

6 *The Odd Women*, ed. by Arlene Young (Peterborough, ON: Broadview, 1998), p. 82.

7 Susan Colón, 'Professionalism and Domesticity in George Gissing's *The Odd Women*', *English Literature in Transition*, 44:4 (2001), 441–58 (441).

8 Kathleen Blake, *Love and the Woman Question in Victorian Literature: The Art of Self-Postponement* (Brighton; Totowa: Harvester Press; Barnes and Noble, 1983), p. 79; Stubbs, p. 143; Ann L Ardis, *New Women, New Novels: Feminism and Early Modernism* (New

Brunswick: Rutgers University Press, 1990), pp. 87–90; Katherine Bailey Linehan, '*The Odd Women*: Gissing's Imaginative Approach to Feminism', *Modern Language Quarterly*, 40.4 (1979), 358–75; Wendy Lesser, 'Even-Handed Oddness: George Gissing's *The Odd Women*', *Hudson Review*, 37.2 (1984), 209–20 (215); Karen Chase, 'The Literal Heroine: A Study of Gissing's *The Odd Women*', *Criticism*, 26.3 (1984), 231–44 (231). See also David Kramer, 'George Gissing and Women's Work: Contextualising the Female Professional', *English Literature in Transition*, 43:3 (2000), 316–30.

9 Patricia Comitini, 'A Feminist Fantasy: Conflicting Ideologies in *The Odd Women*', *Studies in the Novel*, 27.4 (1995), 529–443 (530).

10 Linehan, 373.

11 *The Odd Women*, p. 32.

12 *In the Year of Jubilee*, p. 280.

13 Goode, *Ideology and Fiction*, p. 168.

14 Gail Cunningham, *The New Woman and the Victorian Novel* (London: Macmillan, 1978), p. 151.

15 Cunningham, p. 142 ; Deirdre David, 'Ideologies of Patriarchy, Feminism and Fiction in *The Odd Women*', *Feminist Studies*, 10.1 (1984), 117–39 (119).

16 *The Odd Women*, p. 221.

17 Goode, *Ideology and Fiction*, pp. 153, 158.

18 *In the Year of Jubilee*, p. 102, p. 209.

19 See Fraser, pp. 205–7, on the rise of branded cleaning products.

20 *In the Year of Jubilee*, p. 297.

21 See, for example, Lynn Pykett, 'Portraits of the Artist as a Young Woman: Representations of the Female Artist in the New Woman Fiction of the 1890s', in *Victorian Women Writers and the Woman Question*, ed. by Nicole Diane Thompson (Cambridge: Cambridge University Press, 1999), pp. 135–50; and Gail Cunningham, ' "He-Notes": Reconstructing Masculinity', in *The New Woman in Fiction and in Fact*, ed. by Angelique Richardson and Chris Willis (Basingstoke: Palgrave, 2000), pp. 94–106 (p. 95).

22 *Letters*, V, p. 271; see also p. 260.

23 *In the Year of Jubilee*, p. 335.

24 *In the Year of Jubilee*, p. 199.

25 For an excellent close reading of this novel, see Constance D Harsh, 'Gissing's *In the Year of Jubilee* and the Epistemology of Resistance', *English Literature in Transition*, 34.4 (1994), 853–75.

26 *Letters*, V, p. 295.

27 *In the Year of Jubilee*, p. 428.

28 *In the Year of Jubilee*, p. 413.

29 Barbara Leah Harman, *The Feminine Political Novel in Victorian England* (Charlottesville: University of Virginia Press, 1998), p. 141. For John Goode, if Gissing 'retreats into his own churlish ideology at the end, it is only because he confronts issues which are not, in his terms, soluble'; Sjöholm reads the ending as more open still, identifying the churlish ideology as not Gissing's, but Tarrant's (Goode, *Ideology and Fiction*, p. 170; Sjöholm, pp. 105–6).

30 See *Commonplace Book*, p. 44.

31 On Queen Victoria and advertising, see Lori Ann Loeb, *Consuming Angels: Advertising and Victorian Women* (Oxford: Oxford University Press, 1994), pp. 85–99; Richards, *Commodity Cultur*e, pp. 73–118.

32 *Letters*, V, p. 229. On the victory of the signifier over the signified in modern economic

life, see Guy Debord, *Society of the Spectacle* (Detroit: Black and Red, 1983).

33 *OED*, 1a.

34 *In the Year of Jubilee*, p. 2.

35 *In the Year of Jubilee*, p. 7.

36 *In the Year of Jubilee*, p. 253.

37 Harman, p. 137.

38 *In the Year of Jubilee*, p. 239.

39 *In the Year of Jubilee*, p. 238. Roland Barthes's study of the semiotics of clothing suggests that 'Calculating, industrial society is obliged to form consumers who don't calculate.' *The Fashion System*, trans. by Matthew Ward and Richard Howard (London: Cape, 1985), p. xi.

40 *In the Year of Jubilee*, p. 109.

41 *In the Year of Jubilee*, p. 309.

42 *In the Year of Jubilee*, p. 327. See, for example, Darwin, *Works* XXII: *The Descent of Man*, p. 211.

43 *In the Year of Jubilee*, p. 388.

44 *In the Year of Jubilee*, pp. 410–11.

45 *Critical Heritage*, p. 518.

46 *Routledge's Jubilee Guide to London and its Suburbs*, new edn (London: Routledge, n.d. [1887]), p. 21.

47 For Englishness and rural myth, see Martin J Wiener, *English Culture and the Decline of the Industrial Spirit 1850–1900* (Harmondsworth: Penguin, 1985), pp. 41–80. Wiener cites *Ryecroft* as an example of a 'vision of the country as a shelter from the winds of change' (p. 58). For the actual development of this suburb, see HJ Dyos, *Victorian Suburb: A Study of the Growth of Camberwell* (Leicester: Leicester University Press, 1961).

48 *In the Year of Jubilee*, p. 218.

49 Arnold Bennett, *A Man from the North*, ed. by Nicholas Mander (Stroud: Sutton, 1994), p. 1.

50 Herbert Fry, *London in 1880: Illustrated with Bird's-Eye Views of the Principal Streets; also its Chief Suburbs and Environs* (London: Bogue, 1880), p. 1.

51 Bennett, p. 1.

52 *New Grub Street*, p. 474.

53 Halperin, p. 135.

54 *Letters*, VI, p. 249.

55 'The Novels of Mr George Gissing', *Gissing and H G Wells*, pp. 242–59 (p. 245). Wells also notes the emergence of child-rearing as a new theme for Gissing's fiction in *The Whirlpool* (p. 254).

56 *Critical Heritage*, p. 282.

57 *Life and Labour of the People*, ed. by Charles Booth, 9 vols (London: Macmillan, 1892–7), IX, pp. 177–8.

58 *The Whirlpool*, p. 381.

59 *Critical Heritage*, pp. 290–4.

60 *OED*, 4b, 5, 'engagement', 2b. It can also mean to attract (14) or to entangle (11a, 13a) or, in obsolete usage, to pawn or pledge (1, 2).

61 *The Whirlpool*, p. 114.

62 *The Whirlpool*, p. 5.

63 According to Morley Roberts's unreliable account, Gissing met Edith in the street, although it was in fact in a music-hall (*Maitland*, p. 144).

64 *The Whirlpool*, p. 90.
65 *The Whirlpool*, p. 45. A letter to Algernon indicates that Frothingham's Britannia enterprise was based upon Jabez Balfour and the Liberator crash (*Letters*, VI, p. 127).
66 *The Whirlpool*, p. 91, p. 126, p. 213.
67 *The Whirlpool*, pp. 21–2, p. 208.
68 *The Whirlpool*, p. 208.
69 *The Whirlpool*, p. 217. 'Women think in their hearts that the man's business is to make money and theirs is to spend it' (Schopenhauer, p. 82).
70 *The Whirlpool*, p. 208.
71 *The Whirlpool*, p. 119.
72 *The Whirlpool*, p. 366.
73 *The Whirlpool*, p. 177; see also p. 59, p. 172.
74 *OED*, 1, 2, 5, 10. The *OED*'s citation for meaning 1 genders the word's use thus – 'She spent his money and led him such a life' (*Temple Bar*, 102 (1894), 340).
75 Bowlby pp. 18–34. Cf. *Isabel Clarendon*, II, p. 159.
76 Bowlby, pp. 10–11. See David Trotter, *The English Novel in History*, pp. 20–1.
77 Sally Ledger, 'Gissing, the Shopgirl and the New Woman', *Women: a Cultural Review*, 6.3 (1995), 263–74 (266); Brantlinger, *Fictions of State*, p. 79.
78 *Human Odds and Ends*, p. 190.
79 *The Whirlpool*, p. 34, p. 363.
80 *The Whirlpool*, p. 214.
81 *The Whirlpool*, p. 374.
82 Sjöholm suggests that most readings of this novel are too hostile to Alma and that Rolfe is also culpable: see *The Vice of Wedlock*, pp. 107–31.
83 *The Whirlpool*, p. 136.
84 Greenslade, pp. 134–50; *Letters*, VI, pp. 149–50; *Diary*, p. 396, p. 403.
85 *The Whirlpool*, p. 275, p. 188.
86 *The Whirlpool*, p. 173.
87 *The Whirlpool*, pp. 376–7.
88 *The Whirlpool*, p. 218.
89 *The Whirlpool*, p. 226.
90 *The Whirlpool*, p. 48.
91 See, for example, *The Nether World*, p. 345.
92 Michael Wheeler, *Death and the Future Life in Victorian Literature and Theology* (Cambridge: Cambridge University Press, 1990), p. 202; *Diary*, p. 166. There are four references to Dante in Gissing's notebook *Extracts from my Reading*, and in the *Commonplace Book*, Gissing lists 'a thorough knowledge of Dante' as one of his 'modest intellectual ambitions' (p. 26). Gissing himself was dubbed 'a modern Dante' by the *Court Journal*'s review of *The Nether World* (*Critical Heritage*, p. 137).
93 *The Whirlpool*, p. 320.
94 For Gissing and Orphic myth see Samuel Vogt Gapp, *George Gissing, Classicist* (Philadelphia: University of Pennsylvania Press, 1936), p. 17.
95 *The Whirlpool*, p. 305. Sydney Hillier, *Popular Drugs: Their Use and Abuse* (London: Werner Laurie, 1910), pp. 16–18, anatomizes Britain's new economic insecurity, modern living, the repression of the maternal instinct, concerns about heredity and drug use: 'one perpetual series of engagements producing a chronic state of morbid excitement, nervous strain, and sleeplessness. [...] This decadent tendency of modern society shows itself in various guises. In literature it is very conspicuous, and is instanced by the

demand for a certain kind of fiction, in which the heroine is invariably of the neurotic-erotic type' (p. 17). Hillier also suggests that the artistic temperament is particularly prone to drug abuse (p. 26).

96 Korg, *Critical Biography*, p. 224; *Letters*, VI, p. 155.

97 *The Whirlpool*, pp. 322–3.

98 Introduction, p. xx.

99 *The Whirlpool*, p. 218.

100 *The Crown of Life*, ed. by Michel Ballard (London: Methuen, 1899; Hassocks: Harvester Press, 1978), pp. 48–9.

101 Luisa Villa, 'The Grocer's Romance: Economic Transactions and Radical Individualism in *Will Warburton*', *Gissing Journal*, 36.2 (2000), 1–19 (15).

102 See, for instance, Pierre Coustillas, '*The Paying Guest* and the Praise it Won in 1896', *Gissing Journal*, 32.4 (1996), 20–3.

103 Halperin, p. 274.

104 *The Crown of Life*, p. 90.

105 *The Crown of Life*, p. 138.

106 *The Crown of Life*, p. 130.

107 *The Crown of Life*, p. 145.

108 *The Crown of Life*, p. 25.

109 *The Crown of Life*, p. 2.

110 *The Crown of Life*, p. 54. Bowlby, pp. 29–32. Cf. 'In his present state of mind he cared nothing how disreputable he looked to passers-by. These seedy habiliments were the token of his degradation, and at times he regarded them (happening to see himself in a shop mirror) with pleasurable contempt' (*New Grub Street*, p. 377).

111 *The Crown of Life*, p. 35.

112 *The Crown of Life*, p. 71; see also p. 55, p. 95.

113 *The Crown of Life*, p. 111.

114 *The Crown of Life*, pp. 163–4; for further attacks on London, see pp. 166, 229, 268. Compare *Commonplace Book*, p. 44: 'The "City" is so oppressive to the spirit because it represents the *triumph* of the vulgar man.' See also *Born in Exile*, p. 265.

115 This was an important difference for Gissing between writers and other professionals: 'Enviable are men of business,' he wrote to Algernon, 'who leave their affairs behind them' (*Letters*, VI, p. 143).

116 *The Crown of Life*, pp. 98, 55.

117 I will explore these themes further in an essay on *The Whirlpool* to be published in *George Gissing: Voices of the Unclassed* (London: Ashgate, 2004), ed. by Jenny Bourne-Taylor and Martin Ryle.

118 *The Whirlpool*, p. 15. Gissing read Stevenson's *The Wrecker* and *The Ebb-Tide* in 1895 (*Diary*, p. 393, p. 395).

119 *Letters*, VI, pp. 100–1.

120 *The Crown of Life*, p. 80.

121 See especially Gissing's essay 'Tyrtaeus', *Review of the Week*, 4 November 1899, reprinted in *Gissing Newsletter*, 10.3 (1974), 2–3. See also *Letters*, VII, p. 420.

122 Pierre Coustillas, Introduction to *Our Friend the Charlatan* (London: Chapman and Hall, 1901; repr. Rutherford: Fairleigh Dickinson Press, 1976), p. xiv.

123 *The Crown of Life*, p. 175.

124 *The Crown of Life*, p. 19.

125 *The Crown of Life*, p. 238.

126 Letters, VIII, p. 50; *Critical Heritage*, p. 358.

127 *The Crown of Life*, p. 10.

128 *The Crown of Life*, p. 116.

129 *The Crown of Life*, p. 122.

130 *The Crown of Life*, p. 128.

131 *In the Year of Jubilee*, p. 5; also Grylls, *The Paradox of Gissing*, p. 79.

132 *The Crown of Life*, p. 130.

133 *The Crown of Life*, p. 185, p. 260.

134 *Eve's Ransom* (London: Lawrence and Bullen, 1895; repr. New York: Dover, 1980), pp. 123–4.

135 *The Crown of Life*, p. 270.

136 For Victorian advertising's use of fallen women and classical mythology, see Loeb, pp. 57–71, p. 174.

137 Lowell T Frye, ' "An Author at Grass": Ironic Intent in Gissing's *The Private Papers of Henry Ryecroft*', *English Literature in Transition*, 24 (1981), 41–51.

138 *Letters*, IX, p. 58.

139 Jameson, p. 204.

140 *Ryecroft*, pp. 21, 36–41, 23, 54, 198–9, 3–4, 55, 167–70, 195, 13.

141 *Ryecroft*, pp. 15–16, see also pp. 134–5, 230–1, 287, 33, 201, 196, 97.

142 *Ryecroft*, pp. 261–2.

143 *Ryecroft*, pp. 25, 128–30, 162–3, 197–8, 255–6, 113, 47, 70, 251, 49, 89, 92, 125, 138, 122–4.

144 *Ryecroft*, p. 74.

145 *Ryecroft*, p. 217.

146 *Letters*, VIII, p. 90.

147 Sypher, p. 52.

148 *Ryecroft*, p. 171.

149 *Ryecroft*, p. vii. Introduction, *The Private Papers of Henry Ryecroft*, ed. by Mark Storey (Oxford: Oxford University Press, 1987), pp. vii–xx (p. x).

150 Preface, *Selections*, p. 18.

151 Grylls, *The Paradox of Gissing*, pp. 4–5.

152 *Essays and Fiction*, p. 94.

153 Gisela Argyle, 'Gissing's *The Whirlpool* and Schopenhauer', *Gissing Newsletter*, 17:4 (1981), 3–21 (6).

SELECT BIBLIOGRAPHY

Primary Material

Allen, Grant, *The Woman Who Did*, ed. by Sarah Wintle (Oxford: Oxford University Press, 1995).

Arnold, Matthew, *Culture and Anarchy and other Writings*, ed. by Stefan Collini (Cambridge: Cambridge University Press, 1993).

Bennett, Arnold, *A Man from the North*, ed. by Nicholas Mander (Stroud: Sutton, 1994).

Booth, Charles, ed., *Life and Labour*, 2 vols (London: Williams and Norgate, 1889).

——, *Life and Labour of the People*, 9 vols (London: Macmillan, 1892–7).

Brontë, Charlotte, *Jane Eyre*, ed. by Jane Jack and Margaret Smith (Oxford: Clarendon Press, 1975).

——, *Shirley*, ed. by Herbert Rosengarten and Margaret Smith (Oxford: Clarendon Press, 1979).

Carlyle, Thomas, *Past and Present*, ed. by Richard D Altick (New York: New York University Press, 1965).

——, *Sartor Resartus*, ed. by WH Hudson (London: Dent, 1982).

Darwin, Charles, *The Works of Charles Darwin*, ed. by Paul H Barrett and RB Freeman, 29 vols (London: Pickering and Chatto, 1986–9).

Dickens, Charles, *Bleak House*, ed. by Nicola Bradbury (Harmondsworth: Penguin, 1996).

——, *Christmas Books*, ed. by Ruth Glancy (Oxford: Oxford University Press, 1988).

——, *David Copperfield*, ed. by Nina Burgis (Oxford: Clarendon Press, 1981).

——, *Dickens's Working Notes for His Novels*, ed. by Harry Stone (Chicago: University of Chicago Press, 1987).

——, *Dombey and Son*, ed. by Alan Horsman (Oxford: Clarendon Press, 1974).

——, *Great Expectations*, ed. by Margaret Cardwell (Oxford: Clarendon Press, 1993).

——, *Little Dorrit*, ed. by Harvey Peter Sucksmith (Oxford: Clarendon Press, 1979).

——, *Martin Chuzzlewit*, ed. by Margaret Cardwell (Oxford: Clarendon Press, 1982).

——, *Nicholas Nickleby*, ed. by Paul Schlicke (Oxford: Oxford University Press, 1990).

——, *The Old Curiosity Shop*, ed. by Elizabeth M Brennan (Oxford: Clarendon Press, 1997).

——, *Oliver Twist*, ed. by Kathleen Tillotson (Oxford: Clarendon Press, 1966).

——, *Our Mutual Friend*, ed. by Adrian Poole (Harmondsworth: Penguin, 1997).

——, *Uncollected Writings from Household Words*, ed. by Harry Stone, 2 vols (Bloomington: Indiana University Press, 1968).

Dowie, Menie Muriel, *Gallia*, ed. by Helen Small (London: Dent, 1995).

Eliot, George, *Middlemarch*, ed. by David Carroll (Oxford: Clarendon Press, 1986).

——, *The Mill on The Floss*, ed. by Gordon S Haight (Oxford: Clarendon Press, 1980).

——, *Silas Marner*, ed. by Terence Cave (Oxford: Oxford University Press, 1996).

Fawcett, Millicent Garrett, *Political Economy for Beginners* (London: Macmillan, 1870).

——, *Tales in Political Economy* (London: Macmillan, 1874).

Freud, Sigmund, *The Standard Edition of the Complete Psychological Works of Sigmund Freud*, trans. and ed. by James Strachey and others, 24 vols (London: Hogarth Press, 1953–74).

Gaskell, Elizabeth, *Mary Barton: A Tale of Manchester Life*, ed. by Macdonald Daly (Harmondsworth: Penguin, 1996).

Gissing, George, *Born in Exile*, ed. by Pierre Coustillas (London: A and C Black, 1892; repr. Hassocks: Harvester Press, 1978).

——, *Brownie: With Six Other Stories attributed to Him*, ed. by George Everett Hastings, Vincent Starrett and Thomas Ollive Mabbott (New York: Columbia University Press, 1931).

——, *By the Ionian Sea* (Marlboro: Marlboro Press, n.d.).

——, *Charles Dickens: A Critical Study* (London: Gresham, 1903).

——, *The Collected Letters of George Gissing*, ed. by Pierre Coustillas, Paul F Mattheisen and Arthur C Young, 9 vols (Athens: Ohio University Press, 1990–7).

——, *The Crown of Life*, ed. by Michel Ballard (London: Methuen, 1899; repr. Hassocks: Harvester Press, 1978).

——, *The Day of Silence and Other Stories*, ed. by Pierre Coustillas (London; Rutland: Dent; Tuttle, 1993).

——, *Demos: A Story of English Socialism*, ed. by Pierre Coustillas (London: Lawrence and Bullen, 1897; repr. Brighton: Harvester Press, 1972).

——, *Denzil Quarrier*, ed. by John Halperin (London: Lawrence and Bullen, 1892; repr. Hassocks: Harvester Press, 1979).

——, 'Dickens', in *Homes and Haunts of Famous Writers* (London: Wells Gardner, Darton, [1906]), pp. 107–20.

——, *The Emancipated*, ed. by Pierre Coustillas (London: Bentley, 1890; repr. Hassocks: Harvester Press, 1977).

——, *Essays and Fiction*, ed. by Pierre Coustillas (Baltimore: Johns Hopkins Press, 1970).

——, *Eve's Ransom* (London: Lawrence and Bullen, 1895; repr. New York: Dover, 1980).

——, *Forster's Life of Dickens*, abridged and revised by George Gissing (London: Chapman and Hall, 1903).

——, *George Gissing and H G Wells: A Record of their Friendship and Correspondence*, ed. by Royal A Gettmann (London: Hart-Davis, 1961).

——, *George Gissing at Work: a Study of his Notebook Extracts From my Reading*, ed. by Pierre Coustillas and Patrick Bridgwater (Greensboro: ELT, 1988).

——, *George Gissing on Fiction*, ed. by Jacob and Cynthia Korg (London: Enitharmon Press, 1978).

——, *George Gissing's American Notebook: Notes – G.R.G. – 1877*, ed. by Bouwe Postmus (Lewiston: Mellen, 1993).

——, *George Gissing's Commonplace Book: A Manuscript in the Berg Collection of the New York Public Library*, ed. by Jacob Korg (New York: New York Public Library, 1962).

——, *George Gissing's Essay on Robert Burns: A Previously Unpublished Manuscript*, ed. by Jacob Korg (Lewiston: Mellen, 1992).

——, *George Gissing's Memorandum Book: A Novelist's Notebook, 1895–1902*, ed. by Bouwe Postmus (Lewiston: Mellen, 1996).

——, 'Gissing's Introduction to the Autograph Edition of *David Copperfield*', *Gissing Journal*, 33.1 (1997), 10–19.

——, 'Gissing's Introduction to the Rochester *David Copperfield*', ed. by Richard J Dunn, *The Dickensian*, 77.1 (1981), 3–11.

——, *The House of Cobwebs* (London: Constable, 1906).

——, *Human Odds and Ends: Stories and Sketches* (London: Sidgwick and Jackson, 1911).

——, *The Immortal Dickens* (London: Palmer, 1925).

——, *In the Year of Jubilee*, ed. by Gillian Tindall with notes by PF Kropholler (London: Lawrence and Bullen, 1895; repr. Hassocks: Harvester Press, 1976).

——, *In the Year of Jubilee* (New York: Appleton, 1895; repr. Dover, 1982).

——, *Isabel Clarendon*, ed. by Pierre Coustillas, 2 vols (London: Chapman and Hall, 1886; repr. Brighton: Harvester Press, 1969).

——, *The Letters of George Gissing to Eduard Bertz 1887–1903*, ed. by Arthur C Young (New Brunswick: Rutgers University Press, 1961; repr. Westport: Greenwood Press, 1980).

——, *A Life's Morning*, ed. by Pierre Coustillas (London: Smith, Elder, 1888; repr. Brighton: Harvester Press, 1984).

——, *London and the Life of Literature in Late Victorian England: The Diary of George Gissing, Novelist*, ed. by Pierre Coustillas (Hassocks: Harvester Press, 1978).

——, *The Nether World*, ed. by John Goode (London: Smith, Elder, 1890; repr. Brighton: Harvester Press, 1974).

——, *New Grub Street*, ed. by Bernard Bergonzi (Harmondsworth: Penguin, 1985).

——, *Notes on Social Democracy*, ed. by Jacob Korg (London: Enitharmon Press, 1968).

——, *The Odd Women*, ed. by Arlene Young (Peterborough, ON: Broadview, 1998).

——, *Our Friend The Charlatan*, ed. by Pierre Coustillas (London: Chapman and Hall, 1901; repr. Hassocks, Harvester Press, 1976).

——, *The Paying Guest*, ed. by Ian Fletcher (London: Cassell, 1895; repr. Brighton: Harvester Press, 1982).

——, *The Poetry of George Gissing*, ed. by Bouwe Postmus (Lewiston: Mellen, 1995).

——, *The Private Papers of Henry Ryecroft*, ed. by John Stewart Collis and Pierre Coustillas (London: Constable, 1903; repr. Brighton: Harvester Press, 1982).

——, *Selections – Autobiographical and Imaginative from the Works of George Gissing*, ed. by Alfred Gissing, with an introduction by Virginia Woolf (London: Cape, 1929).

——, *Short Stories and Sketches*, ed. by Algernon Gissing (London: Joseph, 1938).

——, *Sleeping Fires* (London: T Fisher Unwin, 1895; repr. Brighton: Harvester Press, 1974).

——, *Thyrza: A Tale*, ed. by Jacob Korg (London: Smith, Elder, 1892; repr. Hassocks: Harvester Press, 1976).

——, *The Town Traveller*, ed. by Pierre Coustillas (London: Methuen, 1898; repr. Brighton: Harvester Press, 1981).

——, 'Tyrtaeus', *Gissing Newsletter*, 10.3 (1974), 2–3.

——, *The Unclassed*, 3 vols (London: Chapman and Hall, 1884).

——, *The Unclassed*, ed. by Jacob Korg (London: Lawrence and Bullen, 1895; repr. Brighton: Harvester Press, 1976).

——, *Veranilda*, ed. by Pierre Coustillas (London: Constable, 1904; repr. Brighton: Harvester Press, 1987).

——, *A Victim of Circumstances and Other Stories* (London: Constable, 1927).

——, *The Whirlpool*, ed. by Patrick Parrinder (London: Lawrence and Bullen, 1897; repr. Brighton: Harvester Press, 1977).

Gissing, George, *Will Warburton: A Romance of Real Life*, ed. by Colin Partridge (London: Constable, 1905; repr. Brighton: Harvester Press, 1981).

——, *Workers in the Dawn*, ed. by Pierre Coustillas (New York: Doubleday, 1935; repr. Brighton: Harvester Press, 1985).

Hamsun, Knut, *Hunger*, trans. by George Egerton (London: Duckworth, 1921 [1967]).

Hardy, Thomas, *Under the Greenwood Tree or The Mellstock Quire: A Rural Painting of the Old School*, ed. by Geoffrey Grigson (London: Macmillan, 1975).

——, *Tess of the d'Urbervilles*, ed. by Juliet Grindle and Simon Gatrell (Oxford: Clarendon Press, 1983).

Hogarth, William, *Hogarth's Graphic Works*, ed. by Ronald Paulson, 2 vols (New Haven: Yale University Press, 1965).

Jacobs, WW, *The Monkey's Paw* (London: Harper, 1902; repr. Woodbridge: Boydell, 1983).

James, Henry, *The Figure in the Carpet and Other Stories*, ed. by Frank Kermode (Penguin: Harmondsworth, 1986).

Kingsley, Charles, *Alton Locke, Tailor and Poet: An Autobiography*, ed. by Elizabeth A Cripps (Oxford: Oxford University Press, 1983).

Kipling, Rudyard, *Barrack-room Ballads and Other Verses* (London: Methuen, 1892).

Malthus, *An Essay on the Principle of Population; and a Summary View of the Principle of Population*, ed. by Anthony Flew (Harmondsworth: Penguin, 1982).

Martineau, Harriet, 'An Account of Some Treatment of Gold and Gems', *Household Words*, 4 (1851), 449–55.

——, *Illustrations of Political Economy*, 9 vols (London: Fox: 1834).

Marx, Karl, *Capital: A Critique of Political Economy*, ed. by Frederick Engels, 4th edn (New York: Modern Library, 1906).

——, *Economic and Philosophical Manuscripts of 1844*, trans. by Martin Milligan, 4th edn, rev. by Dirk J Struik (Moscow: Progress, 1974).

——, *Theories of Surplus Value*, ed. by Karl Kautsky, trans. by GA Bonner and Emile Burns (London: Lawrence and Wishart, 1951).

Mill, John Stuart, *The Collected Works of John Stuart Mill*, ed. by JM Robson, 33 vols (Toronto; London: University of Toronto Press; Routledge and Kegan Paul, 1963–91).

Moore, George, *'Literature at Nurse', or, Circulating Morals: A Polemic on Victorian Censorship*, ed. by Pierre Coustillas (Hassocks: Harvester Press, 1976).

Morris, William, *Works*, ed. by May Morris, 24 vols (London: Longmans Green, 1910–15).

Ruskin, John, *Works*, ed. by ET Cook and Alexander Wedderburn, 39 vols (London: Allen, 1903–12).

Schopenhauer, Arthur, *Essays and Aphorisms*, ed. and trans. by RJ Hollingdale (Harmondsworth: Penguin, 1970).

Shelley, Percy, *Shelley's Poetry and Prose: Authoritative Texts, Criticism*, ed. by Donald H Reiman and Neil Fraistat, 2nd edn (New York: Norton, 2002).

Sidgwick, Henry, 'What is Money?', *Fortnightly Review*, 31 (1879), 563–75.

Smiles, Samuel, *Self-Help*, ed. by Peter W Sinnema (Oxford: Oxford University Press, 2002).

Smith, Adam, *The Wealth of Nations*, ed. by RH Campbell, AS Skinner and WB Todd, 2 vols (Oxford: Clarendon Press, 1976).

Stevenson, Robert Louis, *The Letters of Robert Louis Stevenson*, ed. by Bradford A Booth and Ernest Mehew, 8 vols (New Haven: Yale University Press, 1995).

Trollope, Anthony, *The Way We Live Now*, ed. by John Sutherland (Oxford: Oxford University Press, 1982).

Wills, WH, 'Review of a Popular Publication in the Searching Style', *Household Words*, 1 (1850), 423–6.

Secondary Material

Ackroyd, Peter, *Dickens* (London: Sinclair-Stevenson, 1990).

'Affable Hawk', Review of *The Private Papers of Henry Ryecroft* and *The Private Life of Henry Maitland*, *The New Statesman*, 24 December 1921, p. 347.

Alden, Patricia, *Social Mobility in the English Bildungsroman: Gissing, Hardy, Bennett and Lawrence* (Ann Arbor: UMI Research Press, 1986).

Allen, Walter, Introduction to *Born in Exile* (London: Gollancz, 1970), pp. 6–12.

Altick, Richard P, *The Presence of the Present: Topics of the Day in the Victorian Novel* (Columbus: Ohio State University Press, 1991).

Anesko, Michael, *"Friction with the Market": Henry James and the Profession of Authorship* (New York: Oxford University Press, 1986).

Arac, Jonathan, *Commissioned Spirits: The Shaping of Social Motion in Dickens, Carlyle, Melville, and Hawthorne* (New Brunswick: Rutgers University Press, 1979).

Archer, Thomas, *Charles Dickens: A Gossip about his Life, Works and Characters*, 6 vols (London: Cassell [1894]).

Ardis, Ann L, *New Women, New Novels: Feminism and Early Modernism* (New Brunswick: Rutgers University Press, 1990).

Armstrong, Nancy, *Desire and Domestic Fiction: A Political History of the Novel* (New York: Oxford University Press, 1987).

Austen, Zelda, '*Oliver Twist*: A Divided View', *Dickens Studies Newsletter*, 7.1 (1976), 8–12.

Austin, Alfred, 'Charles Dickens', *Temple Bar*, 29 (1870), 554–62.

Badolato, Francesco, ed., *George Gissing: Antologia Critica* (Rome: Herder, 1984).

Bakhtin, MM, *The Dialogic Imagination: Four Essays*, ed. by Michael Holquist, trans. by Caryl Emerson and Michael Holquist (Austin: University of Texas Press, 1981).

——, *Problems of Dostoevsky's Poetics*, ed. and trans. by Caryl Emerson, with an introduction by Wayne C Booth (Minneapolis: University of Minnesota Press, 1984).

Ballard, Michel, '*Born in Exile* as an Organic Study in Behaviour and Motivation', *English Studies*, 58.4 (1977), 324–33.

Barthes, Roland, *The Fashion System*, trans. by Matthew Ward and Richard Howard (London: Cape, 1985).

——, *Image-Music-Text*, ed. and trans. by Stephen Heath (London: Fontana, 1977).

——, *S/Z*, trans. by Richard Miller with an introduction by Richard Howard (Oxford: Blackwell, 1990).

Baudrillard, Jean, *The Mirror of Production*, trans. by Mark Poster (St Louis: Telos Press, 1975).

Beckson, Karl, *London in the 1890s: A Cultural History* (New York: Norton, 1992).

Beer, Gillian, *Arguing with the Past: Essays in Narrative from Woolf to Sidney* (London: Routledge, 1989).

——, *Darwin's Plots: Evolutionary Narrative in Darwin, George Eliot and Nineteenth-Century Fiction* (London: Routledge and Kegan Paul, 1983)

Bell, Ian FA, *Henry James and the Past: Readings in Time* (Basingstoke: Macmillan, 1991).

——, ed., *Henry James: Fiction as History* (London: Vision, 1984).

Benjamin, Walter, *Illuminations*, ed. by Hannah Arendt, trans. by Harry Zohn (London: Cape, 1970).

Benjamin, Walter, *Charles Baudelaire: a Lyric Poet in the Era of High Capitalism*, trans. by Harry Zohn (London: Verso, 1989).

Bergonzi, Bernard, 'The Last Heirs of Dickens', *Essays in Criticism*, 12 (1962), 314–21.

Blake, Kathleen, *Love and the Woman Question in Victorian Literature: The Art of Self-Postponement* (Brighton; Totowa: Harvester Press; Barnes and Noble, 1983).

Blench, JW, 'George Gissing's *Thyrza*', *Durham University Journal*, 64.2 (1972), 85–114.

Bloch, Maurice and Jonathan Parry, eds, *Money and the Morality of Exchange* (Cambridge: Cambridge University Press, 1989).

Booth, Wayne C, *The Company We Keep: An Ethics of Fiction* (Berkeley: University of California Press, 1988).

Born, Daniel, *The Birth of Liberal Guilt in the English Novel: Charles Dickens to H G Wells* (Chapel Hill: University of North Carolina Press, 1995).

Bowlby, *Just Looking: Consumer Culture in Dreiser, Gissing and Zola* (London: Methuen, 1985).

Brantlinger, Patrick, *Fictions of State: Culture and Credit in Britain, 1694–1994* (Ithaca: Cornell University Press, 1996).

——, *The Reading Lesson: The Threat of Mass Literacy in Nineteenth-Century British Fiction* (Bloomington: Indiana University Press, 1998).

Bridgwater, Patrick, *Gissing and Germany* (London: Enitharmon Press, 1981).

Brooks, Peter, *Reading for the Plot: Design and Intention in Narrative* (Cambridge, MA: Harvard University Press, 1992).

Brown, James M, *Dickens: The Novelist in the Marketplace* (London: Macmillan, 1982).

Buchanan, Robert, 'The Good "Genie" of Fiction: Thoughts while Reading Forster's "Life of Charles Dickens" ', *Saint Paul's*, 10 (1872), 130–48.

Buckley, Jerome Hamilton, *Season of Youth: The Bildungsroman from Dickens to Golding* (Cambridge, MA: Harvard University Press, 1974).

Cannadine, David, *The Decline and Fall of the British Aristocracy* (New Haven: Yale University Press, 1990).

Canning, Albert SG, *The Philosophy of Charles Dickens* (London: Smith, Elder, 1880).

Carey, John, *The Intellectuals and the Masses: Pride and Prejudice among the Literary Intelligentsia 1880–1939* (London: Faber, 1992).

——, *The Violent Effigy; A Study of Dickens's Imagination*, 2nd edn (London: Faber, 1991).

Caserio, Robert L, *Plot, Story, and the Novel: from Dickens and Poe to the Modern Period* (Princeton: Princeton University Press, 1979).

Chase, Karen, 'The Literal Heroine: A Study of Gissing's *The Odd Women*', *Criticism*, 26.3 (1984), 231–44.

Chatman, Seymour, *Story and Discourse: Narrative Structure in Fiction and Film* (Ithaca: Cornell University Press, 1978).

Cohen, Monica F, *Professional Domesticity in the Victorian Novel* (Cambridge: Cambridge University Press, 1998).

Colón, Susan, 'Professionalism and Domesticity in George Gissing's *The Odd Women*', *English Literature in Transition*, 44:4 (2001), 441–58.

Comitini, Patricia, 'A Feminist Fantasy: Conflicting Ideologies in *The Odd Women*', *Studies in the Novel*, 27.4 (1995), 529–543.

Copeland, Edward, *Women Writing about Money: Women's Fiction in England 1790–1820* (Cambridge: Cambridge University Press, 1995).

Cotsell, Michael, 'The Book of Insolvent Fates: Financial Speculation in *Our Mutual Friend*', *Dickens Studies Annual*, 13 (1984), 125–42.

——, *The Companion to Our Mutual Friend* (London: Allen and Unwin, 1986).

Coustillas, Pierre, ed., *Collected Articles on George Gissing* (London: Cass, 1968).

——, *George Gissing at Alderley Edge* (London: Enitharmon Press: 1969).

——, 'Gissing's Reminiscences of his Father', *English Literature in Transition*, 32 (1989), 419–39.

——, 'Gissing's Variations on Urban and Rural Life', in *Victorian Writers and the City*, ed. by Jean-Paul Hulin and Pierre Coustillas (Lille: Publications de l'Université de Lille), pp. 115–43.

——, *Gissing's Writings on Dickens: A Bio-bibliographical Study*, 2nd edn (London: Enitharmon Press, 1971).

——, 'The Publication of *The Private Life of Henry Maitland*: A Literary Event', in *Twilight of Dawn: Studies in English Literature in Transition*, ed. by OM Brack (Tucson: University of Arizona Press, 1987), pp. 137–52.

——, 'The Stormy Publication of Gissing's *Veranilda*', *Bulletin of the New York Public Library*, 72 (1968), 588–610.

Coustillas, Pierre and Colin Partridge, eds, *Gissing: The Critical Heritage* (London: Routledge and Kegan Paul, 1972).

Cowling, Mary, *The Artist as Anthropologist: The Representation of Type and Character in Victorian Art* (Cambridge: Cambridge University Press, 1989).

Craig, David M, 'The Interplay of City and Self in *Oliver Twist*, *David Copperfield*, and *Great Expectations*', *Dickens Studies Annual*, 16 (1987), 17–38.

Cross, Nigel, *The Common Writer: Life in Nineteenth-Century Grub Street* (Cambridge: Cambridge University Press, 1985).

Cunningham, Gail, *The New Woman and the Victorian Novel* (London: Macmillan, 1978).

Dabney, Ross H, *Love and Property in the Novels of Dickens* (London: Chatto and Windus, 1967).

Daldry, Graham, *Charles Dickens and the Form of the Novel: Fiction and Narrative in Dickens's Work* (London: Croom Helm, 1987).

Daleski, HM, *Dickens and the Art of Analogy* (London: Faber, 1970).

Darwin, Bernard, ed., *The Dickens Advertiser: A Collection of the Advertisements in the Original Parts of Novels by Charles Dickens* (London: Matthews and Marrot, 1930).

David, Deirdre, *Fictions of Resolution in Three Victorian Novels: North and South, Our Mutual Friend, Daniel Deronda* (London: Macmillan, 1981).

——, 'Ideologies of Patriarchy, Feminism and Fiction in *The Odd Women*', *Feminist Studies*, 10.1 (1984), 117–39.

Davis, Oswald H, *George Gissing: A Study of Literary Leanings*, ed. by Pierre Coustillas (Dorking: Kohler, 1974).

Debord, Guy, *Society of the Spectacle* (Detroit: Black and Red, 1983).

Dempsey, Mike, ed., *Bubbles: Early Advertising Art from A. & F. Pears Ltd*, with an introduction by Tim Shackleton (London: Fontana, 1978).

Derrida, *Given Time: I. Counterfeit Money*, trans. by Peggy Kamuf (Chicago: University of Chicago Press, 1992).

Derus, David L, 'Gissing and Chesterton as Critics of Dickens', *Chesterton Review*, 12.1 (1986), 71–81.

Digby, Anne, and Peter Searby, *Children, School and Society in Nineteenth Century England* (London: Macmillan, 1981).

Donnelly, Mabel Collins, *George Gissing: Grave Comedian* (Cambridge, MA: Harvard University Press, 1954).

Dunne, Brian Ború, *With Gissing in Italy: The Memoirs of Brian Ború Dunne*, ed. by Paul F

Mattheisen, Arthur C Young and Pierre Coustillas (Athens: Ohio University Press, 1999).

Dyos, HJ, *Victorian Suburb: A Study of the Growth of Camberwell* (Leicester: Leicester University Press, 1961).

Edmonds, Rod, 'The Conservatism of Gissing's Early Novels', *Literature and History*, 7 (1978), 48–69.

Ellmann, Maud, *The Hunger Artists: Starving, Writing and Imprisonment* (London: Virago, 1993).

Falk, Pasi, *The Consuming Body* (London: Sage, 1994).

Federico, Annette, *Masculine Identity in Hardy and Gissing* (London; Rutherford: Associated University Presses; Fairleigh Dickinson University Press, 1991).

Feltes, NN, *Modes of Production of Victorian Novels* (Chicago: University of Chicago Press, 1986).

Flint, Kate, *Dickens* (Brighton: Harvester Press, 1986).

Ford, George, *Dickens and his Readers: Aspects of Novel Criticism since 1836* (Princeton: Princeton University Press, 1955).

Forster, John, *The Life of Charles Dickens*, with an introduction by GK Chesterton, 2 vols (London; New York: Dent; Dutton, 1927).

Foucault, Michel, *Discipline and Punish: The Birth of the Prison*, trans. by Alan Sheridan (Harmondsworth: Penguin, 1979).

Fox, Richard, and TJ Jackson Lears, eds, *The Culture of Consumption: Critical Essays in American History* (New York: Pantheon Books, 1983).

Fraser, W Hamish, *The Coming of the Mass Market, 1850–1914* (London: Macmillan, 1981).

Fry, Herbert, *London in 1880: Illustrated with Bird's-Eye Views of the Principal Streets; also its Chief Suburbs and Environs* (London: Bogue, 1880).

Frye, Lowell T, ' "An Author at Grass": Ironic Intent in Gissing's *The Private Papers of Henry Ryecroft*', *English Literature in Transition*, 24 (1981), 41–51.

Gapp, Samuel Vogt, *George Gissing, Classicist* (Philadelphia: University of Pennsylvania Press, 1936).

Garrett, Peter K, *The Victorian Multiplot Novel: Studies in Dialogical Form* (New Haven: Yale University Press, 1980).

Garvey, Ellen Gruber, *The Adman in the Parlor: Magazines and the Gendering of Consumer Culture, 1880s to 1910s* (New York: Oxford University Press, 1996).

Gaughan, Richard T, 'Prospecting for Money in *Our Mutual Friend*', *Dickens Studies Annual*, 19 (1990), 231–46.

Gibbon, Frank, 'R H Horne and *Our Mutual Friend*', *Dickensian*, 81.3 (1985), 140–3.

Gill, Stephen, Introduction to *The Nether World* (Oxford: Oxford University Press, 1992), pp. vii–xxii.

Gilmour, Robin, *The Idea of the Gentleman in the Victorian Novel* (London: Allen and Unwin, 1981).

The Gissing Journal, 27–34 (1991–2003).

The Gissing Newsletter, 1–26 (1965–90).

Goode, John, *Collected Essays of John Goode*, ed by Charles Swann, with an introduction by Terry Eagleton (Keele: Keele University Press, 1995).

——, *George Gissing: Ideology and Fiction* (London: Vision Press, 1978).

——, 'George Gissing's *The Nether World*' in *Tradition and Tolerance in Nineteenth-Century Fiction: Critical Essays on Some English and American Novels*, ed. by David Howard, John Lucas and John Goode (London: Routledge, 1966), pp. 207–41.

——, 'Gissing, Morris and English Socialism', *Victorian Studies*, 12.2 (1968), 201–26.

Goode, John and Alan Lelchuk, 'Gissing's *Demos*: A Controversy', *Victorian Studies*, 12.4 (1969), 432–40.

Graham, Kenneth, *English Criticism of the Novel, 1865–1900* (Oxford: Clarendon Press, 1965).

Greenslade, William, *Degeneration, Culture and the Novel 1880–1940* (Cambridge: Cambridge University Press, 1994).

Griest, Guinevere, *Mudie's Circulating Library and the Victorian Novel* (Newton Abbot: David and Charles, 1970).

Gross, John, *The Rise and Fall of the Man of Letters: Aspects of English Literary Life since 1800* (London: Weidenfeld and Nicolson, 1969).

Grylls, David, 'Determinism and Determination in Gissing', *Modern Language Quarterly*, 45 (1984), 61–84.

——, Introduction to *Born In Exile* (London; Rutland: Dent; Tuttle, 1993), vii–xvii.

——, *The Paradox of Gissing* (London: Allen and Unwin, 1986).

——, 'The Teller not the Tale: George Gissing and Biographical Criticism', *English Literature in Transition*, 32 (1989), 454–70.

Guy, Josephine, 'Aesthetics, Economics and Commodity Culture: Theorizing Value in Late Nineteenth-Century Britain', *English Literature in Transition*, 42.2 (1999), 143–71.

Halperin, John, *Gissing: A Life in Books* (Oxford: Oxford University Press, 1987).

Hardy, Barbara, *The Moral Art of Dickens: Essays* (London: Athlone Press, 1970).

——, *Particularities: Readings in George Eliot* (London: Owen, 1982).

Hardy, Florence Emily, *The Early Life of Thomas Hardy 1840–1891* (London: Macmillan, 1928).

Harman, Barbara Leah, *The Feminine Political Novel in Victorian England* (Charlottesville: University of Virginia Press, 1998).

Harrison, Frederic, *Dickens's Place in Literature* (London: Arnold, 1895).

Harsh, Constance D, 'Gissing's *In the Year of Jubilee* and the Epistemology of Resistance', *English Literature in Transition*, 34.4 (1994), 853–75.

Hassam, Andrew, 'The Oscillating Text: A Reading of *The Private Papers of Henry Ryecroft*', *English Literature in Transition*, 28 (1985), 30–40.

Heinzelman, Kurt, *The Economics of the Imagination* (Amherst: University of Massachusetts Press, 1980).

Hepburn, James, *The Author's Empty Purse and the Rise of the Literary Agent* (London: Oxford University Press, 1968).

Heyns, Michiel, *Expulsion and the Nineteenth-Century Novel: The Scapegoat in English Realist Fiction* (Oxford: Clarendon Press, 1994).

Hillier, Sidney, *Popular Drugs: Their Use and Abuse* (London: Werner Laurie, 1910).

Hobsbawm, Eric and Chris Wrigley, *Industry and Empire: from 1750 to the Present Day*, new edn (Harmondsworth: Penguin, 1999).

Hoggart, Richard, *The Uses of Literacy: Aspects of Working-class Life with Special Reference to Publications and Entertainments* (Harmondsworth: Penguin, 1958).

Holdsworth, WJ, *Dickens as a Legal Historian* (New Haven: Yale University Press, 1929).

Hollington, Michael, 'Dickens the Flâneur', *Dickensian*, 77.2 (1981), 71–87.

Hoyas Solís, José Antonio, 'George Gissing's Narrative and Late Nineteenth-Century Narrative Trends', *Anuario de Estudios Filológicos*, 7 (1984), 227–31.

Hudson, Kenneth, *Pawnbroking: An Aspect of British Social History* (London: Bodley Head, 1982).

Hutter, Albert D, 'Dismemberment and Articulation in *Our Mutual Friend*', *Dickens Studies Annual*, 11 (1983), 135–75.

Irwin, Michael, *Picturing: Description and Illusion in the Nineteenth-Century Novel* (London: Allen and Unwin, 1979).

James, Henry, *Literary Criticism: Essays on Literature, American Writers, English Writers*, ed. by Leon Edel and Mark Wilson (New York: Library of America, 1984).

James, Henry, *Literary Criticism: French Writers; Other European Writers; The Prefaces to the New York Edition*, ed. by Leon Edel and Mark Wilson (New York: Library of America, 1984).

Jameson, Fredric, *The Political Unconscious: Narrative as a Socially Symbolic Act* (London: Methuen, 1982).

Jones, Gareth Stedman, *Outcast London: A Study in the Relationship Between Classes in Victorian Society* (Harmondsworth: Penguin, 1984).

Jordan, John A and Robert L Patten, eds, *Literature in the Marketplace* (Cambridge: Cambridge University Press, 1995).

Keating, Peter, *George Gissing: New Grub Street* (London, Arnold, 1968).

——, *The Haunted Study: A Social History of the English Novel 1875–1914* (London: Secker and Warburg, 1989).

——, '*The Nether World* by George Gissing', *East London Papers*, 11.1 (1968), 47–51.

——, *The Working Classes in Victorian Fiction* (London: Routledge and Kegan Paul, 1971).

Kenwood, AG and AL Lougheed, *The Growth of the International Economy: An Introductory Text*, 3rd edn (London: Routledge, 1992).

Kermode, Frank, *The Sense of an Ending: Studies in the Theory of Fiction* (Oxford: Oxford University Press, 1967).

Koike, Shigeru, *Gissing East and West: Four Aspects* (London: Enitharmon Press, 1969).

Korg, Jacob, 'Cancelled Passages in Gissing's *The Unclassed*', *Bulletin of the New York Public Library*, 80 (1977), 553–8.

——, *George Gissing: A Critical Biography* (London: Methuen, 1965).

——, 'The Spiritual Theme of George Gissing's *Born in Exile*' in *From Jane Austen to Joseph Conrad: Essays Collected in Memory of James T Hillhouse* (Minneapolis: University of Minnesota Press, 1958).

Kotzin, Michael C, 'Herbert Pocket as Pip's Double', *Dickensian*, 79.2 (1983), 95–107.

Kramer, David, George Gissing and Women's Work: Contextualising the Female Professional', *English Literature in Transition*, 43:3 (2000), 316–30.

Kucich, John, 'Dickens' Fantastic Rhetoric: The Semantics of Reality and Unreality in *Our Mutual Friend*', *Dickens Studies Annual*, 14 (1985), 167–89.

——, *Repression in Victorian Fiction: Charlotte Brontë, George Eliot and Charles Dickens* (Berkeley: University of California Press, 1987).

Lacan, Jacques, 'Seminar on "The Purloined Letter"', *Yale French Studies*, 48 ([1972]), 38–72.

Langton, Robert, *The Childhood and Youth of Charles Dickens: with Retrospective Notes and Elucidations from his Books and Letters* (London: Hutchinson, 1912).

Leavis, LR, 'George Gissing, Politics and the Chunnel', *English Studies*, 73 (1992), 240–7.

——, 'George Gissing's Life in Books', *English Studies*, 1983 (64), 218–24.

——, 'The Late Nineteenth-Century Novel and the Change towards the Sexual – Gissing, Hardy and Lawrence', *English Studies*, 1985 (66), 36–47.

Leavis, QD, *Collected Essays*, ed. by G Singh, 3 vols (Cambridge: Cambridge University Press, 1989), III.

Ledger, Sally, 'Gissing, the Shopgirl and the New Woman', *Women: a Cultural Review*, 6.3 (1995), 263–74.

Lelchuk, Alan, '*Demos*: The Ordeal of the Two Gissings', *Victorian Studies*, 12.3 (1968), 357–74.

Lesser, Wendy, 'Even-handed Oddness: George Gissing's *The Odd Women*', *Hudson Review*, 37.2 (1984), 209–20.

Levin, Harry, *The Gates of Horn: A Study of Four French Realists* (New York: Oxford University Press, 1966).

Linehan, Katherine Bailey, '*The Odd Women*: Gissing's Imaginative Approach to Feminism', *Modern Language Quarterly*, 40.4 (1979), 358–75.

Loeb, Lori Anne, *Consuming Angels: Advertising and Victorian Women* (Oxford: Oxford University Press, 1994).

Lucas, EV, ed., *The Colvins and Their Friends* (London: Methuen, 1928).

Lucas, John, ed., *Literature and Politics in the Nineteenth Century* (London: Methuen: 1971).

Lukàcs, Georg, *The Meaning of Contemporary Realism*, trans. by John and Necke Mander (London: Merlin, 1963).

——, *The Theory of the Novel: A Historico-Philosophical Essay on the Forms of Great Epic Literature*, trans. by Anna Bostock (London, Merlin, 1971).

Lurie, Alison, *The Language of Clothes* (London: Heinemann, 1981).

McCormack, Peggy, *The Rule of Money: Gender, Class and Exchange Economics in the Fiction of Henry James* (Ann Arbor: UMI Research Press, 1990).

McCracken, Scott, 'From Performance to Public Sphere: The Production of Modernist Masculinities', *Textual Practice*, 15.1 (2001), 47–65.

McVeagh, John, *Tradefull Merchants: The Portrayal of the Capitalist in Literature* (London: Routledge and Kegan Paul, 1981).

Marzials, Frank T, *Life of Charles Dickens* (London: Scott, 1887).

Michaels, Walter Benn, *The Gold Standard and the Logic of Naturalism: American Fiction at the Turn of the Century* (Berkeley: University of California Press).

Michaux, Jean-Pierre, ed., *George Gissing: Critical Essays* (London; Totowa: Vision; Barnes and Noble, 1981).

Michie, Ranald C, *The City of London: Continuity and Change, 1850–1900* (London: Macmillan, 1992).

Miller, Andrew H, *Novels Behind Glass: Commodity Culture and Victorian Narrative* (Cambridge: Cambridge University Press, 1995).

Miller, DA, *Fiction and its Discontents: Problems of Closure in the Traditional Novel* (Princeton: Princeton University Press, 1981).

——, *The Novel and the Police* (Berkeley: University of California Press, 1988).

Miller, J Hillis, *Charles Dickens: The World of his Novels* (Cambridge, MA: Harvard University Press, 1958).

Millhauser, Milton, '*Great Expectations*: The Three Endings', *Dickens Studies Annual*, 2 (1972), 267–77 .

Mitchell, WJT, ed., *On Narrative* (Chicago: Chicago University Press, 1981).

Moretti, Franco, *The Way of the World: The* Bildungsroman *in European Culture* (London: Verso, 1987).

Mull, Donald L, *Henry James's Sublime Economy: Money as Symbolic Center in the Fiction* (Middletown: Wesleyan University Press, 1973).

Murry, John Middleton, *Katherine Mansfield and Other Literary Studies* (London: Constable, 1959).

Musselwhite, David E, *Partings Welded Together: Politics and Desire in the Nineteenth-Century Novel* (London: Methuen, 1987).

Nash, Christopher, ed., *Narrative in Culture: The Uses of Storytelling in the Sciences, Philosophy, and Literature* (London: Routledge, 1990).

Neale, Gywn, *All the Days were Glorious: George Gissing in North Wales* (Iard yr Orsaf: Gwasyg Carreg Gwalch, 1994).

Nevett, TR, *Advertising in Britain: A History* (London: Heinemann, 1982).

Newton, Adam Zachary, *Narrative Ethics* (Cambridge, MA: Harvard University Press, 1995).

Nunokawa, Jeff, *The Afterlife of Property: Domestic Security and the Victorian Novel* (Princeton: Princeton University Press, 1994).

Olmsted, John Charles, ed., *A Victorian Art of Fiction: Essays on the Novel in British Periodicals*, 3 vols (New York: Garland, 1979).

Orwell, George, *The Complete Works of George Orwell*, ed. by Peter Davison, Ian Angus and Sheila Davison, 20 vols (London: Secker and Warburg, 1986–98).

Page, Norman, ed., *Henry James: Interviews and Recollections* (London: Macmillan, 1984).

Patten, Robert L, *Charles Dickens and his Publishers* (Oxford: Clarendon Press, 1978).

Pite, Ralph, 'Place, Identity and *Born in Exile*', in *Rereading Victorian Fiction*, ed. by Alice Jenkins and Juliet John (Basingstoke; New York: Macmillan; St Martin's Press, 2000), pp. 129–44.

Poole, Adrian, *Gissing in Context* (London: Macmillan, 1975).

Poovey, Mary, *Making a Social Body: British Cultural Formation 1830–1864* (Chicago: Chicago University Press, 1995).

Postmus, Bouwe, ed., *A Garland for Gissing* (Amsterdam: Rodopi, 2001).

Propp, Vladimir, *Morphology of the Folktale*, 2nd edn, trans. by Laurence Scott, ed. by Svatava Pirkova-Jakobson, Louis Wagner and Alan Dundes (Austin: University of Texas Press, 1968).

Purdy, Anthony, ed., *Literature and Money* (Amsterdam: Rodopi, 1993).

Reed, John R, *Dickens and Thackeray: Punishment and Forgiveness* (Athens: Ohio University Press, 1995).

——, *Victorian Conventions* (Ohio: Ohio University Press, 1975).

Ribot, Théodule-Armand, *Heredity: a Psychological Study of its Phenomena, Laws, Causes and Consequences* (London: King, 1875).

Richards, Thomas, *The Commodity Culture of Victorian England: Advertising and Spectacle 1851–1914* (London: Verso, 1991).

Richardson, Angelique and Chris Willis, eds, *The New Woman in Fiction and in Fact* (Basingstoke: Palgrave, 2000).

Roberts, Morley, *The Private Life of Henry Maitland: A Record Dictated by J.H.*, (London: Nash, 1912).

Robey, Cora, '*In the Year of Jubilee*: A Satire on Late Victorian Culture', *Tennessee Studies in Literature*, 17 (1972), 121–7.

Routledge's Jubilee Guide to London and its Suburbs, new edn (London: Routledge, n.d. [1887]).

Ruskin, John, *Works*, ed. by ET Cook and Alexander Wedderburn, 39 vols (London: Allen, 1905).

Russell, Norman, *The Novelist and Mammon: Literary Responses to the World of Commerce in the Nineteenth Century* (Oxford: Clarendon Press, 1986).

Sadrin, Anny, *Parentage and Inheritance in the Novels of Charles Dickens* (Cambridge: Cambridge University Press, 1994).

Said, Edward, *Culture and Imperialism* (London: Chatto, 1993).

Scheick, William J, *Fictional Structure and Ethics: The Turn-of-the-Century English Novel* (Athens: University of Georgia Press, 1990).

Schneider, Daniel J, *The Crystal Cage: Adventures of the Imagination in the Fiction of Henry James* (Lawrence: Regents Press of Kansas, 1978).

Schwarzbach, FS, *Dickens and the City* (London: Athlone Press, 1979).

——, 'Victorian Literature and the City: A Review Essay', *Dickens Studies Annual*, 15 (1986), 309–35.

Selig, Robert L, *George Gissing* (Boston: Twayne, 1983).

——, 'A Sad Heart at the Late-Victorian Culture Market; George Gissing's *In the Year of Jubilee*', *Studies in English Literature*, 9 (1969), 703–20.

Seltzer, Mark, *Henry James and the Art of Power* (Ithaca: Cornell University Press, 1984).

Shatto, Susan, *The Companion to Bleak House* (London: Allen and Unwin, 1988).

Shell, Marc, *The Economy of Literature* (Baltimore: Johns Hopkins University Press, 1978).

——, *Money, Language and Thought: Literary and Philosophical Economies from the Medieval to the Modern Era* (Berkeley: University of California Press, 1982).

Simmel, Georg, *The Philosophy of Money*, trans. by Tom Bottomore and David Frisby (London: Routledge and Kegan Paul, 1978).

——, *The Sociology of Georg Simmel*, ed. and trans. by Kurt H Wolff (New York: Free Press, 1950).

Simpson, David, ed., *Subject to History: Ideology, Class, Gender* (Ithaca: Cornell University Press, 1991).

Sjöholm, Christina, *The Vice of Wedlock: The Theme of Marriage in George Gissing's Novels* (Uppsala: Uppsala University Press, 1994).

Sloan, John, *George Gissing: The Cultural Challenge* (New York: St Martin's Press, 1989).

——, 'The Literary Affinity of Gissing and Dostoevsky: Revising Dickens', *English Literature in Transition*, 32.4 (1989), 441–553.

Smith, Grahame, *Dickens, Money and Society* (Berkeley: University of California Press, 1968).

Spiers, John and Pierre Coustillas, *The Rediscovery of George Gissing: A Reader's Guide* (London: National Book League, 1971).

Stone, Harry, *Dickens and the Invisible World: Fairy Tales, Fantasy and Novel-Making* (London: Macmillan, 1980).

Storey, Mark, 'Introduction' to *The Private Papers of Henry Ryecroft* (Oxford: Oxford University Press, 1987), pp. vii–xx.

Stubbs, Patricia, *Women and Fiction: Feminism and the Novel* (Sussex; New York: Harvester Press; Barnes and Noble, 1979).

Sutherland, John, *The Longman Companion to Victorian Fiction* (London: Longman, 1988).

——, *Victorian Novelists and Publishers* (London: Athlone Press, 1976).

Swann, Charles, 'Sincerity and Authenticity: The Problem of Identity in *Born in Exile*', *Literature and History*, 1984 (10), 165–88.

Swinnerton, Frank, *George Gissing: A Critical Study* (London: Secker, 1912).

Sypher, Eileen, *Wisps of Violence: Producing Public and Private Politics in the Turn-of-the-Century British Novel* (London: Verso, 1993).

Taine, Hippolyte, *History of English Literature*, trans. by H Van Laun, 4 vols (Edinburgh: [n.p.], 1874).

Thomas, JD, 'The Public Purposes of George Gissing', *Nineteenth Century Fiction*, 8 (1953), 118–23.

Thompson, James, *Models of Value: Eighteenth-Century Political Economy and the Novel* (Durham, NC: Duke University Press).

Thompson, Nicole Diane, *Victorian Women Writers and the Woman Question* (Cambridge: Cambridge University Press, 1999).

Tindall, Gillian, *The Born Exile: George Gissing* (New York: Harcourt Brace Jovanovich, 1974).

Tindall, Gillian, 'The Haunted Books of George Gissing', *Essays by Divers Hands*, 43 (1984), 62–74.

——, Introduction to *Born in Exile* (London: Hogarth, 1985), unpaginated.

Tintner, Adeline R, '*Denzil Quarrier*: Gissing's Ibsen Novel', *English Studies*, 64 (1983), 225–32.

——, *The Twentieth-Century World of Henry James: Changes in his Work after 1900* (Baton Rouge: Louisiana State University Press, 2000).

Todorov, Tsvetan, *The Poetics of Prose*, ed. by Jonathan Culler, trans. by Richard Howard (Oxford: Blackwell, 1977).

Tolkien, JRR, *The Monsters and the Critics and Other Essays*, ed. by Christopher Tolkien (London: Allen and Unwin, 1983).

Torgovnick, Marianna, *Closure in the Novel* (Princeton: Princeton University Press, 1981).

Toynton, Evelyn, 'The Subversive George Gissing', *American Scholar*, 59 (1990), 126–38.

Lionel Trilling, *Beyond Culture: Essays on Literature and Learning* (Harmondsworth: Penguin, 1967).

——, *Sincerity and Authenticity* (London: Oxford University Press, 1972).

Trotter, David, *Circulation: Dickens, Defoe and the Economics of the Novel* (Basingstoke: Macmillan, 1988).

——, *Cooking with Mud: The Idea of Mess in Nineteenth-Century Art and Fiction* (Oxford: Oxford University Press, 2000).

——, *The English Novel in History 1895–1920* (London: Routledge, 1992).

Turner, ES, *The Shocking History of Advertising*, rev. edn (Harmondsworth: Penguin, 1965).

Veblen, Thorstein, *The Theory of the Leisure Class* (New York: Dover, 1994).

Vernon, John, *Money and Fiction: Literary Realism in the Nineteenth and Early Twentieth Centuries* (Ithaca: Cornell University Press, 1984).

Villars, P, *London and Its Environs: A Picturesque Survey of the Metropolis and its Suburbs*, trans. by Henry Frith (London: Routledge, 1888).

Walkowitz, Judith, *City of Dreadful Delight: Narratives of Sexual Danger in Late-Victorian London*, (London: Virago, 1992).

——, *Prostitution and Victorian Society: Women, Class and the State* (Cambridge: Cambridge University Press, 1980).

Ward, AC, *Gissing* (London: Longmans, Green, 1959).

Ward, AW, *Dickens* (London: Macmillan, 1882).

Waters, Catherine, *Dickens and the Politics of the Family* (Cambridge: Cambridge University Press, 1997).

Watt, George, *The Fallen Woman in the Nineteenth-Century English Novel* (London: Croom Helm, 1984).

Watts, Cedric, *Literature and Money: Financial Myth and Literary Truth* (Hemel Hempstead: Harvester Wheatsheaf, 1990).

Weiss, Barbara, *The Hell of the English: Bankruptcy and the Victorian Novel* (London; Lewisburg: Bucknell University Press; Associated University Presses, 1986).

Welsh, Alexander, 'Blackmail Studies in *Martin Chuzzlewit* and *Bleak House*', *Dickens Studies Annual*, 11 (1983), 25–35.

——, *The City of Dickens* (Oxford: Clarendon Press, 1971).

——, *From Copyright to Copperfield: The Identity of Dickens* (Cambridge, MA: Harvard University Press, 1987).

West, WJ, *George Gissing in Exeter* (Exeter: Exeter Rare Books, 1979).

Wheeler, Michael, *Death and the Future Life in Victorian Literature and Theology* (Cambridge: Cambridge University Press, 1990).

White, Arnold, *The Problems of a Great City* (London: Remington, 1886).

Wicke, Jennifer, *Advertising Fictions: Literature, Advertisement and Social Reality* (New York: Columbia University Press, 1988).

Wiener, Martin J, *English Culture and the Decline of the Industrial Spirit 1850–1980* (Harmondsworth: Penguin, 1985).

Williams, Raymond, *The Country and the City* (London: Hogarth Press, 1993).

——, *Culture and Society* (London: Hogarth, 1983).

——, *The English Novel from Dickens to Lawrence* (London: Chatto and Windus, 1970).

——, *Keywords: A Vocabulary of Culture and Society* (London: Fontana, 1988).

——, *The Long Revolution* (London: Chatto and Windus, 1961).

——, *Problems in Materialism and Culture: Selected Essays* (London: Verso, 1980).

Winnifrith, Tom, *Fallen Women in the Nineteenth-Century Novel* (London: Macmillan, 1994).

Wolff, Joseph J, *George Gissing: An Annotated Bibliography of Writings about Him* (De Kalb: Northern Illinois Press, 1974).

——, 'Gissing's Revision of *The Unclassed*', *Nineteenth-Century Fiction*, 8 (1953), 42–52.

INDEX